the graphic designer's guide to clients

second edition

ellen shapiro

ALLWORTH PRESS
NEW YORK

Copyright © 2014 by Ellen M. Shapiro
All Rights Reserved. Copyright under Berne Copyright Convention,
Universal Copyright Convention, and Pan American Copyright Convention.
No part of this book may be reproduced, stored in a retrieval system, or
transmitted in any form, or by any means, electronic, mechanical, photocopying,
recording or otherwise, without the express written consent of the publisher,
except in the case of brief excerpts in critical reviews or articles.
All inquiries should be addressed to
Allworth Press, 307 West 36th Street, 11th Floor, New York, NY 10018.

Allworth Press books may be purchased in bulk at special discounts for sales
promotion, corporate gifts, fund-raising, or educational purposes.
Special editions can also be created to specifications.
For details, contact the Special Sales Department,
Allworth Press, 307 West 36th Street, 11th Floor, New York, NY 10018
or info@skyhorsepublishing.com.

17 16 15 14 13   5 4 3 2 1

Published by Allworth Press, an imprint of Skyhorse Publishing, Inc.
307 West 36th Street, 11th Floor, New York, NY 10018.

Allworth Press® is a registered trademark of Skyhorse Publishing, Inc.®,
a Delaware corporation.

www.allworth.com

Cover design by Laurie Rosenwald
Book design and page composition/typography by Ellen Shapiro

Library of Congress Cataloging-in-Publication Data is available on file.
ISBN: 978-1-62153-401-3

Printed in the United States of America

My wish

May you prove — as the designers included in this book have— that making clients happy and doing great work are not mutually exclusive activities.

how do
clients think?

are they
hearing
you?

what do they
see when you
present
your work?

do you
understand
what they're
saying?

will your
idea fly?

does your
work touch
their hearts?

contents

part I
What I've Learned about Clients

part II
Corporate Clients

part III
Retail and Entertainment Clients

part IV
Institutional Clients

acknowledgments

My thanks to:

Allworth Press. To Tad Crawford for his vision and professionalism and to Thornwell May for his astute proofing and editing.

*Communication Art*s editor and publisher Patrick Coyne and managing editors Robin Alyse Doyle, Rebecca Bedrossian, and Anne Telford for their continuing support.

Laurie Rosenwald for her fab cover design.

Felix Sockwell for his icon set and handshake drawing.

The designers all around the country who, by graciously allowing me to interview them and their clients, made this book possible.

author's note

My first book, *Clients and Designers*, published by Watson-Guptill in 1990, led to a long-term assignment from *Communication Arts* magazine: two "Clients and Designers" pieces each year. Of the eighteen interview chapters in the second edition of this book, twelve appeared in *CA*. This 2014 edition, incorporates much new material and was edited and updated to reflect client-company ownership changes, relevant events, and much more.

for more than two decades I've been heading my own design practice as well as covering graphic design and visual culture for design magazines and blogs. I've had the privilege of talking to the clients and designers who've been responsible for some of the most effective visual communications ever produced—branding, web sites, annual reports, retail environments, books, catalogs, packaging, product design, posters, ad campaigns.

How do successful business people and creative professionals find each other, work together, make decisions, and evaluate the effectiveness of what they produce? What are their secrets? How do they resolve conflicts? How do they team up to produce work that is both creatively innovative and achieves the client's objectives?

The purpose of this book is to take you inside their minds and show you how they do it—and how you can, too.

What I've Learned about Clients

Financial matters aside, we graphic designers need clients to give our work purpose and structure. If we didn't have clients, we wouldn't be making fine art. We'd be out and about looking for clients.

Sometimes clients put their own needs above yours.

1 The Client: Elusive, Difficult, Coveted

graphic designers are fairly predictable. We usually want the same things. The opportunity to do good work is at the top of our lists.

Yes, there are differences and debates. Over the last decade or two, there have been philosophical rifts about legibility versus memorability, classicism versus innovation. But we are usually in agreement on what constitutes great design. We love to admire the latest expressions of creativity, beauty, wit, insight, and technical wizardry. How did the designer do it?

All of us want to do something of that quality and impact, too. Not just for ourselves or to be admired by our peers.

But for our clients.

A Service Business

In the twentieth century, the art world, as it had functioned since the Middle Ages, was transformed. Church and state no longer dictated appropriate subject matter and style. The artist was freed to make art to please him or herself (and at the very top of the market, to please gallery owners and wealthy art buyers). This paradigm shift not only changed painting, drawing, sculpture, and photography, it changed architecture and even cooking. Celebrity chefs can be tempermental *artistes*. If you don't like a dish, choose a different restaurant. Or perhaps something is wrong with you, with your unsophisticated taste buds and lack of appreciation.

Are graphic designers the last remaining vestiges of the old paradigm? Maybe so. Whatever we produce always has to please our patrons, the clients. If it doesn't, they'll ask us to change it. In the worst cases, they won't pay for it—and then hire someone else.

Like it or not, we work in a service business.

The purpose of graphic design is not to express our feelings about the universe (which doesn't mean we shouldn't believe in what we're doing). Our work isn't created for exhibition in museums and galleries—although if we're very good, it sometimes ends up there. It is used, to give just a few examples, to brand a product or service, to tell a company story, to give people a positive experience, to unite them behind a cause, to entertain, to announce an event, to raise money, to recruit, to sell, to inform.

Not Just Any Clients. Great Clients

If we didn't have clients, we wouldn't all be painting and sculpting and creating nouvelle cuisine. We'd be out and about looking for clients. With a great client, the process is a partnership. We don't feel like hands for hire. There is no servitude. There is joy and excitement in the process. We work in concert with individuals of vision to bring success to their organizations.

Designer April Greiman, whose work often blurs the boundaries between fine art and graphic design, says that she needs clients to give her projects structure and purpose. "When you work with a visionary," she says (see chapter 20), "there is a conceptual collaboration, and from that you grow tremendously." Pentagram partner and AIGA medallist Paula Scher also calls her best clients great collaborators. "The best collaborators in my career have been George C. Wolfe and Oskar Eustis, artistic directors of the Public Theater," she says. "They've allowed me to do fantastic work because they have vision."

A great client has a vision, a great story, and a great budget. Okay, maybe not a great budget, but an adequate budget, or at least an understanding of what it takes to get things done.

Why Aren't They All Great Clients?

If all clients were like Wolfe and Eustis, we'd all be doing work as awe-inspiring as Paula's Public Theater posters. Right?

What's the matter with the rest of them?

After all, you and I have the talent and the skill to produce work of that caliber, don't we? The only thing that comes between us and all that great work, all the awards and recognition, is the client.

At first, I was going to say, let's skip the horror stories. But, alas, there are too few great clients.

There are few great anythings in this world. Just look around. Millions more people shop at Wal-Mart than at that cool boutique you just discovered. Most companies cater to a least-common-denominator mentality. Their marketing managers are folks with jobs to do, office politics to worry about, budgets and sales quotas to meet. Groundbreaking design might not be the number-one priority on their agendas, as you've perhaps learned the hard way. One almost-great client said to me, while choosing a safe, plain-vanilla design over two much more interesting options (and, I guess, noticing the look on my face): "Ellen is seeing all her design awards fly out the window." A perceptive guy. He put the tastes of his future investors, or at least what he envisioned they would respond to, first. Some clients have less noble motivations. A few are far from tactful or respectful.

Yes, there have been the legendary Olivettis, Container Corporations of America, Knolls, and Herman Millers. There have been the legendary CEOs like Thomas Watson, Jr., of IBM, who were, in fact, patrons of the arts—at least of the "commercial" arts of product design and packaging design, exhibition design, and advertising. Contemporary design patrons include some of the same august corporations, as well as companies like Nike, Apple, Nickelodeon, Target, and many entrepreneurs, publishers, and arts organizations. Sometimes a small business, like a bakery or toy store or garage band, becomes a great client, offering a designer creative freedom and the opportunity to do fun, interesting, meaningful work.

The number of organizations that are committed to design as an integral part of their mission or culture is increasing, and that's encouraging.

Can Your Clients Be Great Clients?

Helping you make that happen is the purpose of this book. With the right tools, ranging from suggested questions to ask potential clients to examples demonstrated in the eighteen case studies of long-term relationships between successful design firm principals and their clients, you can help your clients become, if not great clients, at least clients with whom you can produce successful, satisfying work.

"Knowledge is expanding at an exponential rate," maintains Jon Esser, coordinator of arts recruitment programs at Purchase College, State University of New York. "There is good reason for designers to be optimistic. Clients are content providers, and content providers are increasingly in need of images and text that excite and compel the reader or user. The overwhelming flow of information must be given shape, and designers are content navigation enablers. That means more opportunities for more designers. The constant need to win market share will motivate clients to take more risks," he continues. "They will no longer define their needs as, 'Make us look just like our competition.' They are taking a bolder position: 'Make us look better than our competition.' That means more satisfying work for more designers."

More opportunities for more designers. More satisfying work. The potential is there, *if* you take the right approaches to meeting clients, establishing relationships with them, and keeping them happy.

Clients Are Much Less Predictable than Designers. Or Are They?

I can predict that Zevvie, our German shepherd dog, will go ballistic when another dog and owner walk down "her" street. And when company comes, she'll hide under the table and then emerge to be petted. Our former German shepherd, who had a different temperament, behaved much the same way. A guide to German shepherd dogs could be relatively easy to write.

But a guide to clients? I can't predict what my own clients will do from one day to the next. Much less yours, whom I've never met.

Or can't I? If your clients are of the old-school variety (and that doesn't mean they're old; they could be young and inexperienced), they'll demand an unreasonable amount of work in a ridiculous amount of time, for a fee that's much too low. They'll keep you waiting for half an hour, but if you arrive five minutes late, they'll be sitting around the conference table looking at their watches. They'll never have anything organized; won't take enough time to thoroughly explain their needs; will wait weeks before responding to a proposal, and then call and say, "We need the job tomorrow." When there's a tiny typo, they'll immediately point it out. But when you come up with an excellent solution, they'll barely acknowledge it or try to change it. They'll nit-pick and haggle over every detail but ignore the big picture. They'll insist that you cram enough copy for a well-paced twenty-four pages into half that many, and then make you use a photo that ruins the whole thing. No amount of arguing and pleading and rational demonstrations of superior alternatives will cause them to change their minds. Then they'll try to get an agreement that stipulates they will own all the rights in perpetuity.

Okay, maybe I'm exaggerating. But it all goes with the territory of being a client. After all, they are the ones paying the bills.

The Competition Is Ever-Growing

If you don't agree to their requirements, they might take their business somewhere else. And that might not be a bad thing. It will free you up to work for clients whose requirements are a better fit. There will always be someone else willing to do the job. Clients' inboxes are filled with promise-filled pitch letters and links to their online portfolios. And don't even let met get started talking about crowd-sourcing sites where competitors work on spec for fees so low they could be for a tank of gas, not a brand identity.

No one knows more about the competition than Ed Gold, former executive vice president and creative director of the Barton-Gillet Company, specialists in institutional marketing, and professor at the School of Communication Design at the University of Baltimore. Ed interviewed 300+ designers around the country for his seminal book, *The Business of Graphic Design*. Every year, he says, 15,000 to 20,000 students graduate from the more than 2,000 graphic design programs in US art schools, colleges, and universities. "The number of new people in the field is impossible to quantify," he adds, "because people are coming into graphic design from areas like mass communications and media studies, from computer graphics programs, and by creating their own curricula from online offerings. The only sure thing is that the competition is much more intense than ever before."

Every year, new business plans are written and new partnerships and firms are formed. Public relations and marketing firms and printing companies "cross-sell" design services to their existing clients. Big ad agencies add more and more "design boutiques" to their mix of offerings, and they're often willing to lowball graphic design services or even provide free work in order to get or hold on to lucrative advertising and PR accounts.

"Fortunately," says Allen Kay, chairman of the New York ad agency Korey Kay & Partners, "there's no Home Depot for do-it-yourself advertisers." There are, though, plenty of Home Depots for do-it-yourself designers. They're called FedEx Office, AlphaGraphics, VistaPrint. Every year, more and more potential clients, heeding the claims of software makers and template publishers, are trying to figure out how to do it themselves.

Our mission is to keep convincing clients to use *us*. We have the education, the experience, the talent, the insights. We can see things they can't, come up with solutions they could never conceive of, use the power of images and words to make their business dreams come true.

Then why can they be so difficult?

Some Great Clients Are Difficult, for Good Reasons

Clients who are difficult can sometimes be the best kind to have. They challenge you to do your finest work. They don't want anything mundane. They don't want an imitation or something they've seen a million times before. They know that in order to sell their products or services, they must have a unique selling proposition, one that is visualized by a unique, effective design solution. They seek out designers who have distinctive voices and who can give voice to their vision.

Martin Zimmerman of LFC Capital offers the most articulate explanation of this that I've ever heard (chapter 9). "Why would I want an imitation of what my competitor already has?" he asks. Zimmerman gives designers creative freedom within the structure of carefully articulated business objectives. "The whole idea is to create a feeling of success and sophistication," he explains. "There are lots of problems out there, but there are not too many fresh ideas on how to solve them."

It's much harder to create an original solution that satisfies requirements like Zimmerman's than it is to follow explicit directions, to do a formula design, or to merely lay out a client's text and pictures so they fit on a page.

Sandra Ruch, who for many years was responsible for Mobil Corporation's brilliant Masterpiece Theater posters, prided herself on being demanding. "I could be very blunt and say, 'This doesn't work,'" she said, describing her working relationship with Ivan Chermayeff and with other top designers and illustrators. "There were times when it took us four or five months before we came up with the right image. Four or five months of working it over and over. Ivan went back to the drawing board many times when he didn't come up with something we felt was what we wanted, and so did Seymour Chwast of Pushpin Studio. There's nothing wrong with that."

When the client is knowledgeable—and fair—the designer rises to the occasion.

Bad Clients Are Difficult, Too. How to Tell the Difference

"We do our best work for the clients who understand the most about design," asserts Marcia Lausen, principal of Chicago's Studio/lab. "They are the ones who trust us. We've also done good work for difficult clients," she adds, "and those difficulties usually result from their lack of understanding about the design process and/or issues of trust. To do good work for difficult clients means an extraordinary investment of time and effort spent on education and confidence-building. These are things that you can't bill for—can you imagine a proposal with these line items?—but they are keenly important."

My personal definition of a bad client is someone who wants a globe.

Several years ago, I worked with the marketing director of a Silicon Alley upstart that characterized itself as a company of young, nimble, quick problem solvers. The marketing director told me she had sole responsibility for design decisions (how wrong they often are about this). "These are great!" she said upon previewing comps of an identity based on collages of photographic images. My assistant and I had worked hard on them and thought they were pretty cool, too. I don't remember exactly what her boss, the company president, said when I presented them in his office. But I do remember (a) feeling like I'd been punched in the stomach and (b) suggesting that if he thought the concept was so out of sync with his vision, we could start over and revisit Phase I. "We'll think about it," he said in a tone of voice that meant "You're out" just as clearly as Michael Corleone dismissed his father's *consigliore*, Tom Hagen, in *The Godfather*. And then I was back on the street, a tear running down my cheek. Several months later, I visited the company website. The new solution: a globe. And not even a nice one at that.

A bad client is someone who claims to delegate responsibility, but really doesn't, or then takes it away. Over the years, I have seen the authority pulled out from under many, many women (and a few men) inside corporations, professional service firms, and nonprofit organizations. It's a sad commentary on American business.

A bad client notices that other companies that are making money have globe logos (or swooshes or elliptical orbits) and wants one, too. A bad client bosses designers, as well as his or her underlings, around. A bad client thinks the software does the work, so it should be easy to throw together a dozen more layouts overnight. A bad client has fonts and Photoshop and thinks he or she can put stuff together as well as you—or if not quite as well, for a lot less money—and that it will be good enough.

I still wonder if I could have turned that Silicon Alley guy into a good client if I'd been a little more patient, diplomatic, and inquisitive. If I hadn't gotten emotional, I could have figured out how to engage him in a conversation to find out what he, not the marketing director, really wanted to communicate. Surely, there must have been a better solution than a globe.

Advises Pentagram partner Michael Bierut: "The biggest trap is to believe that the brief you're first given is the whole story. It never is, and I repeat, never is the whole story. Moreover, the information that no one tells you up front is often the most important thing you need to know. Don't worry, it will come out eventually, usually when your first idea is being rejected. It's important to keep an open mind when you're presenting. Don't assume you know it all, just shut up and listen."

It's Easier to Sell Good Design to a Company that Already Buys It

Early on in my career, I met Arthur Michaels, a salesman for one of the top-flight printing companies. An erudite, literary type who always wore a suit and bow tie, Arthur was fond of saying, "It's much easier to sell good printing to a company that already buys good printing." Why? His answer: "If they've only bought bad printing, they'll never understand the difference or want to pay for good printing." I've thought about that principle a lot over the years.

"Educating the client" is an essential part of our work, but designers bandy the phrase around as if somehow we could teach all the Philistines (and every other heathen tribe) the difference between good design and bad. Once enlightened, they would never buy bad design again. Everyone who's successfully sold anything knows that not all potential buyers are qualified. When evaluating each potential new client, ask yourself:

 I Will this client be a good fit for me and my business?
 I What might this engagement lead to (no idle promises or fantasies, but a realistic assessment)?
 I Will it provide the opportunity to do work of the highest quality of which I am capable?
 I If not, what is its potential value?

Making an unwise choice can set you up for long-term frustration. The same time and effort (or less) that is put into courting and nurturing an unqualified client can be spent establishing a relationship with an organization that is, or can be, committed to good design. Ah, you say, the Apples and Nikes of this world already have designers coming out of their ears. They won't even return my call. My advice is, keep trying. Not necessarily them, but other organizations that, at least in some small way—whether it's an ad campaign, the design of their products, the way their website works—demonstrates that someone there cares about design.

Remember, It's Supposed to Be Fun. And It Is

Sure, we could have chosen to open restaurants or antique shops (and sell stuff made by other people). We could be leading tours of Macchu Pichu or designing dresses or interiors. Maybe we would make more money and have less angst if we did something else. After all, if we were very talented (and very photogenic) fashion designers or interior designers, we could have our own TV shows, or at least have the chance to compete on one.

We chose graphic design because we love type and images. We love print media and ink on paper and electronic media and moving images. We love to change minds and influence people and add joy and interest to the environment. We want people to be better informed, have an easier time finding their way around, support worthy causes, and be visually delighted. There's a whole bunch of reasons, each as individual as every one of us.

Mostly, I cherish the opportunities graphic design gives me to keep learning. Over the years, I've learned, as just a few examples, how bone fractures are healed, how independent films are distributed, how premium credit cards are marketed, how tax-exempt revenue bonds are issued, and how maritime law is practiced. I've had the privilege of working with development professionals at Israel's leading technology university and at the American Baptist Church, and with psychologists, scientists, financiers, management consultants, and academics. I've art directed photography at medical centers where cancer is treated, at plants where network computers are manufactured, at luxury hotels, and at facilities where people with disabilities learn skills to lead more fulfilling lives.

I've been able to contribute to visually identifying and marketing my clients' organizations. I've helped motivate kids not to start smoking, and created and sold my own products that help kids learn to read. And I'm not all that special.

It's what graphic designers do.

2

How to Meet Clients

Jonas Klein, longtime design manager at IBM Corporation, encouraged designers he didn't know—strangers—to contact him. He advised that they phone first to introduce themselves, then send a package of printed samples. He wanted to see work that was relevant to IBM's business. If the right project came up, he would give the designer a call. "Most of us traditionally answered our own telephones," he said. "And I'm talking about senior executives."

Try doing that today. There is no way to get the phone number of any IBM design manager. Or even an email address. A recorded message explains "the central procurement process for vendors."

Clients Are People Who Know How to Make Themselves Scarce

Voice mail has made telephoning a lost art. I recently received a direct-mail invitation to a $1,200 seminar: "Voice Mail Messages That Get Answered." Hmmm. Nothing can feel more humiliating than cold calling and leaving messages. CEOs and managers do not want you to bother them. And even if you get through? It sometimes doesn't get you anywhere. Laura Yamner, who's been responsible for high-profile projects at American Express and Condé Nast Traveler, is a typical client who hates getting cold calls. "If I talked to everyone who called trying to sell services I would never get any work done," she says. She has a point. After all, you are someone's target market, too. What would your day be like if you took all those calls from people who want you to change to their brand of phone service?

The clients we'd love to have, as we all know, claim that they are happy with their current suppliers and aren't changing firms, reviewing portfolios, taking calls, or opening unsolicited mail.

If Men Are at Ball Games and Women Are in Yoga Classes, Where Are the Clients?

If they're not answering their phones, and your emails are going right into their spam folders, how will you find them?

It depends on the state, region, city, and industry. Clients belong to certain organizations, like chambers of commerce, associations of business communicators, and societies of public relations professionals. They are listed in industry directories. They attend networking events, trade shows, and conferences (and, of course, some do open mail and pick up the phone; successful sales calls are made every day). Speaking at conferences is a tried-and-true way to market services. It's important to get on the roster of conferences that clients attend, not only those that designers attend, and to attend such potentially fruitful events as holiday parties at other clients' offices. Especially if they're service firms, like attorneys, accountants, and management consultants, entertaining their own clients.

And some potential clients are actually trolling around the Internet looking for the right designer (more about that later).

Getting as specific as you can to pinpoint places where the particular clientele you are looking for are congregating can pay off big time. Jeffrey Everett, of El Jefe Design in the suburban Washington, DC area, who's known for posters for entertainment clients, says he makes the best business contacts at art fairs and popular culture conventions. "I see those events as a way to meet people who like my work as well as to make money by selling posters. I'm doing New York Comic Con this year," he notes. "I'll be able to sell my designs and meet art directors from every industry I'm interested in working with—TV, movies, games, publishing. When you have 100,000 people see your work over the course of four days and can make around $6,000, it's the best of both worlds."

Designers meet clients in all kinds of unexpected places, too. Not only on the proverbial golf course and tennis court, but at airport lounges (flying first-class does have its advantages, I hear), college reunions, and pancake breakfasts. New York parents have been quoted as saying they choose their children's private schools based on whether the other parents might be good client material (after all, that's whom they'll be hanging with at birthday parties and play dates for the next six or seven years).

A stranger sitting next to me on the Metroliner joined my firm's client list a few years ago. He was talking on his cell phone, and the conversation seemed to be about closing a financing deal for a new company. It sounded intriguing, and he probably hadn't hired Pentagram—yet. Well, I thought, I can sit here and keep reading my *Vanity Fair*. Or, I can try to turn him into a client. I had two hours and forty-seven minutes. What was there to lose? The worst thing that could happen? He could get up and flee to another seat.

"So," I smiled at him, "it sounds like you're in the XYZ business." We chatted for a while. He handed me a card that looked like it was put together at the local copy shop. "That's a great company name," I said. "You could use a great logo to enhance your message." I told him a little bit about my firm. When the train pulled into Penn Station, we shook hands and I gave him my card. A few days later, I sent him a letter (a real letter on company stationery, in an envelope with a nice stamp: "It was a pleasure meeting you . . ."). A few weeks later, I got an email: "How much would you charge for a logo?" Notice that money, alas, is almost always the first question.

My firm submitted a proposal and got the job. I can't say that things would go as well with every stranger on a train. But a big part of being a design firm principal is seizing every chance to cultivate client relationships.

Do Those Clever Self-Promotions Work?

A few years ago, I was only too happy to have been assigned a magazine article on those 3-D holiday promotions designers love to send. You know, elaborately packaged goodies with rice-paper wrappings and raffia bows. I had created a few myself, some of which even got published in magazines and books, and which clients seemed to appreciate. But when it came to getting new work, a more direct approach, like spending a day or two on the phone calling clients to get referrals—instead of affixing hand-lettered labels to jars of barbecue rub—seemed to be a more effective use of time and resources.

I was ready to write an exposé. I was going to do for handmade designer gifts what Jessica Mitford's *Poison Penmanship* had done for Famous Writers' School and the American funeral industry. I called designers whose promotions had appeared in books like *The Best Seasonal Promotions* to get the lowdown on how those things eat up huge chunks of time and money while enlarging the designer's ego more than the client list.

But, according to the designers I interviewed, boy, was I wrong. "I've gotten calls as much as five years after a promotion was received," reported New York design firm principal Mary Pisarkiewicz of Pisarkiewicz Mazur + Co., who told me that a client she hadn't heard from in years called to say, "I want to work with you again" after getting a clever holiday gift. Other designers' responses included: "These things keep your name in front of clients"; "They're great showcases for design and production techniques"; "They maintain our client base"; "They have a reenergizing effect on creativity"; "They give you the opportunity to have fun, to create something meaningful"; and "They always pay off."

Not everyone agrees that this approach will work. "They're all lying," claims one of the country's most successful designers. I won't go as far as to concur with him; I'll only say that gifts are a meaningful thank-you for clients you already work with. Just don't count on them to bring in new business as effectively as they did for Pisarkiewicz. If it happens, it's like getting a bonus.

I haven't given up the idea entirely, but instead of bottling edibles and doodads, I spend some of my so-called free time creating small, limited-edition books. The subjects have been travel, food, gardens—things that are personally meaningful to me. The layouts illustrate my approach to typography, unencumbered by someone else's identity standards (even standards I developed). Writing and designing the books is a welcome break from client work, and at holiday time, clients really seem to welcome them.

Even if you never get business from doing self-initiated projects, they are great opportunities to flex your personal creative side and to remind yourself that, yes, you are a very good designer. Other designers I've spoken to take a similar approach. The promotions and gifts they mention most frequently, and that might work for you, include signed and numbered posters, boxed note cards, and apparel like T-shirts and caps—your coolest designs, of course.

And, how about this idea: after a project is completed, send the client a thank-you note handwritten on beautiful stationery you've designed—a much-appreciated touch these days.

What Approach Best Distinguishes You?

Early in my career I had a big success with a mailing to the public corporations in the New York area listed in *Inc.* magazine's "top 100 fastest growing US companies" issue. I researched the names of the marketing directors and investor relations managers and sent them a brochure with a cover that read: "Finally, annual reports that make growing companies look like a billion." The inside spread was illustrated with nicely faked covers and spreads of annual reports for fictitious companies. That promotion led to half a dozen meetings and annual reports for three companies on *Inc.*'s list.

What industries do you want to target? And once you have the contact information, what, actually, do you want to say to them (other than, "I do good design")? What will people in your target market respond to?

Pretend you have three minutes on the *Today* show—three minutes to make your case to the people you'd most like to work for. You've been coached by the best image and public-speaking consultants in the business. What, exactly, will you say when Matt Lauer asks, "Why should a client hire you and not somebody else?" Build a mailer or an e-newsletter around that concept. Test it with a few members of your target audience. Ask, "How would you respond to this?" and "What could I do to generate a better response?"

And when your marketing idea is successful, consider *not* publicizing it on "design community" websites. Designers can be a bit too eager to show off their clever promotions to their peers (read: competitors). If you do so, your concept may not be your own any more. Other people may start doing it better than you. My quality-annual-reports-for-small-companies idea was overtaken by powerful competitors pretty quickly.

What about Stories in the Press?

You open a design magazine, and there's an eight-page feature about you and your work. It's one of life's peak moments. You'll get congratulatory calls and emails from colleagues and friends, and lots of résumés. You hope that the article will also bring inquiries from potential new clients. Maybe. But don't count on it. "I'm delighted to have been profiled in *CA*," says Richard Poulin, partner in New York's Poulin + Morris. "But our clients — architects and real estate developers—don't read graphic design magazines."

What *do* they read? The newspapers and industry and business magazines and websites. Publications that—unless you've designed something revolutionary that changes people's lives—are unlikely to run a story about graphic design. The "Form and Function" column in the *Wall Street Journal*, for example, will report on industrial design: bicycles for the handicapped and design innovations in software and hardware, but not on what the editor has told me he deems "marketing fluff."

There *is* news in what we do: signage and wayfinding systems that help people get around; packaging that doesn't just make goods look appealing but informs people of the benefits of what's inside; information graphics that make content accessible. The more design work is presented as solutions to environmental, social, economic, and other problems, the more newsworthy it will be to the business and general press.

I was very pleased to see a recent story on the front page of the *New York Times* business section on how a young Oakland, CA, company was challenging market leader Kraft Foods' "Lunchables"—with clean, informative package design that is a shelf-level billboard for the healthier product inside. That story, about Revolution Foods Meal Kits and their design firm, Addis Creson, became chapter 12 of this book. Since then, Revolution Foods has been featured in *Bloomberg Businessweek* and its founders profiled in *Fortune*.

It's important that we designers get our stories out there. The more graphic design-creates-client-success stories get in the news—and in magazines like *Bloomberg Businessweek* and *Fortune*—the more graphic design will be recognized as an essential strategic component of business success.

Today, when most people hear the word "designer," they think interiors or fashion. Let's help change that, and make communication design part of their vocabularies.

If you believe you have a story, send samples of the relevant work to the managing editors of the most appropriate publications. You can find the right people to contact in *Writer's Market*, an annual directory that lists every publication and what the editors are looking for (and not looking for). Poulin + Morris's elegant work for medical centers, banks, and universities has been the subject of articles in *Sign Business*, a trade journal with an estimated circulation of 18,000 management-level decision makers. The firm's work for Sony was featured on the cover of *Identity*, a magazine that showcases corporate graphics and signage. Stories like that build business.

Design stories are often part of a trend or cultural phenomena: what people are wearing, playing, eating, reading, buying. If you're not the whole story, perhaps you can be part of a story. Editors and writers often have an idea based on something they've seen, a trend they've noticed, and are looking for examples to illustrate it.

Because of this, a few graphic designers have become minor celebrities, and, like other celebrities, are in the news more often than we regular folks. When Milton Glaser's "I ♥ NY more than ever" logo with a burnt bottom edge was rejected by the New York State Department of Commerce after 9/11, it made international headlines. Today, more than twelve years after the event, a Google search for "Milton Glaser burnt I heart NY" turns up 102,000 results, and "I heart NY" alone gets 126 *million* results.

Great work is evergreen.

Some designers spend $2,000 to $5,000 or more a month on a retainer for public relations services. A PR professional knows the editors, how to frame an article, the exact format to send it in, and how to act quickly if a story relates to breaking news. In a Small Business Special Report in *Crain's New York Business*, a story on Susan Karlin, principal of Suka Creative, described how she used cold calling to rebuild her business after one of New York's economic meltdowns. "Pitched" by her PR professional, the story reportedly brought her several more inquiries. "Three days after it ran, I got a call from a major university with the opportunity to bid on a project," she said.

If you are featured in a magazine, or if your opinion is part of a trend story, that is something to tweet about. Put a link on your site and make sure you get reprints or a PDF to send to clients and prospects.

How Important Are Design Awards?

Awards are important. To launch a firm. To keep your name in front of your peers. For self-esteem. To reward employees who contributed to important projects. However, I have never met a client who admitted that he or she looked through an awards annual or went to an awards dinner. But then, maybe I've met the wrong clients. April Greiman points out that awards are important to organizations in the business of design—fashion, entertainment, architecture, design stores, furniture, and high-tech. "Design clients are great," she says. "They do pay attention to the magazines and are very aware of who's doing the best things."

There are even a few clients, I've heard, those with hot new youth-market products, for example, for whom being on the crest of the trends is apparently so important they'll count the number of awards in an annual and zero in on the biggest winner.

Even if you don't do the kind of work that will attract the attention of the kind of clients who count awards, winning awards—in competitions that really mean something—will put your name in front of thousands of other designers. And being known by other designers can lead to getting clients. "Word of mouth begins with design awards," Ed Gold maintains. "Win awards, and your peers spread your name around in mysterious ways you don't even know about."

Awards have built the reputations of some of the most prestigious films and of global agencies like Fallon, whose strategy in its beginnings as Fallon McElligott Rice was to let big-time awards for ads for small local businesses and nonprofit organizations (chapter 21) catapult the firm to national and international fame.

No Matter What, Referrals Will Be Your Number-One Source of New Business

If you do good work, the word gets around, both to colleagues within the organization and at other companies.

Most design firm principals report that the majority of new business comes from referrals from existing, satisfied clients. Poulin + Morris are known in the tightly knit architecture and real estate communities because developers and building owners swap war stories about who's done outstanding work for them (and whom to keep away from). So do company presidents, chairmen, and marketing directors. In chapter 9, financial services CEO Marty Zimmerman describes his quest to find the right designer: he called fellow CEO Gordon Siegel of Crate & Barrel and asked, "Gordon, who do you use for design? Who's terrific?"

That's how it usually works. One recommendation from a respected colleague can be worth more than scores of self-promotions, PR releases, and design awards—and zillions of tweets. "The kind of work that you do attracts clients. Period," asserts architect Michael Rotondi, founder of the Southern California Institute of Architecture (chapter 20). "Those who do not grasp this simple relationship continue to wonder how to get better projects. If you do cheap, crummy work you attract cheap, crummy clients. If you do great work you attract great clients," he says.

Referrals can come from public relations firms and ad agencies. A big job to you may not be worth doing for them. Especially in smaller local markets, it's wise to make sure that the account executives and creative directors at the largest regional agencies know about you.

Referrals can also come from other designers. A prestigious web design project for a high-end bicycle company was referred to Liska + Associates (whose work for a real estate Internet start-up is profiled in chapter 6) by fellow Chicago designer Rick Valicenti, who already had a bike account and didn't want a conflict of interest. Valicenti thought that Liska's pristine, highly organized style would be a good fit for the client. Explains Steve Liska: "No one's sitting around with a big design job in their out box. Clients are very cautious right now. It's hard for them to get a decision from above. But word of mouth is still the most important way we get new business."

Reputations build referrals. When I came to New York to work for the late Herb Lubalin, he had the deserved reputation of being the very best with type. Lubalin, Smith, Carnase's eclectic clients ranged from cosmetics companies to publishers to industrial corporations, all of whom wanted letterheads and packages, ads and book jackets adorned with beautiful letterforms, ligatures, and swashes. Some of the studio's biggest projects, in addition to lots of shampoo bottles for Loréal Paris, were a poster campaign for a series of filmed plays, logos, and ads for a big-three automaker, and annual reports for a *Fortune* 50 oil exploration company.

I'm not sure a reputation for doing beautiful things with type would be enough to have a client list like that today. More of an industry specialization and results orientation is usually needed. What works now is a reputation something like this: XYZ design firm manages corporate identities that unite disparate brands; knows how to communicate with extreme-sports aficionados; creates ads and promotions that can sell out an entertainment event.

But a reputation for doing beautiful things with type might boost the client list of designers of book jackets, museum catalogs, and invitations to arts-related events. Ariane Spanier, headquartered in Berlin, Germany, serves an increasingly international group of clients by creating handcrafted type treatments; type that splits into fragments, organically morphs into new forms, or peels open, revealing something different underneath. Spanier's clients are in what she calls "the cultural sector": museums, galleries, architects, galleries, artists, curators. Organizations that have found her online include the Indira Gandhi National Centre for the Arts in New Delhi and Brodno Sculpture Park in Warsaw. They were seeking something unique, with extraordinary production values.

If what you have to show are tri-fold, 4-by-9 brochures using old photos from the client's files, think about reinventing yourself. It might require some reeducation and deep thinking about how you need to position yourself for the clients you want to attract now.

Good News Spreads Quickly

Today, fifteen years after the phenomenal launch of its groundbreaking campaign for the musical *Rent*, Drew Hodges's agency, SpotCo, creates the posters and campaigns for more than half the shows on Broadway (chapter 17). Hodges's expertise, knowledge of which has spread quickly from one entertainment mogul to the next, helps sell up to eight thousand tickets per show per week.

A referral can also come from a client's colleague or acquaintance in a different industry, but one with a similar need. Liska + Associates got an important client, makers of IT management software, through a referral from a client in a different industry. Says Steve Liska: "The founders called and said, 'We heard you're really good at helping people get businesses going.' They needed everything—product naming, identity, print literature, ads, their website, the interface design with icons—in a month." A reputation built on that kind of expertise (and speedy service) builds repeat business and more referrals.

Over the years, my firm got a lot of new business from clients changing jobs. You did a good job for them at Company X, and they call you when they're settled in at their new job at Company Y. Remember the ditty you sang as a child, as a round at camp: "Make new friends and keep the old. One is silver and the other is gold." Being a rainmaker can sometimes involve fortuitous showers of new business that come when re-orgs and downsizings send talented people to other organizations.

Your Website

Study the sites of the design firms featured in this book. They're clean, organized, and a bit provocative. By that I mean they don't show and tell everything. They give a deliciously brief taste of the firm's work and capabilities. Then, it's up to the interested party to make the next move, to pick up the phone or hit that "contact" tab.

Need I say that spending the time it takes to design an effective site is one of the best investments you can make? Your site should have an effortless navigation system that guides the visitor through a portfolio of a dozen to twenty projects that present compelling reasons to work with you. And, ideally, it should be designed using a content management system that allows you to easily make changes and add new work.

Boston design firm principal Michael Weymouth (chapter 10) says that when weymouth.com was launched, it was ranked by a European magazine as one of the ten hot websites in the world. "It is my opinion, though, that 'hot' does not get you much work," he says, "so our new site is more utilitarian. All we expect is that people will think highly enough of it to put us on their design review list." And then he adds, almost unnecessarily, "But if we had an ugly, dysfunctional site, we would not get that call."

Before you launch your site, test it. Upload the files to an FTP site and direct your friends and relatives there. Let them look at it on Macs and PCs, large monitors and small, tablets and smartphones, Firefox and Safari. Let them tell you if there are any problems with the navigation, the fonts, the images and the spelling—before it's out there in the world.

When it's ready to launch, your email sign-off can promote the site and invite current and prospective clients to visit. So can a low-key email campaign—to people you already know or know of. It's not spam when it's a personal "hello" from you to a former or current or potential client who might even enjoy hearing from you.

"The word 'promote' is key here," advises Rick Landers of LandersMiller, a hip New York design office whose clients range from a kids' magazine to hospitals and pharmaceutical companies. "We always have to explain this to clients when we build sites for them. Just because you build it doesn't mean that anyone will see it. You have to promote it. When we post new work, we make a social media post linking to the work. We also send an email to our clients and collaborators announcing the work. Updating our site map through Google has been super helpful in keeping the content recent, also updating our various page metadata helps with Google searches. We can't put a percentage increase of traffic or give a factual statement that this helped get new business," he says. "But in looking at our site's analytics, we can see an increase of traffic over time once we started making those efforts more consistent."

They Just Might Be Looking for You

More and more designers who do innovative, distinctive work are reporting that the right clients are finding them online—and expanding their influence globally. Ariane Spanier is in Germany, but clients in Scandinavia, Poland, the UK, and India have found her and commissioned major projects.

In Monterrey, Mexico, Anagrama, which characterizes itself as a brand intelligence group, has grown from three to thirty people in just four years and is serving more than one hundred clients throughout Latin America and around the world. They have two full-time employees who do nothing but answer phone and email inquiries from potential clients. Founding partners

Sebastian Padilla and Gustavo Muñoz attribute this phenomenal success to their online portfolio. First of all, they say, they choose clients carefully, turning down work that doesn't have the potential to get them noticed. Then, every project, from a business card to a full branding program or retail environment, is beautifully staged and photographed. "That has been our biggest investment," Muñoz attests. "Two designers work only on the portfolio, location scouting, prop styling, art directing photography, and post-production. This strategy has paid off. Anagrama's site has attracted so many Asian clients, they're planning to open an office in Japan.

"When people contact us out of the blue, it's usually because they've seen our site, agrees Stuart Rogers of New York's RED, Rogers Eckersley Design. The site of this firm, founded by two 2004 SVA MFA graduates, shows off their work for the Downtown Alliance Canyon of Heroes; the spring gala at Harlem's famous Apollo Theater; and the branding for Super Bowl XLVI.

If you're wondering why the right clients aren't finding you, take a look at landersmiller.com, arianespanier.com, anagrama.com, and red-nyc.com, and see if your site has that kind of wow factor. And please check out rosenworld.com, the site of Laurie Rosenwald, the cover designer of this book.

The Social Network?

Yes, it's important to have a great site and to send timely emails when you've got good news, but if you listen to the consultants who (for a fee) will develop and implement your social media strategy, all you have to do is have the right mix of Facebook, Twitter, Pinterest, Instagram, Dribbble, your own blog, etc., etc.—and business will come pouring in.

Sometimes it seems like everyone is spending hours and hours posting status updates and tweeting and pinning. In between all that, and downloading apps, texting, blogging, making and watching YouTube videos, getting deals on Groupon, reviewing restaurants on Yelp and hotels on TripAdvisor, buying and rating stuff on Amazon and eBay, when is any real work getting done? It's all fun, it's all good, unless you're wasting time that otherwise could be spent on productive work—and ah, don't we all?

And, truly, do you know practicing designers who have attracted major clients with real projects and real budgets via their Twitter feed? I don't.

To make sure my instincts were right about this, I recently surveyed a bunch of successful young designers, and of the few who claimed that they got work through social media, when asked for specifics, not one could actually point to a real client or a real project that came to them that way. Other designers expressed a healthy dose of caution and issued warnings such as: "The only people who will look at your work on sites like Dribbble are other designers looking for 'inspiration.'"

"I know some people really work Pinterest," reports designer-illustrator Jeffrey Everett. "I pin my own work from my blog, but I have never really seen a benefit. Same with Dribbble, which seems like an excellent way to have a lot of other designers see your work and copy it," he warns. "Designers are not going to hire you, so why show off to them? I get a little antsy belonging to any site where people can leave comments and you can't edit them away," he says. "The positive comments are rarely useful and are more for ego stroking. The negative ones usually are in the vein of 'you suck,' which doesn't help, either."

To test the social media waters more deeply, I responded to a pitch from a consultant who sends out "thirty ways to get clients through social media" e-newsletters. When I asked him for specifics on what kind of projects his designer clients get by using his tips, there was a lengthy silence and a quick sign-off. I hope the answer isn't "none."

Rick Landers advises that while the primary audience of most design-related social networking sites is other designers, not clients, the more traffic or views they get, the more prominent your work can become in an online search. And that could be their greatest value.

Many designers are having more success with Behance, a well-designed, easy-to-use portfolio site. The Anagrama partners attribute a lot of their success to the buzz started via Behance "appreciations."

"Behance takes the guesswork out of how to organize work and concentrates the focus on the visuals and accompanying copy/explanation, the thinking behind the work," says Esteban Pérez, who recently earned his MFA in communication design from Pratt Institute and is now a senior designer at Suka Creative. "The interface fades back, so the actual work becomes the point of focus. But what really has made Behance work for me," he adds, "is the ability to view the plethora of creative talent, share the creative process with peers, comment on other's work, and 'appreciate' projects." Pérez says that he's gotten more than half a dozen inquiries from qualified clients.

Specific Platforms for Specific Needs

Without Facebook, how would we know what our friends around the world are doing? And wish them happy birthday? But does posting a clever status update bring in new clients? I wouldn't count on it.

Facebook, however, can spread a great idea like wildfire.

In Johannesburg, South Africa, Mohammed Jogie and Jacques Lange, organizers of the Mandela Poster Project, hoped to get ninety-five designers to submit posters in honor of Nelson Mandela's ninety-fifth birthday in July 2013. They started a Facebook group and a Google+ community and posted their own designs and those of a few colleagues. Posters started pouring in.

"Facebook was an ideal platform to create excitement and participation because designers could follow the project 'live' and see how it unfolded in a very transparent manner," Lange says. "Because of the general high standard of work posted, each new contribution inspired another. We could clearly see that the most exceptional submissions immediately sparked a flood of more contributions." In a few weeks, more than 700 extraordinary posters expressing themes of freedom and social justice in homage to "Tata Madiba" had come in from around the world. The exhibition, created to raise money to build a children's hospital in South Africa, attracted worldwide media attention and is traveling to six countries.

Graphic designer, game developer, and "geek's geek" Michael Pinto is considered one of the founders of Silicon Alley. He paused from working 24/7 on a new PBS Kids game site to tell me about his social media philosophy, which is that each platform can open up doors if you are offering the right kind of service and can find the right kind of audience.

"The key with any social media site is to identify what works well on that platform," he explains. "As a visual designer, I get frustrated with Twitter because it's all about text and they do a good job of hiding photos from casual viewers. However, if you're an aspiring copywriter (or politician or movie star), you may find Twitter the perfect vehicle for sharing snappy text updates that get the attention of the people you want to interact with online. Instagram is a good platform if you do photography, fashion design, or fine art that has a street-art attitude. For those creatives, it's a way to build a mass following of fans who may buy products directly from you. But due to the limitations of the faux-retro format, it could be a poor tool for a designer who is promoting web design, information graphics, or anything that involves a great deal of detail."

"And don't forget old-school digital tools like e-newsletters," Pinto adds. "They are a great way to do client outreach and tickle prospects who might not have worked with you in a while." Pentagram and other top firms send out an e-newsletter with "new work" every month. "Many designers make the mistake of spending too much time being distracted by shiny new objects before they attend to the basics," he warns, "which is building your own site, a platform over which you have 100 percent control, which looks professional, and to which you can easily add new work."

Linking In

One thing for sure: a LinkedIn profile does help. It is your bona fide résumé and a valuable reference source. Without it, it's almost like you don't exist. As a design journalist, I use it almost daily to check affiliations and job titles. And I've been noticing for a long time that potential clients do check you out before asking for a proposal. "In the digital world we live in, potential clients like to do their homework before reaching out to contact you in person," says Rick Landers, "so having positive reviews or endorsements on LinkedIn can help build your reputation and give you additional credibility."

But even LinkedIn is not a magic bullet. As Pinto notes, "LinkedIn is a great research tool if you want to identify clients who work at specific companies. But it's a poor outreach tool. If you network on LinkedIn enough, you may find the name of a marketing director at a large company who could use your services. However, that's only the starting point; you'll need to find a way to contact him or her by sending something via snail mail or by making an old-fashioned cold call."

Why Not Just Pick Up the Phone?

For many people, cold calling is terrifying. Why open yourself up to rejection? Other people learn to enjoy it and make it part of their routine. "I'm never too busy to make ten calls a day," says Sue Karlin, whose successful cold-call techniques were the subject of an article in *Crain's*. And as Michael Pinto just pointed out, even if you identified a prospect online, you've still got to take the direct route and pick up the phone.

In his columns as editor of the late, lamented *Critique* magazine and in speeches at conferences, Marty Neumeier, director of transformation at Liquid Agency, a San Francisco brand consultancy, excoriates designers for wasting time doing "indirect" things that he says don't work—like designing fancy capabilities brochures for themselves—instead of just picking up the phone and asking for an appointment.

"Marty," I said, "I have several questions. First, people are fed up with cold calls, so how can you get through their lines of defense? Second, how do you determine whom to call? Third, what do you say when you finally get the prospect on the phone? That can be a paralyzing moment."

Neumeier is one of the smartest and most experienced people around when it comes to these things. "There's a huge difference between telemarketing and legitimate introductory phone calls," he says, "Sure, there's voice mail and the spam filter, and a million other ways to screen you, like a receptionist saying 'We don't give out that information.' I take that as a challenge," he asserts. "I go to the company's site and find out who's who. I call and ask for that person. I keep trying until I catch him or her. One secret is 'super Thursday.' We've found that you can get through to more people on Thursday than on any other day of the week.

"And when you do get through, have your story ready," he advises. Here is a story that Neumeier has found effective:

"You don't know me, but I think we may have some common ground. I

called you specifically because your company is one of the organizations we want to work with. There's no hurry, but in the future, I'd like to present some research we've done on your category/industry/market. I think you'll find it eye-opening."

He says, "The whole idea is to connect the dots between your design capabilities and your prospect's business goals."

Before founding *Critique*, Neumeier made his mark by designing packaging for companies like Apple, Hewlett-Packard, and Symantec. In those days, his firm's presentation was a slide show called "22 Ways to Sell More Software." He maintains: "Design means nothing to clients. Demonstrate how your work will lead to concrete business outcomes. If you can't tell that story, it's probably because you don't have it straight in your own mind. You need to start there."

Have a Focus, Real Work that Proves It, and Show It to Them in Person

How can you get their attention? Get that meeting? What if you've never done anything like design packages that jump into consumers' shopping carts? "Have a focus, a specialty," advises Neumeier. "The last thing anyone needs is another generalist. Build your pitch around what you have done or can do that is unique."

"Find a niche," echoes Providence, Rhode Island, designer Tyler Smith, who made his mark in the men's fashion industry (chapter 16). "Focus on a vertical niche, whether it's menswear like me, or design for restaurants or travel companies. Then you'll have a fighting chance."

Then, if you do get through to the right person on the phone, the likely response might be, "Send me something."

Is "send me something" just a way of blowing you off? Maybe. But do it anyway. Email your "best of the best" PDF—a tantalizing taste of what you can do—and a link to your site. Then ask for that meeting. It's so tempting these days to start working without even meeting the client.

I can't emphasize enough that, if it's at all possible, get in the car, on the train, or, if the job's important enough, on a plane, and meet the client in person. Establishing that personal relationship will make all the difference—even if, later on, almost all your communication is via email. In fact, I was once in competition with the very same Tyler Smith for a project for a Boston professional services firm. I FedEx'd our proposal. Tyler got in his car, delivered his in person, and met the partners. Guess who got the job.

And when you get there, show real work that relates to their industry, stuff that shows in more detail what you've already demonstrated online—whether it's marketing materials for other companies with similar business issues or a laptop presentation of your interactive work. I've found that if potential clients like what they see, you can end the show-and-tell after three or four pieces. They've seen enough of what you've done for someone else. If they like you and your work, they want to know right away what you can do for them. "Focus on the project as soon as possible," stresses Neumeier. Quit selling and start listening.

What about Salespeople?

It's every designer's fantasy. Someone else will do all this. You stay in your atelier all day long, *creating*, while an experienced, persuasive yet sensitive account executive/salesperson scopes out all the big projects at major client organizations and brings in the bacon. He or she knows exactly how to research the opportunities, set up meetings, show work, write proposals, price, close sales, and manage projects. If you find the right person, your firm will grow and prosper like gangbusters. It just takes a little patience and an initial investment.

I've tried it—twice—and can only, sadly, report that it didn't work. To make a very long story short, salespeople (at least those I carefully interviewed and had high hopes for) are expensive, spend a lot of your money, and don't bring in enough work or even the right kind of work. Why not? The straight answer (and many designers have found this to be true): clients want to meet *you*. They will accept account executives at big ad agencies and the largest branding firms. They hire smaller design firms precisely because they want to work directly with "creatives." In fact, they feel insulted if the person whose name is on the door doesn't personally come in to meet them.

Taking the time to meet a qualified new prospect doesn't mean that you look too hungry for work. It means that you care. "What you have to do back at the office perhaps can be delegated to someone else," advises Kathleen Zann, former manager of marketing communications for James River Corporation. "But I insist on meeting the principal."

The late, great New York multimedia phenomenon Hillman Curtis, author of *MTIV (Making the Invisible Visible): Process, Inspiration and Practice for the New Media Designer*, told me that he was never too busy to go out and meet prospects himself. His advice: Get major clients on board at initial meetings by discussing themes that express the essence of what they are trying to accomplish. Bring a laptop presentation with examples of past successes, which could include a style guide and a motion spot. "What I focus on is the client's current site or ad campaign," he said. "I talk about their identity, their story, their brand, and suggest ways we might support them, about thematic directions we might take."

No one else could do this for him.

A salesperson can only "present." You can provide a taste of what it's like to work with you—something only you can do.

Getting Started (Here's When Volunteer Work Is a Good Idea)

What if you're just starting out? You've been working for a design firm or ad agency or in-house for a few years and think you're ready to strike out on your own. The problem is, you haven't been totally responsible for designing anything you could claim actually helped any organization accomplish anything. Everything in your portfolio is still school assignments or projects you assisted on . . . and maybe you don't even like the stuff anymore. But, hey, that job paid the rent. What to do?

I always keep my eyes open for a deserving nonprofit organization with a horrible logo. It won't be too hard to find. It could be a health-related charity or a local arts organization. Redesigning the logo will be given as a class assignment. The client will be contacted and informed that the organization can get a new, student-designed logo—if they provide a short, honest critique of each of about twenty logos, and, should one of them be chosen, pay the student an honorarium of at least $250 (this teaches both the client and the students that work is never "free"). I lead the students through the identity process, from defining image characteristics based on the client profile through creating and presenting an effective symbolic mark to designing collateral—letterhead, signage, home page, T-shirt.

This assignment ensures that each graduate has at least one valid designer-client experience and "real"-appearing assignment in his or her port-folio. It was developed in response to the continuous lament: "Everybody is looking for experience. How can I get it?"

Creating an opportunity where none existed is a smart way to get it.

If you are lacking in experience (but not in talent or drive), take the initia-tive. You don't have to be a student and get a class assignment! Create work for yourself. Don't wait for it to come to you.

Demonstrate What You Can Do

Somebody you know, or whom your parents or friends know, runs a business or organization that could use your services. Show them a mix of your best school assignments and fantasy projects you've created to show what you can do. Listen, really listen, to what they need. Offer your work at an irresistible price (but again, not for free). Show what you can do with type and royalty-free images and black-and-white photocopies. Start growing your reputation the way Fallon McElligott Rice did (chapter 20): do a knockout newspaper ad for the laundromat or barbershop or a compelling poster for the food bank or day-care center. If it's a religious or charitable organization or other cause you believe in, volunteer your services. Take former Fallon art director Dean Hanson's smart advice: "That strategy has worked since the beginning of the industry. I've never met a good creative that didn't follow this route to some degree."

And make sure your portfolio is consistent. Yesterday, I got an emailed portfolio that contained a few of each of the following: typography class assignments, costume designs for the theater, arty black-and-white photos, fake ads, and pencil drawings from Life Drawing I. We've all seen portfolios like that. They will never get you the job or the client you really want. If you truly want to be a successful graphic designer, roll up your sleeves and get to work. Make sure those fake ads look like they came from the pages of the art directors club annual (why not? there's no client holding you back). Make those costume designs into posters for the Metropolitan Opera. Turn the photos into CD jackets. Ditch the pencil drawings.

And please, show what *you* can do. Not what your instructors, your last boss, your roommate, or your partners in a group project can do. Make sure that the work you present is yours and yours alone. Make sure it represents what you are capable of doing without the previous boss, instructor, class-mates, or roommate. If you fake your way in, you'll soon be found out. Be honest and save your next boss or client—and yourself—the anguish of deal-ing with a difficult and embarrassing situation.

Why Not Become a Design Entrepreneur?
What if you think you can go it alone? You've got a great idea that can change the world. Why not, in addition to serving clients, become your own client? Find a need and fill it.

For more than ten years, I've been selling a line of manipulative materials that help teachers, tutors, and parents help kids—especially kids with learning difficulties—learn to read. I've made more money from the sale of Alphagram Learning Materials than from the total income from my firm's largest client. This has required, in addition to intensive research, meeting with experts around the country, sending mailings to targeted lists of districts and schools, and attending literacy conferences—actually manning a table, meeting teach-ers and parents, and direct-selling.

If you have the fortitude to engage in activities like those, you might want to join the growing number of graphic designers who are becoming entrepre-neurs, in addition to doing their client work. As just one example, Lizzy Showman, a 2013 graduate of the MFA Design ("Designer as Author") program at the School of Visual Arts, is starting two companies, a nonprofit dedicated to inner-city youth athletics, and blueprintregistry.com, an innovative wedding registry platform.

Taking a different but equally valid road, Janet Cummings and Peter Good (chapter 23) transformed a decrepit piece of real estate in the village of Chester, Connecticut, into a stop on the tourist itinerary that includes their design studio, a gallery where they sell their posters, calendars, note cards, and other printed ephemera, and a chic fashion and accessories boutique.

The most successful new companies grow out of a need, and if there is a real need you think you can fill, a good starting point is the book, *The Design Entrepreneur: Turning Graphic Design Into Goods That Sell* by Steve Heller and Lita Talarico, founders and cochairs of the SVA MFA Design program.

Be Upbeat, No Matter What

There have been outstanding years for this business. And horrible ones. My firm and many others survived at least two stock market crashes. Many of us rode through the dot-com boom (when it seemed as if the MBAs and techies were getting a lot of the big-paying business that graphic designers didn't know how to sell). Then we rode through the dot-com crash (when some of the interactive-design companies that had done so spectacularly went bankrupt, along with their clients). We were just entering a slow, hopeful recovery when 9/11 happened. And then came The Recession.

If there's any immutable truth about business, it's that things are always changing. Fifteen years ago, we couldn't have predicted that every organization in the world would need a website and a design firm to develop and launch it, and that they would now need tablet and phone apps. Who knows what will happen next?

Attitude has a lot to do with getting business. Even in a down market, project a positive attitude. Get out there. Take credit for your successes. Let them think your calendar is full. After all, it might be, tomorrow.

Once You've Met Them, How to Get Clients to Give You Work

(and How to Get Paid for That Work)

If this book had been written a few decades ago, the word "money" would rarely appear. One did not mention money when discussing the august design firms of the 1970s and '80s. When a client engaged the services of a designer, the "deliverables" were quality and originality. In design classes at UCLA, when we learned about the work of Charles and Ray Eames and Alexander Girard and Saul Bass, it was understood that their clients were looking to capture a unique talent and vision.

Today, a client's first question is usually, "How much will it cost?" And it's not just for informational purposes. It's to see if you're willing to do it at a low price—or to begin a competitive bidding or bargaining session. A guide to clients, by definition, has to be a guide to positioning and pricing your work so you will *have* clients.

You Have to Provide Something They Can't Do In-house

Quite simply, in order for you to get business, clients have to believe in you. And believe that you can do something that they can't do—or shouldn't spend their time doing.

More and more, in the quest to save money, clients devise in-house "solutions" that involve using administrative staff and standard templates. It's not uncommon to see the owner of a small company trying to make ads, and the founder of a nonprofit attempting to lay out the newsletter. A wise management consultant might suggest that their time would be better spent growing the company, marketing products, contacting and cultivating donors—fulfilling their core missions. Most larger organizations have a staff for in-house layout and production. To justify hiring you, they have to believe you can do something that no one else can.

"Today, we've got to do the hard stuff," claims Peter Farago, principal of

Farago + Partners, a New York advertising and branding agency. "Clients will only pay for what they can't do themselves." Farago, whose clients call him one of the smartest and most creative people they've ever met (see chapter 12), realizes that these days everybody can (or thinks they can) design a page, use a template to make a simple website, get a picture from an online stock photo agency, or get a logo designed via a crowdsourcing site for $99. What can't they do? Create interactive experiences that will keep users coming back. Brand every aspect of a consumer's experience.

"We've got to keep doing the same things we've always done," says Farago. "Tell stories. Tell the client's stories. But in new ways, with new tools."

Competing in the Crowdsourced World

If you offer a service they can do in-house, price is usually the biggest consideration. Or, put another way, the usual reason not to use in-house people is price: "If outsourcing is cheaper, let's go with a vendor," clients reason. If you provide a commodity item, like page layout, you can find yourself working cheap. And being treated like a vendor. Or worse, like a lackey. Meaning you're expected to sit at your computer and make corrections all day.

Google "web design" and you get 1,580,000 results. Google "logo design" and you get 995,000 results, including many like this (a few details changed):

> **$24.95 - Logo Design - 24 Hrs   1(800)123-4567**
> www.logo.com/Custom-Logo-Design
> **Unlimited Custom Logo Designs By 240 Designers in 24 Hours!**

How do you compete with that? I don't need to tell you that at any given time, dozens of potential clients are soliciting online bids for identity and stationery and web design, for prices that are more in line with dinner for two than for a significant design project.

Why should clients do anything more than visit crowdsourcing sites and sit back until they're "100 percent satisfied?" All in the anonymous, faceless, universe of the Internet. No temperamental artists to deal with, who'll want to argue or might leave the office in tears if a design is rejected.

Here's the thing, though. What they're getting is probably not original art. Most evidence points to the fact that many crowdsourced logos are made from stolen parts. And stolen parts can mean lawsuits from the copyright owners. Honestly, what smart client wants that?

Jeff Fisher, a veteran Seattle-area designer and principal of Jeff Fisher LogoMotives, has been the victim of numerous rip-offs. He uses Facebook and blogs to speak out against the ills of crowdsourcing. He writes:

> With online crowdsourcing or "contest" activities, submitted designs are posted for all to see. I've often seen those presented ideas blatantly appropriated by other

participants and then submitted as their own "original" designs. Some less-talented designers simply rip off existing, published designs of other design professionals and submit the designs as their own. Through Google Image Search, or the keen eyes of other design professionals, rip-offs of my logo designs—including my logos with no alterations at all—have been found on crowdsourcing sites. I've also seen many cases of participants merely changing the name or colors of a design that was rejected in one "contest" and resubmitting it in another one. How can any of these scenarios be in the best interest of the designer or the client? For the vast majority of participants, there is no compensation at all. And these "clients" are getting exactly what they should expect for trying to have their design projects produced on the cheap and the quick.

There's room in our economy for work done at all levels, and some people get started or keep busy by "competing" to "win" by doing many small projects posted online. But the general consensus is that the vast majority of the work is done in South Asian logo mills where technicians have access to huge libraries of clip art, much of it consisting of stolen parts from work that was published in design annuals, books, and legitimate sites like logolounge.com.

And if the parts weren't stolen, maybe the concept or style was. Someone very close to me, who shall remain anonymous, recently crowdsourced the logo design for his Internet start-up. Yes, he said, it was a time-consuming process, and he had to wade through a lot of junk. But he ultimately got something that at first appeared to be a well-drawn, charming, lime-green character. I was pleasantly surprised. Until I saw the character "Mike" in ads for "Monsters University." The "designer" had ripped off Disney and Pixar.

Beware. Don't set yourself up for a costly infringement lawsuit.

Here is the answer. If you truly are a professional designer, you *can't* compete in the crowdsourced world. No one interviewed for this book, even the fresh-out-of-school designers, ever does. If someone you know is thinking about crowdsourcing, report the facts. He or she wouldn't ride a bicycle made of stolen parts. Why identify the organization they're working so hard to build with stolen ideas? And why hire "a pair of cheap digital hands," as Michael Pinto puts it, rather than someone who will be an essential player on the strategic and creative team?

Some brave designers are actually doing something about it. Felix Sockwell, the creator of the icons in this book, recently noticed that the logo of a favorite local café looked suspiciously like a famous Louise Fili restaurant logo. Yes, he learned, the owners had paid $24.95 to an overseas company that promised dozens of options—and delivered a knockoff. Rather than complain about it, Felix sat down with the owners, explained the process, presented options, and ultimately designed a distinctive, original identity. "We all learned a lesson here," he says. "They got swindled at first, but they came around and even paid my full fee, some of which I'll spend at the café." Bravo, Felix!

Ask for the Money!

Superstar attorney Gerry Spence, author of *How to Argue and Win Every Time*, writes, "Everywhere I go, lawyers ask, 'How do you get those big-money verdicts?' I reply that I simply ask for the money. I tell the jury what I want. It seems that the more we want something, the more hesitant we are to ask for it."

You've got to ask for the money in this business, too. Okay, it's not the big money personal injury lawyers ask for. But why not at least ask for enough to keep the business running and make a little profit? Why are we so reluctant to do it? We love what we do. We are still amazed sometimes that people pay us. We will do almost anything for the opportunity. And then we get angry and feel exploited when we realize we've made a bad deal.

My son, Alex Miller, spent a summer in New Orleans soliciting donations door-to-door for the Sierra Club. They taught him to ask for the money. He and other college students went there for the food, jazz, and beer, but they learned lessons about life and doing business, doled out in daily, two-hour, role-playing sessions. Before the students knocked on the first door of the day, the trainers corrected their mistakes from the day before and made sure they had the pitch down cold: "It's great to know you feel the same way we do about big oil companies polluting the Gulf of Mexico," they were coached to say. "We really appreciate your $25 membership in the Sierra Club. But, you know, if you gave $50 or $75, we could accomplish so much more."

You're already there. You have a willing, sympathetic customer. Seven people have slammed the door in your face. This one believes in your cause. He or she is on your side. The checkbook is out. The pen is poised. Ask for more money! What's there to lose?

But in design, if you ask for too much, they could go somewhere else. They very likely will, in fact, if your fee is too high. It's not like getting the $50 instead of the $25. It could mean getting all the way there, to the proposal stage, and getting nothing.

First, Find Out What They Want

Before you ask for the money, you have to know what they want and how much they are willing to spend. This isn't always easy. But remember what Gerry Spence advises: "Tell them what you want."

"I want to do this job for you."

"I will do an excellent job."

"Here's how much I need: $10,000." Or "$50,000."

Ah, but the client wants to spend $5,000. Or $25,000. The budget is set. And they haven't told you because it's a competitive bidding situation.

Here's a typical (losing) scenario: You meet a potential new client team. You show your work. You seem to hit it off. They seem interested, too. Great! You find out as much as you can about what the company is trying to accomplish. They describe their aspirations and goals. You can visualize the solution in your head. It will be beautiful! You can already see it on the pages of the design magazines. Everyone on Behance will "appreciate" it. It's not only a splendid design idea, it will make the client billions of dollars. A win-win situation. You offer to write a proposal and have it delivered the next week. They agree. You leave the meeting aglow. You spend three days on what you think is a dazzling proposal. Then you never hear from them again. Or, if they are unusually etiquette-conscious, they write: "While we appreciate your most interesting proposal, we've decided to utilize the services of another vendor."

What happened?

You forgot to ask how much they had to spend. I know it's tough. I know they don't want to tell you. But don't operate on hopes, wishes, fantasies. Get as much real information as possible. Here are some questions to try (before wasting days of your life):

"Do you want to work with me?"

Maybe the answer is no, as they discovered upon meeting you, for one of a dozen reasons. But they politely agreed to the proposal. Why not? Company policy requires three proposals. Why not get one from you, since you offered?

"Is this a competitive bidding situation?"

Find out.

"Who else are you talking to?"

Maybe they'll tell you.

"What do I have to do to get this job?"

You really want the answer to that one.

"Are you looking for the best price, or are there other considerations?"

Face it. Almost everyone is looking for a good price, as long as their other considerations are met. Maybe they want a larger firm, a smaller firm, someone with more experience in their industry, or even (to avoid any perceived conflict of interest) someone with less experience in their industry.

How Do You Know What to Charge?

That's always the toughest question, a challenge for even the most seasoned designers. It's a combination of instinct, figuring out what the market will bear, and setting rates that will cover your overhead and maybe even make a little profit.

If your prices are too high, especially in smaller markets, you won't get enough work to stay in business. And if your prices are too low, savvy clients won't think you're experienced enough to be working for them.

Why aren't we as valued as the legendary Paul Rand, who reportedly charged Steven Jobs $100,000 for the logo for the NEXT computer. Rand gave Jobs one solution, neatly documented in a hand-bound book that demonstrated how he arrived at the solution. Obviously, to some clients, low price is not the goal. Thankfully, an increasing number of them do consider design an essential service, like law, accounting, and management consulting, for which they pay professional hourly rates, retainers, and consulting fees. Other clients are still learning. And we have to help teach them.

Formulas for determining prices are beyond the scope of this book, but you can consult a number of reliable sources, including the *Graphic Artists' Guild Handbook of Pricing and Ethical Guidelines*, which lists projects by type and client size and suggests a range from "low" for smaller, newer firms to "high" for larger, more established firms. That's because when you're first starting out, you can't charge what the big guys do.

"It's never easy," admits a talented designer who started her firm just three years out of school. "I look at the client's budget and the value of the project; whether it will be good creatively and give me good experience. Later on, I might be able to be a little more demanding."

For more specific direction, Tad Crawford, publisher at Allworth Press, recommends his imprint's *The Graphic Designer's Guide to Pricing, Estimating, and Budgeting* by Theo Stephan Williams.

Set Your Limits

It's important to set your threshold and not go below it, no matter how much the economy has tanked or how seductive the client and project seem. If $1,500 is the lowest price you can charge for a logo design, stick to it. It's a matter of self-esteem, as well as what economists call the "opportunity cost." The time you spend slaving on the $300 logo can be better spent looking for the client who will pay five times that much. You want a client who will come back for more of the right kind of work, not for more too-cheap work. You want the client's colleagues and friends to know about you—that you do great work, not that you charge low prices. You want them to know that your fees are fair and reasonable, given the effort you expend on their behalf and the value you bring to the table. Thus, it's just as important for you to qualify the client as it is for the client to ensure that you meet his or her organization's qualifications.

Keep asking questions:

"How much do you want to spend?"

"We don't know. We're waiting for bids." That might mean they're waiting to see if they can get the dazzling Jaguar S-Type-R for the Honda Civic price.

"Will you go for the lowest bid?

If the answer is really yes, policy requires we go with the lowest bid, this might be the right time to shake hands and part company, even if it hurts. There will always be a lower bid.

What is your range?

This is probably the most important question. Let them know, gently and tactfully, if you are out of their range. If they are impressed by you and your work, maybe there will be a higher range for the next project.

Not long ago, I neglected to ask the "What are you looking for?" question of a glamorous New York nonprofit organization that called about a public-awareness campaign. I spent several days on a "brilliant" proposal, which I presented in person. I never heard from them again. Why? I didn't ask that key question and make sure I got an honest answer. They were looking for a pro bono agency that would work for free, ostensibly in order to get samples for their portfolio. The client kept their cards hidden, as smart players do. Right now, there might be a dozen brilliant proposals on the director's desk, chock-full of ideas they can get their pro bono agency to execute for free.

Are you shocked? Please. The media are packed with news about the illegal and unethical activities of corporations, including manipulating accounting procedures to show profits when there are losses, creating elaborate ruses to avoid paying taxes or to boost the value of stock, and falsely stating profits to lure or mislead investors. And then hiding the truth and the evidence of their wrongdoing. And let's not forget companies like the toy and clothing and tobacco makers that exploit third-world labor, or market products that cause illnesses and injuries.

And you expect them to be 100 percent forthright and honest and fair with you, one of their *graphic designers?*

Make Sure You're Getting Paid Before You Start

"Before I begin working" are the key words. The biggest disappointments I've had in this business, the most emotional moments, happened when I thought I was working for a client (and should have been getting paid) and the client thought (or said they thought) I was merely marketing services, a part of the "free" process of generating new business.

There are a lot of tactics used to get you to start working before they commit to pay you. And even more tactics for backing out of the "promise" afterward with a sincere-sounding explanation that circumstances have changed beyond their control:

"Don't worry. Your contract is in legal, but we need to see something by next week."

"I'm sure you'll be the one, but I need you to meet another group of managers. Can you just bring along something to show them what you have in mind?"

"If you do it this time, there will be a lot more work down the road."

"I just need something visual I can show my boss."

"I'm leaving for Mexico City tomorrow and need to take it with me. We'll sign your agreement when I get back."

Boys in high school didn't have nearly as many successful pickup lines. Clients know how to seduce us. We should be the ones seducing them.

And it's not limited to graphic designers. A management consultant profiled in *Crain's New York Business* said that her biggest problem was making sure she didn't end up spending three hours in a Starbucks every day telling potential clients everything she'd learned over her entire education and career. "I tell them I provide one hour of complimentary consultation," she said. "After that, my time is billed."

We're in The Zone the minute we hear about an assignment. We live and breathe design 24/7. We want to transmit that excitement to the client. It's so tempting to include just one little comp in the proposal, to sketch an idea at the meeting table. It can be even more tempting when a potential client dangles the promise of a big, exciting, juicy new job in front of you—if you agree to provide a few free ideas first.

The rules of thumb (repeat after me) are: Ask for the money. Never work on spec. Get one-third up front; one-third after you make your initial creative presentation, and one-third when the project is completed.

As Grandma Used to Say, They'll Never Buy It If You Give It Away

Sure, big ad agencies invest many thousands of dollars in speculative presentations to get new business. But (a) they have research departments; (b) they often get paid for the presentation; and (c) millions of dollars in fees and commissions are usually at stake. Whether design clients are capitalizing on this "industry practice" or are just curious or greedy, they will sometimes ask design firms—who might be paid $3,000 to $30,000 for the entire job—to undertake a similar speculative process.

Don't do it. Just say no.

I am telling you this from personal experience, and from many other designers' personal experiences, as reported in magazine articles, letters to editors, conferences, workshops, and anguished late-night phone calls. It just doesn't work. Even if you "win"—i.e., get the job, which is questionable —

it won't work out. Why? Quite simply, the client knows you can be pushed around. If you do this much for free now, you will do that much more for free later. Everything that happens in the relationship will be a problem. Besides, the most likely reason the client cooked up the spec competition in the first place was to get a bunch of free ideas to execute in-house. And by execute, I mean kill, butcher, exploit.

"Designers have to be very clear about how much of a solution they're willing to give before the client can make a decision," advises Robert Mouthrop, a marketing and communications specialist at leading financial service firms and nonprofits for more than twenty years. "You have to put a realistic price tag on yourself and your time," he says. "From the client's point of view, if you can get it for free, how much can it be worth?"

AIGA, the Professional Association for Design, has developed standards to "reflect conduct that is in the best interest of the profession, clients, and the public." The AIGA Standards of Professional Practice state:

> A designer shall not undertake any speculative projects, either alone or in competition with other designers, for which compensation will only be received if a design is accepted or used. This applies not only to entire projects but also to preliminary schematic proposals.

This language was developed after lengthy debate and a skirmish with the US Department of Justice, which objected to "possible restraint of trade." But restraining trade is not what this is about at all. It's about the value of professional services. It's about having the opportunity to gather all the information needed to develop an appropriate solution, not a superficial one.

According to AIGA executive director Ric Grefé: "Designers deserve the respect of their clients as trusted advisors on solving communication challenges with effect and creativity. The only way designers can achieve this is to share a common set of values that communicate the value of their work. Spec work undermines this ethic. The creative services that many advertising agencies give away in spec work is simply bargaining at the margin, not with their core intellectual property, like it is with ours. The only solution is for each designer to live up to the shared values and, together, educate the clients."

Even a proposal can be speculative, if too much is asked. On larger projects, designers should be expected to write a proposal that includes a fee estimate for professional services. It's unfair for clients to expect a total project price with detailed line-item production costs. Providing those numbers forces us to virtually design the job—before we've been given the opportunity to do the research that will lead to the right solution. Just say no to that, too. Indicate that you'll develop two or more approaches within the client's stated overall budget—after you receive the signed agreement and retainer.

That Doesn't Mean Money Is Always the Object

None of us want to be too hard-nosed. Money isn't the only object. There are times when, with the right client, a lower-paying or even pro bono project can be a meaningful, satisfying opportunity, worth more than a big fee.

"All of us must be dreamers," notes Jon Esser. "But we must also remain responsive to material constraints. The client engages you because of your knowledge and creative abilities. If you don't produce solutions, you won't last long in the field. But if you can't derive satisfaction from your work, you won't last long, either."

One of my firm's best-known projects, the "Channeling Children's Anger" logo, a scribble that transforms itself into a heart, designed by Terri Bogaards, was donated to the Institute of Mental Health Initiatives. We did it—as well as the invitations, posters, and T-shirt—for love, satisfaction, and to help a worthy cause. With a grant from Sappi Paper North America, we produced "Every Child Reading" guides for the International Dyslexia Association that were distributed to parents and teachers in the nation's most disadvantaged school districts. Every year, Sappi awards "Ideas That Matter" grants to designers who submit the best proposals for projects for nonprofit organizations. If there's anything that members of the design and advertising community have in common, it's willingness to donate their talents to worthy causes.

A Contract Is Essential

Whether you're doing a major project for a *Fortune* 500 corporation or a small job for a local nonprofit, a contract or working agreement is essential. It doesn't have to be long and complicated. It can be short and sweet. It can be part of your proposal, a page that sets out the terms and conditions of the relationship that, in retaining you, the client has agreed to.

Contracts are covered in detail in many other books, including *Business and Legal Forms for Graphic Designers* by Tad Crawford and Eva Doman Bruck, which has a CD-ROM of fifty-three customizable forms. Choose and use one of them. Tailor it to your own needs, but keep it simple and in plain English. If it looks like a commercial lease full of legalese, you might get a response like, "We have to send this to our attorneys for review." The idea is to use a document that clients will sign without protest or delay.

It's important that at least the following are covered: A description of the work you'll provide. The fee. What items are not included in the fee, such as out-of-pocket expenses, and how they will be billed. How the client will pay, and when. Who owns the rights. Clauses like client's responsibility for errors and omissions and for getting copyright clearances are important, too.

At a HOW Design Conference, I devoted a full session to explaining a model contract for services. Most of the audience members managed to stay awake, and actually followed attentively through an explanation and discussion of fifteen paragraphs, one by one. The questions afterward were revealing: "This is great, but how do I present it to my clients?" and "How do I get them to sign?" Many designers, apparently, are scared or embarrassed to be proffering something as crass as a contract. Suggestions like "send it to them" and "ask them" were met with resistance.

I suggested standing in front of a mirror and repeating:

"I need you to sign this before I begin working."

It sounded like more than a few people were too shy to do that. I hope they're getting paid.

Remember, You Are the Owner of the Work

Your contract doesn't need to cover every point that could possibly arise, and you shouldn't even try to go into that much detail. But the one paragraph you should never leave out, according to Julius Rabinowitz, an intellectual property attorney (and my husband), is the following:

> Upon payment of fees and expenses in full, [design firm name] will assign the copyright to the design you have selected, and any other copyrightable materials that we prepare, for any and all uses related to [describe the agreed-upon use], no geographical or time limitation [or describe the agreed-upon limitations]. You agree that our work under this agreement is not a Work Made For Hire.

Why is this paragraph so important? Without it, if the client doesn't pay, it's breach of contract, not so easy to prove. If you take the case to your local civil court, the client might start pointing out things about your work or service he or she is unhappy with, and you might end up settling for less than you deserve. With the paragraph in your contract, you own the copyright to the work until the client pays in full. Violating it, i.e., not paying for the work, is copyright infringement and potentially subjects the client to a significant amount of monetary damages and perhaps more importantly, to an injunction against further use. No client wants that.

Here's another, even more sure-fire way to get paid, especially if you do interactive work. Don't deliver until the money is in your bank account. Follow the lead of Cody Schatzle, head of Query Creative, in New Paltz, NY. Cody is a very accommodating web designer and programmer, except for one thing. He gets 50 percent up front and none of his clients' projects go live until the fee is paid in full. "My work is scratch-coded with HTML, CSS, PHP, MySQL, and Javascript," he says. "And I know my way around PayPal, too." The client approves the site on Query's server, and as soon as the second 50 percent arrives in Cody's PayPal account, the site gets migrated to the client's server. It's as simple as that. Who's got time to chase after the money, he asks. Not him. And not you, either, I bet.

And Yet, It's All Based on Trust

Julius recently reminded me about the conclusion of one of the first cases he won. When he asked the judge to rewrite the contract with "tighter" clauses so the infringer wouldn't be tempted to breach it again, the judge shared this bit of wisdom: "The greatest contract in the world can't take the place of the trust necessary in a successful relationship." If you don't trust that the other party will honor the contract, advises a much more experienced Julius, you shouldn't enter into it in the first place.

Before you send over your agreement, pay attention to what your gut is telling you. If you have any concerns about a client's take on certain issues—such as whether he or she really intends to pay in thirty days—don't conclude that a "tight" agreement will solve the problem. The client will conveniently forget the provision or say that he or she thought it meant something else.

Sit down and talk again, and try to establish that trust.

Be Fearless

Here are wise words from former AIGA president Debbie Millman. You've heard them from me, but they're even stronger summarized by the founder and chair of the Masters Program in Branding at the School of Visual Arts and president of the design division at Sterling Brands, where she advises such leading companies as Gillette, MTV, Nestle, and Pepsi.

Debbie's Top Ten List for Getting The Business You Want

1. Be fearless when asking people for business.
2. Find lots of potential clients . . . it's impossible to know which ones will be the best fit for you.
3. Work harder than anybody else that you know.
4. Never give up if it's something that you really want.
5. Don't lie about what you know and what you've done.
6. Don't be afraid to want a lot.
7. Things take a long time; practice patience.
8. Avoid compulsively making things worse.
9. Finish what you start.
10. Often people start out by thinking about all the things they can't do. Once you take that path, it's very hard to get off it. Shoot high and shoot often.

Keeping Clients Happy (and Coming Back for More)

you can get this far and still lose.

The contract can be signed and something can go wrong.

"They just didn't give us what we wanted," clients say.

"They got locked into one design idea, which we didn't think was right for us."

"After all that selling, they put junior people on the job."

"They didn't listen."

"The work was incomplete."

"It was late."

"There were too many surprises."

"They kept trying to sell us stuff that was too expensive."

"They didn't tell us what the changes would cost."

"There were problems with the fabrication (or functionality)."

Your bill (or a portion of it) gets paid and the client is already working with someone else.

Be Prepared to Meet All of Their Expectations

I created a teaching aid entitled, "What Design Directors and Firm Principals Do." It's a chart with five rows of boxes.

The top row is labeled "Preliminaries" and includes a box labeled, "Meet with client to discuss project and define audience, communications objectives, budget, delivery date." Another box is: "Ask probing questions; write and deliver or present proposal; negotiate proposal terms; get retainer and signed agreement." The second row is called "Concept Development" and includes "Research and determine specific, ideal content, format, look and feel, materials, and production techniques that will accomplish client's goals." I tell the students that this is all about understanding the client's business; not just doing what you think looks cool, expresses your personal feelings, or might win an "A" or the admiration of other designers and awards-show judges. The third and forth rows, "Design and Art Direction," includes "Select photographers, illustrators; give creative direction." The last row, "Production Supervision," includes boxes labeled, "Deliver errorless files to vendors," "Make sure the project gets fabricated or programmed correctly," and "Follow up on delivery."

"Where Do You Fit In?" asks the headline.

Many students are a bit stunned. For four years their efforts had been solely focused on the activities described in one or two boxes out of twenty-eight—creating designs with images and type, designs that please them and that express their feelings and opinions.

Clients expect more, I explain. You can't even begin designing until you understand the client's organization, what they're trying to accomplish. Then, if you screw up one or more of these other areas, the client may go somewhere else anyway, even if your creative concepts are excellent. (That's one reason it's a smart idea to start your career working at a firm where you can learn from experienced people, rather than as a freelancer.)

To keep clients happy—and keep them coming back for more—you have to meet or exceed expectations in all of these areas.

"If you don't have extraordinary, towering competence as a designer, you will not only not attract clients, you will lose the ones you have," warns Brian Collins, chief creative officer of COLLINS, a New York design and advertising firm that creates branded experiences for clients ranging from Hersheys to the New York Knicks. "Crowdsourcing sites are just the tip of the iceberg. In this emerging economy, you must be astonishing or you simply won't exist. Graphic design is becoming a commodity, but clients can and will go anywhere for great ideas."

Remember Who the Audience Is

Says Pentagram partner Michael Bierut: "When I was starting out, I thought I was the audience and the goal was to please myself. Then I got some experience and realized that clients were the audience and the goal was to please them. Of course, both these things are sort of true, but basically wrong. I finally realized that the real audience is the people out there in the real world who are going to be stuck with whatever it is that I'm designing. Often, there is no one to speak for those people during the design process. The more you can be their advocate, the better your design will be."

One technique I personally find helpful is to do informal market research to find out what resonates with the real audience that Michael is referring to. When I'm working on a logo project, for example, I'll take the six most promising concepts out into the field and gauge the responses. If the logo is for the local bank, I'll ask commuters waiting on the 8:16 a.m. train platform, "Which of these designs do you think is most appropriate for Local Federal Savings?" If it's for a company that runs farmers' markets, I'll send a PDF showing half a dozen potential solutions to the people I know who cook and appreciate produce that's fresh from the farm. The feedback helps me delete the concepts that aren't working and more finely hone those that are. When I present the two or three recommended directions, I'll have solid evidence to back them up, and can do so with conviction and passion.

In fact, besides talent and experience, passion is the word clients use most often when describing why they chose their designers. When asked why she chose Addis Creson (chapter 12), Revolution Foods chief experience officer Kirsten Tobcy responded, "The combination of their fantastic talent, their passion for our mission, and their experience with food packaging made it a really easy decision for us to work with them."

Talk the Talk

Students spend four or more years learning to talk about juxtapositions, imagery, irony. I surprise them when I suggest that they read the business press. The pages of the *Wall Street Journal, Bloomberg Businessweek*, and *Inc.* are where you learn to talk client talk. A senior designer or firm principal should be almost as comfortable discussing return on investment and sustainable competitive advantage as Garamond versus Caslon and Wordpress versus Drupal CMS.

You were hired to make the right choices. You should be able to justify those choices. And the answer should make business sense. It should not be about decoration. If the question is, "Why did you choose this approach?", "Because it looks cool" or "It's like this really awesome piece I saw" will always be the wrong answer. "Because it communicates the following characteristics of your organization" is more like it.

Impress them with your research. Show that you're on their team, that you've used the product or service (at the least, that you understand why the target market needs it), and that you will be a loyal champion and advocate.

And please don't fall into clichés associated with "flaky creatives." Don't miss deadlines. Show up on time, no, ten minutes early. Be prepared. Have the points you want to make down cold. Look and act businesslike.

But Don't Lay It On Too Thick

It's a long way from "because it looks cool" to "dynamic sensibility of vision" and "coherent yet multilayered visual message." Where did all the designer jargon come from? Once upon a time, in order to communicate with high-level executives and charge higher fees, proposal-writers at big-time corporate identity firms must have taken a look at *The Harvard Business Review* or *Artforum* and said, "Ah ha, here's how to do it." Great visual communications masters like Herb Lubalin and Saul Bass, if they were still among us, might not be able to recognize the epidemic of verbiage that resulted. As just one example, I found this in an article about a new institutional logo:

> The contemporary and dynamic geometric asymmetry of the color planes sit in contrast to the elegant academic tradition of the classic typeface. Distinct negative/positive relationships invite the viewer to complete the message by attributing form and meaning to negative space. This exchange makes the mark more memorable. The chosen colors … achieve a pleasant, yet energetic high-contrast interaction that communicates clarity and determination.

Heaven help us. I mean, it's an okay logo. And sure, a successful solution needs a bit more documentation than "Because we dig the way it looks." But let's not gag clients with pages of purple bureaucratese. Graphic design is a visual art. Most intelligent people can see if something works or not, looks good or not, right away. That's the whole point. The flowery rationale isn't going to be there when a future customer looks at the thing, scratches his head, and asks, "What the hell is that supposed to be?"

And, by the way, the correct grammar is: "*asymmetry* (singular) *sits.*" I don't mean to sound cantankerous, but when you write, make sure your subjects and verbs agree. Try to follow the advice of Strunk and White in their classic *The Elements of Style*, a must for every reference shelf:

> Write in a way that comes naturally. Omit needless words. Do not overstate. Do not explain too much. Do not inject opinion. Be clear.

Presentations That Speak for Themselves

The most successful designers know how to present work in a way that is not only clear, that not only "sells," but that begins and continues a dialogue with the client.

Ed Gold has identified what he calls "the ten common characteristics of great designers."

After "talent" ("their work flat-out looks good"), Ed ranks "advocacy" as the number-two necessary characteristic. "A designer who can't sell an idea is probably not going to be very successful," he says, adding, "I'll go a step further. A designer who can't sell an idea will never be a great designer." Ed advises all designers to take courses in persuasion and presentation.

As you've probably experienced, there is nothing less inspiring than a portfolio presentation in which a job candidate recites in a monotone: "This is a piece I did for so-and-so; this is a piece I did for so-and-so." It's equally depressing to clients when designers start explaining how they used type or images. The results are there right in front of their eyes.

As Hillman Curtis cautioned in *MTIV*, "Never, never, never sell your design. You should be able to lay out your comps in front of clients, and if you have heard them, stayed true to their desires, and included them in your creative process, the designs will speak for themselves. You can stay quiet, answer their questions if necessary, and listen to their feedback. Take notes and bring it closer on the next rev[ise]." Curtis wrote that he always tells his designers that if they find themselves saying things like, "We used Helvetica because it's simple yet strong," they haven't done their jobs.

I have been preaching the same thing for years. You, the designer, won't be there when the reader opens the brochure, turns the page, clicks on the link, or sees the logo or ad for the first time. Like the student portfolio, if it needs an explanation, something's wrong. Verbal pyrotechnics and even reams of support documentation can't transform an unsuccessful design into one that works.

What about Lunches, Dinners, and All That?

Taking clients to lunch used to be part of my routine. From The Four Seasons to Asia de Cuba, sushi bars to Indian buffets, I was out at least twice a week with clients and prospective clients. Not any more. No one has time. Me included. Expensive lunches might seem almost decadent in this environment. Before I decided to move my office out of New York City, I kept a diary of how I spent my days: At my computer ten hours a day, five days a week. Six of the ten talking on the phone and emailing stuff back and forth. A few client meetings a week—at their offices. A quick bite at a salad bar, sandwich place, or my desk. Could do that from anywhere and save all that commuting time—and rent.

Is there a place in business today for wining and dining? Some designers and clients say yes. Others no. "I might be more successful if I did more of that," muses Drew Hodges. "But it seems like nobody wants me to take them to lunch. Everyone's too busy."

Michael Mabry, identified in one national survey as "the most influential graphic designer in the United States," says that he wouldn't even want to have lunch with most clients he's met over the years. "Clients should be people you want to go to dinner with. But it's very, very rare." Mabry, who moved his office from San Francisco to Emeryville, California, to be closer to home and family, has been somewhat pessimistic on the subject of clients for years. "Companies that I thought I liked disappointed me too much," he confesses. "Once you get into the inner workings, you see arrogance, lack of vision, fear of the CEO, unwillingness to try new things." He found happiness, though, working for children's furnishings retailer and cataloguer The Land of Nod. He even likes to have lunch with the principals. "The company was founded by two friends," he explains. "It's a joy to work with them and go out with them. This has never happened before, but it's a real natural thing to spend time with them, to share a meal, to watch TV with their kids. In a perfect world, that's what all client relationships would be like."

Foes or Friends?

True, in a perfect world, more clients and designers would be friends, rather than wary adversaries, each trying to hold onto his or her vision of the project while the other tries to "ruin" it.

In the Chicago suburb of Dundee, Illinois, Samata LLC principal Pat Samata says that she and husband/partner Greg Samata work hard to nurture client relationships that turn into friendships. "I can't tell you how many times I've said, 'This friend of mine, she's a client, she's also a friend,'" says Pat. Instead of traditional client entertainment based on wining, dining, and tickets to sports events, clients might be invited to supper at the Samata home, sharing a bottle of wine that Greg uncorks while the kids are running around the table. "We wouldn't want to work with anybody we wouldn't want for a friend," Pat adds, describing how the partners chose to resign the firm's highest-billing account because the client was "chewing up the staff for breakfast." She explains, "Nobody wanted to pick up the phone. Life is too short for that."

Adds Marcia Lausen, "Design is a life-consuming business. I can't think of a good friend who is not a colleague or a client. The client who becomes a true friend is easy to talk to about difficult things, such as money issues or a return to the drawing board. And because we're friends, we do talk. If I need money, I can say how much and why. They know I wouldn't ask if I didn't have to, and will give a short, straight answer like, 'Okay, that sounds fair,' 'Sorry, I can't get it,' or 'I'll see what I can do.' Business is great when it's like that."

A new client friendship can be tricky to handle at first. Should you extend that invitation to a Saturday-night dinner at your home or to your end-of-summer barbecue, or not? Will stepping over that line muddy the waters? Will knowing that the client has been in your kitchen, used your bathroom, or seen your three-year-old have a tantrum make it more or less difficult for you to bring up such issues as the invoice is fifteen days overdue? You have to feel your way through every situation. Occasionally, "very-good-friend" clients do give once-favored designers the brush-off after there is a business disagreement or "management decides to change vendors." Don't fool yourself; friendship is no guarantee you'll get all their work forever. And that can hurt. But many designers think it's worth it to attempt to become friends. Because, as

Lausen says, design is a life-consuming business and we want our good clients to become part of our lives.

Pamper Them

Consultants to the graphic design business claim that the number-one secret of success is to make clients feel pampered. And that doesn't just mean wining and dining them when appropriate. It means making them feel like you're 100 percent there for them.

Business consultant Maria Piscopo writes: "Clients are sometimes like children who need hand-holding. Indulging them without doing yourself a disservice promotes a relationship where they feel you are on their side." Adds Don Sparkman, a Washington, DC, design firm president and the author of *Selling Graphic and Web Design*, "A certain amount of coddling encourages clients to become repeat customers. Clients want to feel that you are their special designer, even if they work with other designers."

Correct. Clients also want to feel like they are your special client—even like your *only* client, while you're engaged in their projects—even though they know that isn't true, or even possible.

If it were only up to clients, you would always be at your desk when they call. They would get 100 percent of your undivided attention. You would never be in a hurry (except when doing something for them, of course). When the call is a request, the work would be finished and delivered, if not by 5:30 p.m. that day, by 8:59 a.m. the next morning. Every email would be answered within five (no, make that two) minutes. If a meeting is requested for tomorrow, your calendar would be wide open. Overall, you'd put in twice as much effort and attention as anticipated, and the bill would be 30 percent less than the estimate.

Realistic? Not exactly. But those designers who are able to create that illusion might be enjoying the greatest success.

Perhaps the interview in this book that comes closest to unlocking the secret is the one (chapter 14) that explores the relationship between Kit Hinrichs and the late Tom Wrubel, founder of The Nature Company. This client-designer partnership seemed to have it all. Hinrichs's identity, packaging, and catalogs for The Nature Company not only won a zillion design awards, they used the power of design to help build a single Berkeley store that sold field glasses and books about insects into a $90 million, international empire. The secret ingredient? Hinrichs and Wrubel drove around the Bay Area together and talked about life. Hinrichs was not a "vendor" or a "service provider" or even a "creative," but a trusted confidante and advisor. Nature Company merchandising and marketing manager Kathy Tierney has stated, "We won't have a meeting without him." Was that unique? Not for Hinrichs.

"It's not unique to the Nature Company," he says. "Tom and I spent a lot of time together. I was on retainer as a consultant, and we used to drive around to the stores together and spend hours talking. You can always do better work if you know the top person well. And, sure, you can be dedicated to more than one client."

What If the Client Really Needs Help?

Most clients are not like Tom Wrubel. Some, as you've probably learned, might not even know whether something is doable or even legal or advisable.

"Educating clients" is something we hear and talk about all the time. Accomplishing that successfully while keeping them happy is not easy. Most clients are pretty sure that they know what they're doing, and they resist being "educated," especially about basic stuff they don't know (the number of pages in a book has to be divisible by four), which would embarrass them, or stuff you think they should know (that in order for you to prepare an accurate estimate, they really do have to pin down how they need the site to function).

Even if you do everything right, sometimes it seems as if they don't appreciate the value of what they're getting. "An oxymoron is a grateful client," grouses agency chairman Allen Kay. His compatriot Peter Farago agrees, "Your clients can be just like your children, resentful, unappreciative." Adds Kay: "If we still had all the clients we had over the years, we'd be billing $2 billion."

But looking at things in a more positive light is the only way to keep sane—and to move forward. Les Daly, for thirty-three years vice president for public affairs at Northrop Corporation (chapter 11), advises that clients and designers are in a teamed situation, whether they like it or not, whether their experience levels are equal or not. Daly, who worked with many top design firms, says that designers who want to show clients the "right" way to do things should take it slowly.

"Let's look at the struggle of a designer with an average client who knows little or nothing except what he or she may be afraid to like," Daly advises. "Decisions in a bureaucracy are more often made by fear than conviction. Respect that fear. Move in small steps. Take the client by the hand at every turn. This may not be the right moment or project for leaping to the edge. And get rid of attitude. Too many designers arrive excessively alert to any signal that their design integrity may be threatened. Remember that you aren't in some kind of contest," he warns. "Ideally, a design project is an opportunity for the client and designer to both expand their experience and learn from each other how to achieve the company's objectives."

Daly is not alone in feeling this way. "Make sure your ego isn't out of line with your talent," says Connie Ryland, former brand manager at Klein Bicycles in Waterloo, Wisconsin, who challenged Liska + Associates to create an online community of hard-core bike aficionados. "There has to be the right balance between good creative work and attentive customer service," Ryland adds. "A lot of firms give you good creative but fall off on the service."

Let that be a word to the wise. As I said in chapter 1, we are in a service business.

Hang In There

Many projects these days involve teams, committees, boards of directors. Everyone has a say. And often that say in not in sync with your vision at all. Maybe the concepts behind the mockup you thought had been approved by that "great" client are now in jeopardy because he or she is bending to committee wishes. Being able to weather those storms with equanimity is what separates the really good designers from those whose end products reveal the struggle and end up looking compromised.

To every request I personally think is unreasonable, I strive to uncover the underlying cause. What problem is not being solved? What issue hasn't been dealt with? In what situation will what I've presented not be doing its job for you? Tell me more!

Situations such as inconsistent expectations, lack of clear inputs, and late-breaking requirements could fill a whole book. And in fact they do. *Designing Together: The Collaboration and Conflict Management Handbook for Creative Professionals* by Dan M. Brown is a bit academic in tone, but the section on "situations" lays out thirty-two common scenarios and provides convenient lists of bullet-pointed dialogue suggestions. Example: if someone on the marketing team tells you, "Now that I think about it, we're also going to need X." Instead of fighting, panicking, criticizing, you could say, "X impacts our plan; here's how we can revise the plan to accommodate these new requirements." Or you could say, "Let's sketch out how these new require-ments impact the design; I don't think we can make it work given our other constraints. And we'll have to increase the budget."

Rehearsing Brown's dialogue suggestions may help turn you from a "creative" lacking in self-confidence to a businesslike, professional peer on the same level as your clients. They may have MBAs. You probably don't. But sometimes it doesn't hurt to sound like you do.

And then hang in there. Revise the plan. Sketch out how the new require-ments impact the design. Show them. Sometimes, when committee members see their idea visualized, they realize that it's not as strong as they imagined it would be, and you will be able to revert to your original concept. And some-times, your original concept will be improved. Design is a process, a verb. These things take time. Being able to manage the process is what you've been hired to do.

Let Them Know How Much the Changes Will Cost

If referrals are the number-one source of new business, not letting clients know the cost of changes could be the number-one source of lost business.

And there are always changes. The chairman wants to see more ideas. More meetings are required. Pages are added—more products, more copy, more pictures. What is the assumption? That you love to work so much that it won't cost any more? This would never happen with a plumber ("Just fix the pipe in the *other* bathroom"), an auto mechanic, a dentist. Why should it happen with a graphic designer? Maybe the answer is because we've let it.

Let's not, any more.

Technology has made billing issues more complex. Even issues as simple as photo post-production. You agree to a fee to design, say, an alumni magazine. The client then sends the event pictures as color JPEGs, many of dubious quality. One way to "save" the images is to make them black and white. Forty pictures need color information removed and to be sharpened, straightened; curves, brightness, and contrast adjusted. It's a time-consuming process. Don't include all that work in your fee—in essence doing it for free—and be angry about it. Calculate a number that covers your costs, then send the client a memo. *Before* he or she gets the bill. Explain that the work was not anticipated in the proposal. If the client is a reasonable person, you will get an initialled okay or an emailed confirmation and there will be no unpleasant surprises for either of you later.

Several years ago, I moderated two panels for the AIGA New York Chapter: "Marketing Design Services from the Client Perspective" and "Effective Billing and Collecting." Both the panel of esteemed clients and the panel of esteemed designers agreed: there are always changes, and changes cost money. "Let us know how much. Let us know right away!" cried the clients, almost in unison. No client wants to be in the position of having to get the boss's approval on an invoice that's 30 percent higher than the estimate— even if the boss is the one who requested the changes. You might be under tremendous pressure to finish a job (it's especially crucial if that's the case), but still take ten minutes to write and send the memo, before you commence the extra work.

Part of your role is to make your client into a hero. Heroes don't get bills that put them in difficult positions. That five minutes may save your relationship, and maybe even your client's reputation within his or her organization.

Stay in Control of the Project

For all the designer self-promoting, sometimes we "forget" what experts we are. When it really counts—in a new business pitch or creative presentation— we are often too modest about our accomplishments and value. We do know more about the design process than the client. (If you don't, you should still be working for someone who does, and learning from him or her.) Yet, when it comes to how the project should be managed, we often let clients intimidate us. We let them tell us what to charge, how we should organize our working phases, how to make a presentation ("just email us a PDF"), and what the results should be, aesthetically.

The client's job is to tell us what results are needed, businesswise, and to let us present the correct solution and methodology.

If you have achieved successes in the past, say so. Tell them. Ask them to follow your lead. You are the expert. That's why they hired you and are paying you. It's appropriate to say things like this:

"This is how the job needs to be managed if you want the result you are looking for." [Describe exact steps.]

"I need all people who have veto power to be present at the meeting."

"It's worth it to wait a week until the chairman/president gets back to get his or her input before we start working/move to the next phase."

"If that doesn't happen, we may have to redo the phase and you will be charged for it." [Works like a charm.]

"I need you to do this [whatever it is] *for me before we move on to the next phase."*

"This [whatever calamity you foresee] *has happened to me before and I want to ensure it doesn't happen with your organization."*

"If that's the situation, maybe you should find another designer."

"Maybe you should find another designer" is not a threat. It's a simple statement of fact. It can open a valuable discussion. You have certain expertise, insights, and talents to offer. If the client is not listening to you, perhaps another designer will be a better fit. On the other hand, that statement may bring to the client's attention the fact that they have chosen you and that it would be in their best interests to follow your lead.

But you had better know what you're doing.

What If the Client Hates Your Idea?

You and I are not the only ones who have this problem. Far from it.

Stefan Sagmeister is one of the most admired graphic designers in the world. He can pick and choose his clients. And Sagmeister's clients are not your run-of-the-mill marketers or brand managers. They're often stars of music or media or fashion who've engaged a kindred spirit to help craft an image and transmit a message to the people who will have the most affinity with it. Nevertheless, Sagmeister still has to fight for his ideas. "I fight for things all the time," he says. "I cry and beg."

Let's say you show three concepts in the order in which you think they work best to transmit the message. Naturally, the client picks number three, your least favorite. You don't hate it, but it's obviously not the caliber of numbers one and two. "The full-bleed photograph is much more dramatic in number two," you might venture, trying to sell your rationale. "I like number three," the client replies, in a tone of voice that clearly means: "I made my decision. Don't even think about crying and begging."

What would Sagmeister do in that situation? His answer: "It would never happen. As a rule, we show one thing. Our clients know from the beginning that the presentation will have one solution. Even if they are marketing people used to seeing three or five comps, I tell them that if we did that, the overall quality would be lower. After all, it's the job of the designer to pick the best solution." Sagmeister says that he only breaks the rule when the solution is something that would require a tricky manufacturing process that might be too difficult or expensive to pull off. And what if the client doesn't like that one solution? "We talk about it," he says. "I ask questions. Why don't they like it? What's bothering them. Our second presentation incorporates what they did like about the first one. There is almost never a problem then," he says. "Actually, crying and begging is a last resort."

Is one good idea enough? Or should you present a range? To some clients, one concept that hits the mark is enough. Others do need to see a range, and many designers want to explore the choices with the client. "This is a full-service agency," asserts Drew Hodges of SpotCo. "I am not a personal visionary. My clients want to be choosy. They want to have a role in the choice. I always say, 'I think this is the one,' but I show at least half a dozen. There are always different ways to solve something."

One word of advice: Never, never show a design that you do not want the client to choose. For obvious reasons, that is always a mistake.

Know When Not to Delegate

Clients want "principal attention." One of the first, and best, lessons I learned was from Joyce Cole, former communications director at *Fortune* 50 company W. R. Grace & Co., where they gave design firms the opportunity to "try out" on small projects before trusting them with bigger and more significant ones. This was more than twenty years ago, and my firm was assigned the employee newsletter for the division that made plastic film for the meat-packing industry. Entertaining a belief that the subject matter (snapshots of shrink-wrapped pork butts coming off the assembly line) was beneath me, I gave the assignment to a junior designer, who did a not-great, but I thought good-enough, job. When I brought the comps to Joyce, she looked at them, pulled her glasses down on her nose, looked at me, and said, "Ellen, *you* didn't do *these*, did you?" When I admitted I hadn't, she said, "Let me give you some advice. Don't let this happen again." I didn't. I redid the newsletter and we went on to produce several very significant projects together. In fact, Joyce, now head of a custom knitwear company, is still a client.

Clients hire *you* because they want *your* designs. I know it's a tough position to be in, but your clients' wishes are more important than your employees' feelings. Employees can redo the work—under your direction, learning from you, their mentor, how it should be done—but a lost client is most likely gone forever. As a boss, you have to make sure that everything that leaves your office is as good as if you'd done it yourself.

How Important Is Personality?

Very. Sagmeister credits the late Tibor Kalman of M&Co., a fearless wit who challenged all prevalent stylistic notions, with showing him how to make clients fall in love with designs they thought they hated.

Make clients fall in love with designs they thought they hated.

Isn't that the secret we're all looking for? If we knew that, we'd all be rich and famous and ecstatically happy.

How, exactly, I asked, did Tibor accomplish that?

"He overwhelmed the clients," is Sagmeister's answer. "He had more personality than the minyan of ten marketing people in the room. He spent an incredible amount of energy making sure things got through the process and produced the way he wanted them. He built elaborate presentations. He was honest. With all the ass-kissing going on in this business, clients thought it was refreshingly honest when Tibor called them idiots. If a client was cheap, Tibor might lay a row of pennies or dollar bills from the front door to the conference room. And he was willing to fight, to pull the job. He would threaten: 'Okay, we'll stop working for you.'"

Is this the way Sagmeister operates? "No. Not at all," he says. "It makes no sense for me to emulate that. I have a different kind of personality."

I never fail to be amazed by Tibor stories. He died in 1999, but his reputation endures. An up-and-coming entertainment client told me that Tibor thought his company's logo should be a rowboat going upstream. I was not only struck by the offbeat brilliance of the idea, but by the reverent tones the client used. Len Riggio, chairman of Barnes & Noble (chapter 13), changed agencies on the strength of Tibor's recommendation.

How can I project that kind of confidence, you are probably wondering?

How can I get that kind of respect and attention? What should I say or do to make it happen? All of us wonder that all the time.

"These are very individual occurrences," says Milton Glaser. "They're based on personal chemistry." He admits that his then-radical ideas for Grand Union Supermarkets (chapter 15), such as European-market-style environments for selling fresh fish, cheese, and herbs, would have gone nowhere if it weren't for his friendship with the client, Sir James Goldsmith. "We liked each other," Glaser says simply.

Perhaps the real secret is taking the time to find the clients with whom the chemistry will happen for you.

Get Referrals to Their Friends and Colleagues

Okay, you've done everything right. The project is wildly successful. You've even gotten paid. Now what?

Keep in touch with your client and ask for referrals.

There is a fine line between keeping in touch and being a pest. Learn where that line is, and stay on the good side of it. Call once in a while to say hello and find out what's going on at the organization. Send holiday greetings. Assume that the client is happy and that you will continue to be "their" designer. Ask for referrals, too. As attorney Gerry Spence has said (chapter 3), "It seems that the more we want something the more hesitant we are to ask for it." There's nothing wrong with calling every once in a while to ask:

"Is there anything else I can help you with?"

"Are there any projects coming up in the next six months or year?"

"Is there anything happening in other divisions of the company I should know about?"

"Can you introduce me to your colleagues in other departments?"

"Can you give me the names and numbers of people who might be interested in my work?"

If you've truly met the client's needs, it's likely you'll be getting more work, both from the client and from his or her colleagues, both inside and outside the organization. It may not happen immediately. But it will happen. The phone will ring. It will be the marketing director in another department or at another company. Ask:

"Where did you get my name?"

And don't be surprised when you hear it was from that client you made into a hero.

The People
Who Do It Right

the clients and designers featured in this book are big names for a reason. The following eighteen chapters will show you why.

The Secrets of Success Are Between the Lines

Over the years, I've had the privilege of interviewing many of the top players in this business—the people who've made this elusive, collaborative, client-designer partnership work best. Up to now, you've read mostly about what I've experienced, sprinkled with experiences of other designers. From now on, you'll hear directly from some of the world's smartest clients (and their designers) in a question-and-answer format.

Q&As are honest and revealing. The writer doesn't provide a narrative or interject a point of view.

Why a focus on superstars of the business? Let me answer that by relating this anecdote: one of the first talks I gave, sort of a disaster, introduced my first book, *Clients and Designers*. The organizers of a conference invited me to talk about the book, and I took the request much too literally. I showed slides of pages of the book, which was highly illustrated with color photography, spread by spread. After a few minutes, one audience member got up and announced, "If you're going to show us a book, I want my money back!" If that weren't bad enough, another said, "I don't want to hear about those famous people! Tell me what I can do, not what Ivan Chermayeff has done."

Actually, I shouldn't have gotten ruffled. It was true then, and still is now, that the way we learn is from the masters. Not only how to design, but how to work with clients so that your designs live to see the light of day.

"What they have done *is* what you can and should do!" I insisted that day—and still insist.

They Are All Great Designers

According to Ed Gold, all great designers share ten common characteristics. Numbers one and two, as mentioned before, are *talent* ("their work just seems to look better; when we look at it we say, 'Gee, I wish I'd done that'"), and *advocacy* or sales ability. Ed identifies the other characteristics as *curiosity; dissatisfaction* (defined as the determination to do things that haven't been done before); *perfectionism; energy; confidence* (the belief that they can design anything, in any medium); having the right balance of *idealism and realism; wit*, and the fact that great designers just *love their work*.

I hope you'll be inspired by the designers interviewed for this book, especially by their confidence. They can't be pushed around. They expect clients to listen to them. And for the most part, they do. In the words of Mike Weymouth, "Clients who come to my firm tend to know they're going to get 'new and different,' and they actually listen to us. They ask us for our advice and, by and large, they take it." April Greiman characterizes herself as "shy," but she's not too shy to say this about her clients: "Having identified with my aesthetic, ideologically, they give me freedom. My clients have done their homework in terms of which designer they've chosen. I don't interfere with the way they manufacture their products or run their organizations. They don't question my aesthetic or interfere too much with my design."

These designers are the ones who have positioned themselves as experts worthy of clients' trust and respect. They haven't merely "positioned themselves." They *are* the experts.

They Are All Great Clients

In the following chapters, you'll also be hearing from some of the world's most successful clients. All, as you'll see, also share common characteristics:

They have *vision*, a vision of their organizations and an understanding of how design can help bring about that vision.

They *trust* their designers. They give the designer the opportunity to do his or her job without interfering or micromanaging.

They can do this because of their *professionalism*; these are people who articulate their needs masterfully and present clear, intelligent design briefs. They push, when a design isn't working, in a way that inspires the designer to do better, not that ridicules or belittles.

Interestingly, great clients share many of the traits of great designers: *curiosity, dissatisfaction, perfectionism, energy, confidence, idealism, wit*. And they also *love their work*.

And They Are Real

This book is not about doing business online with faceless virtual clients who don't know your name. After all, you are not a faceless virtual designer. It's about doing business face-to-face (at least sometimes) with real human beings with whom you can have a meeting, share a meal, and celebrate the results of a job well done together.

There is room on this planet for every kind of business model, including one where certain kinds of clients who want the cheapest, the fastest, and the most impersonal can easily get it. And, sure, most of us work at our computers all day and send PDFs via email to even our closest and dearest clients. But this book is about a different kind of business model, an old-fashioned one in which there are personal relationships and mutual respect.

Archetypes, Not Stereotypes

Even though I've given the clients who graciously allowed me to interview them titles like "The Visionary," "The "Financial Wizard," and "The Tycoon," they are all unique individuals. Yet each represents an archetype of the most positive kind, one that is worthy of emulation. I hope that by absorbing what each client—and each designer—has to say, by reading between the lines a bit, you'll feel as if you are having a series of private meetings with some of the smartest people around.

Only a Diamond Lasts Forever. This Is Business.

As anyone who reads the advertising columns knows, clients change agencies all the time. There are "incumbents." Agencies are "in review." Sometimes it's because sales are down. Sometimes there's a new management team. Sometimes it's a personality thing. Sometimes the client just wants a different approach. The same thing happens to design firms. It just isn't reported in the papers because the millions of dollars spent on public media aren't at stake.

Your best client today may not be there for you when you call three years from now. What happened? Did you do something wrong? Probably not. It's business. Companies are merged and acquired. Business strategies change.

Some of the legendary relationships chronicled herein—Grand Union and Milton Glaser, The Nature Company and Kit Hinrichs—did not last forever, as noted in the introductions to those chapters. While they lasted, though, a lot of extraordinary work got done. The fact that they are historic doesn't make what we can learn from them any less valid.

Maybe Not Forever, But for a Really Long Time

If there's anything I've tried to emphasize in this book, it's that doing good work for satisfied clients—work that creates value and customer loyalty for them—will lead to more work for them, their organizations, their colleagues, friends, and others who are impressed by your work—and who hear good things about you.

All of us want to make clients happy and do great work. I wish there were ten easy steps guaranteed to make that happen. Although every situation is different, here are the key things I've learned from these interviews:

Ellen's Top Ten List for Being a Designer Who Gets and Keeps Great Clients

1.   Don't just start designing. Do research.

2.   Don't reinvent yourself as a marketing consultant. But do use your clients' products, talk to their customers. Learn what makes them different and better.

3.   Take things slowly. Don't come to a first meeting and tell potential clients how to run their organizations. These relationships take months or years to develop.

4.   Collaborate; involve the client in the process.

5.   Dealing with big (or any size) clients sometimes means dealing with big egos. Some clients like to take credit for the creative work. Let them.

6.   Develop your own working style. Some designers like to show one solution that they've determined is best. Others show a range of solutions. Do what works for you, and adapt it to the needs of each client.

7.   Listen more than you talk.

8.   Have the confidence to stick up for what you believe in. But also have the confidence to be flexible when circumstances warrant it.

9.   Study the best work out there. Don't copy it, but figure out what makes it great. Then strive to produce work of that caliber for every one of your clients.

10. You don't get too many big opportunities in life. Take full advantage of those you do get.

Applying What They Have to Say

I invite you to sit down with a cup of your favorite beverage and read the interviews in the following eighteen chapters.

Because every client relationship is different, you've got to figure out the how-to yourself. This is not a book with checklists of exact instructions. Instead, you are invited to read between the lines: What is this client really saying? How does he or she think? What was expected of the designer, and how was the expectation met? What was the insight behind the designer's solution that created value for the client? How can I apply this wisdom to my own client relationships and be more successful at what I do?.

In this second edition, to make things clearer, I've added boxes with my interpretations of the interviewees' "takeaway messages." I hope you will take away a lot that is helpful to you.

I can always be reached at ellen@visualanguage.net

part II

Corporate Clients

Some corporate clients make products, like bicycles, airplanes, and artificial hearts. Others provide services, like real estate brokerage, consulting, and investment banking. Whether it's a meal kit for kids or an ergonomic chair, the focus is equally on the design of the product and on the way it is packaged, launched, and advertised—and how customers interact with it.

Will your idea fly? Will it create value for the client?

The Internet Start-Up

Domu
AND Liska + Associates

Noah Schatz is president and CEO of **Domu**, a Chicago online apartment-listing site. Domu is an offshoot of Schatz Development, founded in 1948 by Noah's father, real estate developer Jack Schatz. Before launching Domu, the company enjoyed a lengthy and successful run of new-construction projects, culminating in 600 North Fairbanks, a 227-unit luxury condominium designed by internationally acclaimed architect Helmut Jahn.

Liska + Associates is a nine-person, Chicago-based brand and communication design consultancy founded by **Steve Liska** in 1980. The firm's watchword is "making things clear across all media for all audiences." Active in the AIGA, Society of Typographic Arts, and Society for Environmental Graphic Design, Liska has taught in masters programs at several leading design schools. In addition to real estate, Liska + Associates serves clients in varied industries, including beauty, health care, and hospitality.

Design director **Kim Fry** shares responsibility for client contact, creative direction, and production supervision on the Domu project.

A seasoned real estate developer has a concept for a start-up. To launch it, everything is needed, including design of the site itself and creation of newspaper and transit advertising that will inform the target audiences—renters and landlords—and turn them into users. The project goes to Liska + Associates, a firm the client learned to respect when they produced successful interactive and print marketing materials for a more traditional real estate project. "We learn who you are and what you do," says Steve Liska about his firm. "We gain an understanding of your brand essence, audiences, existing assets, challenges, and opportunities. We distill large amounts of complex information and design branded components that work across all media to create a consistent image. We direct all aspects of the design process, ensuring that all components run smoothly and are completed on time and on budget." The Domu project illustrates how all those words translate into real-time success—for the designer, for the client, and for the customers and users, the public.

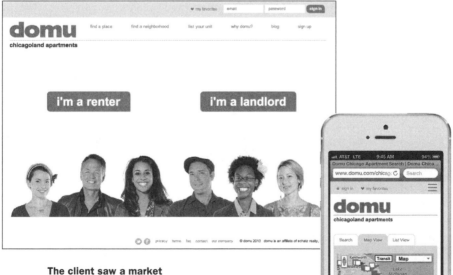

The client saw a market need: a map-based site that connects renters and landlords. The designers did everything needed to turn that vision into reality.

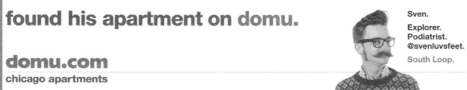

A simple logo, a clean, uncluttered website, and humorous ads were seen by the client as elements that would stand out in "a disjointed, old-fashioned industry that has struggled to adapt to the Internet age."

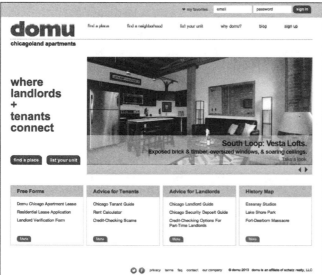

Now, client and designers agree, the site practically runs itself.

[The conversation began with a Q&A with Steve Liska and Kim Fry.]

Q: Steve, this is a project that uses every resource of a design firm: thinking, art direction, copywriting, web and print advertising design and development, even bus posters. And it's fun and out there in the public realm. How did Domu find you and get in touch with you?

A: Liska: Domu was started in 2009 by an existing client of ours, a real estate developer that saw the need for a better apartment-finding experience. We first worked with them on marketing their latest condo development: producing the website, signage, sales gallery, and print collateral for the project.

How was the assignment presented? Because the developer was an existing client, did you need to submit a proposal?

Liska: It started out as a conversation about the need for this type of online service, how would it work. Together, we defined the scope of the project, which included naming, logo, site design and development, marketing, advertising, and more. We were asked to submit a proposal outlining our involvement in detail and to work within an initial start-up budget.

After you got the job, what was the first thing you did?

Liska: We analyzed the competition. The need was obvious. There was no trusted, free resource for apartment-seekers or landlords. At the time, most people found apartments by using Craigslist or the *Chicago Reader*, a free local paper. Neither was always reliable, and neither was focused on apartments only. Other companies had been getting into the online rental market, and some of their sites looked good on the surface, but they were usually backed by people with goals other than helping you find a place to live. Most of them were run by real estate developers trying to rent their own properties or get a commission, usually one month's rent. That kind of site has controls over what is listed and how their own properties show up. You contact them and they conveniently "don't have that apartment available any more," but "will be glad to help" by steering you to a different property. People who'd been using those services were frustrated.

If you think this is too much business strategy, think again. All effective design firms need to ground their work in strategy and goals. Otherwise we are merely decorators.

After analyzing the competition, we helped the client define the brand—Chicago's hip apartment resource—and what it stood for: trust. We wanted the new site to be the first place people check, to be the Chicago apartment-rental resource they trust and use. Then we worked on naming. Everyone liked the name Domu, derived from the Latin word for home. Everything marketing-wise evolved from that.

Did the client express what they wanted the look and feel to be like?

Liska: I think they came to us because we tend to make the complicated appear simple—and this is a very complicated site. We went through lots of layouts, options, and directions. But the general direction was that everything needed to evoke a simple "you can trust us" attitude. That strategy worked out great. Domu is now the go-to site for almost everyone looking to rent a place. That's because using the site is an honest, clear, friendly experience.

Are you bringing all-lower-case Helvetica and lots of white space back in style?

Fry: That would be nice. Open and friendly is important, and having a clean, neutral aesthetic was part of their brand. And this is a client who appreciates the minimalist visual approach.

Is it fair to describe this as a low-budget program in terms of no illustration and very little photography?

Liska: Many things of quality that look simple are not. It is not a low-budget site or marketing campaign. It is just approached minimally and judiciously in relation to imagery. The real estate world is full of bad stock photos of people laughing in their kitchen with a glass of wine, walking their cute little dog, and frolicking by the pool. Our client understood that their market would not buy into the trite, conventional real estate style, so images were carefully shot with real people, not models, to look editorial. The ads stand out partly because they are so simple. And they reflect the site. In the end, it is the apartments that people go to the site to see, and that has always been the focus.

It looks like your firm is taking on an ad agency role, including writing the copy. Are you also placing the ads?

Liska: The copywriting tends to be a collaborative process. The copy is fun, quick, and humorous, and makes the point. The media is handled in-house.

Fry: We design the prototypes and help with visual direction and copy. The client produces and buys the media, which works out great for both parties.

How was the site launched? Did the ads and bus posters come first, building anticipation for the new service?

Liska: The site was created first. It had to be live to prove how user-friendly and content-rich it was. The hard part was getting it populated with available rental units. At first, they offered free listings to landlords—who were initially skeptical. They also used condo listings they had access to. After checking them out to ensure they were real, they copied ads from other sites. And they just hustled hard to get the site as content-rich as possible. Then came the newspaper ads, billboards, buses, subway platforms, doorknob hangers, for-rent signs, and marketing at neighborhood events. There was a cool old Domu Volkswagen bus and Domu bicycles, all intended to reach the audience to make this the top-of-mind resource. And all for that one week every couple of years when you decide to look for a new apartment! We produced web ads and a series of videos, but the bus posters were so popular that they started appearing on people's blogs. So they're what we've stuck with.

Does someone actually go around and physically check each listing to ensure that it's real and represents the apartment accurately?

Liska: They check out the listings, not by physically going to them. They review them and have a feedback loop on the site if there are any issues. There have been very few complaints about listings.

How and how often is the site updated?

Fry: The site is updated hourly, but most of it happens automatically through the templates we designed. The owners and landlords add new content through a Drupal-based CMS, a content management system that defines all style. And we keep an eye on it. We recently went through a site design update; the Domu team removed things to make the experience more stream-lined. The basic visual concept remains the same, but we continue to make evolutionary changes based on technology. For example, we've been able to take advantage of the advances in Google maps and are changing the site to be responsive for phones.

Liska: Check out the new Domu on your iPhone and see how well it works.

[Later, I spoke with the client, Noah Schatz.]

How did you determine the right time to launch the site?

Schatz: The housing market was steadily deteriorating, and in 2009 it was becoming increasingly evident that considerable time would pass before another really attractive major real estate development opportunity would arise. With ongoing turbulence in the home-lending industry, we were aware that Chicagoans were defecting to the apartment market.

We were also aware of the inefficient nature of the apartment-finding process: With the sale of each new smartphone and tablet, classified ads in legacy media like newspapers were falling out a favor. Craigslist was beset with blind and misleading ads posted by brokers posing as landlords, and it lacked a user-friendly, map-based interface. Retail apartment locators did not present the entire market to their clients, but only those properties where the landlord promised them a commission. And the multiple-listing service, with its cooperating-broker model, imposed transaction costs too heavy to justify its widespread use in the apartment sector. When I hatched the idea, the model was simple: put tenants in direct contact with landlords, allowing both parties to reduce transaction costs and increase efficiency.

How did you first meet Steve Liska? And what design projects did you work on with Liska + Associates before starting Domu?

To land clients like this:

You must be able to provide a wide range of capabilities and gain trust by demonstrating that you share their vision.

Schatz: I met Steve at the inception of our last high-rise development project, 600 North Fairbanks, when we were seeking his help with the design of the digital marketing operation, including creation of the website and the operation of the computers at the sales center. We were impressed by his firm's client list, and the graphic design, branding, and logo work they produced for those clients, as evidenced in their own promotional materials. When we first approached Steve about Domu, we discussed our vision for a user-friendly, intuitive, map-based apartment search website with a clean, design-driven aesthetic, free of advertisements and other forms of screen clutter.

To quote a review in an online business newsletter: "For the most part, Domu removes the annoying and frequently dubious middlemen from the picture, instead allowing you [the tenant] to negotiate directly with landlords." If Domu puts the renter directly in touch with the landlord, how do you generate revenue?

Schatz: Domu generates revenue by charging landlords a nominal fee to list individual apartment units and by charging property management companies monthly fees to list entire buildings. The landlords create their own listings through our easy-to-use content management system. They write their own copy, upload their own images, and select all the applicable amenity parameters. Tenants search for free and find these listings using a variety of neighborhood, unit type, and rent filters, and contact the landlords directly, exactly as they would have done a decade ago when they combed through the classified section of their local newspaper.

In the Internet world, many good ideas ultimately do not succeed. But you have. Was there a written business plan? Did you need to raise outside capital?

Schatz: We invested significant time researching the concept. We attempted to define the size of the apartment market, the total number of vacancies, the seasonal peaks and valleys, the number of potential landlord customers, and the total potential revenue based on assumed percentages of market share.

We also conducted extensive analyses of Craigslist, attempting to determine the percentage of ads that qualified as bona fide—rather than blind—listings, the period of time that listings remained at the top of the first page, the number of times per day that the same listings were re-posted, and the overall efficacy of the site. We used our data to create revenue estimates, then compared those estimates to projected start-up and operating costs to draw conclusions about economic viability. No outside capital was sought or required. Today, the site practically runs itself.

What was the process of coming up with the name like? How many names did you go through before agreeing on Domu?

Schatz: The process of selecting a name was occasionally frustrating, but enjoyable and exciting. At first, we searched for a name directly related to apartment living, figuring it would instantly explain our product and increase SEO, search engine optimization. It soon became apparent that variations on words like "pad," "crib," and "nest" were tired and clichéd. Ultimately dispensing with that notion, we focused on creating something portable, minimalist, and unique. I just liked the ring of "domu," which is the Latin root for "home," and soon there was consensus that its brevity and originality would be hard to beat.

Of course, we weren't out of the woods yet. An Internet squatter in a remote Canadian village had purchased the name many years ago in the hope that someone would someday pay a premium for it. Fortunately, it was a modest premium that fit within our start-up budget.

What about the clean look and feel of the site and of the ads and marketing materials? And the red and black color scheme with lots of white space? Did you consider various design schemes before making a decision?

Schatz: We articulated a vision of our concept: A simple logo; a clean, uncluttered website; and an appropriately modern feel. We viewed these as critical elements in a disjointed, old-fashioned industry that has notoriously struggled to adapt to the Internet age. Steve understood and presented us with a handful of excellent ideas. He devised a simple logo we instantly fell in love with, and from there we merely looked over his shoulder and toyed with color schemes. Steve's team conceived both the design and the meme of the ad campaign. We created the names, occupations, and taglines, but the overall advertising scheme, which reflected the simplicity and minimalist feel of the site, was the product of Steve and Kim's creativity.

Not every client agrees to not filling up every square inch of white space, especially ad space they're paying for, with clutter. Are you ever tempted to ask

for more stuff—more copy, more pictures, testimonials—in an ad or poster?

Schatz: Never. The Domu design aesthetic is clean and minimalist. Everything from the website itself to the advertising copy reflects that aesthetic. Apartment-finding should be easy and intuitive, and ads should be easy to read and understand. Clutter is uninviting and counterproductive.

A little Googling shows that not everyone in Chicago loves your ad campaign. What do you say to bloggers who have no sense of humor?

Schatz: Our initial advertising campaign was steeped in irony and absurdity. We found it funny and at times hysterical, but a number of Chicago's bloggers and tweeps either failed to understand the humor or didn't care for it. Our objective was simply to avoid implementing a marketing campaign based on ads resembling brochures created by banks and pharmacies—ads with generic photographs of smiling people in a state of veritable utopia. We were not deliberately courting controversy, of course. Instead, we were hoping to create a buzz, something that would stimulate the average pedestrian or commuter.

As for our advertisements' detractors, we're delighted that they've seen fit to notice us. In the meantime, our taglines have inspired a series of parodies in the Twittersphere and spawned an instantly recognizable local meme, which we view as a sure sign of success.

What capabilities do you think a designer needs in order to successfully complete a project of this magnitude?

Schatz: Working extensively with Steve and his team, we have developed great respect for their opinions on a wide range of branding issues. We have come to view Steve not just as a graphic designer, but as a confidante who understands our aspirations and dispenses valuable advice on how to achieve a position of trust, respect, and authority within our industry.

Can you sum up your thoughts about the value of design to your business?

Schatz: Our mission was to improve the efficiency of apartment search and to simplify the online experience. Knowing these objectives could not be met without a proper design aesthetic, and we were prepared to spend whatever was needed, within reason, to get it right from inception. In hindsight, our instincts were correct. We have been repeatedly complimented on the design of our website, and we strongly believe that our design aesthetic, from page layout to logo, has created significant, intangible value to our business. ■

The Design Icon

The Knoll Group
AND Tom Geismar

In 1940, Hans and Florence Knoll opened a design studio and shop on Madison Avenue that changed the face of commercial interior design. In the tradition of the Bauhaus, they commissioned renowned architects to design office furniture to complement Modern architecture. And they commissioned Massimo Vignelli and other noted graphic designers to produce catalogs and brochures that mirrored the spirit of the furniture designed by Bertoia, Breuer, Diffrient, Noguchi, Saarinen, van der Rohe, and many others, that became icons of Modernist graphic design and product photography. In 1972, an exhibition at the Louvre celebrated the company's achievements in product, showroom, interior, and graphic design. Several years ago, a newly intriguing Knoll look and spirit began to appear, including collateral with a multicolored, layered look and a small-space newspaper ad campaign with clever headlines and copy ("Designer Recliner") that made me want to run right out and buy a Frank Gehry Power Play Club Chair for $1,653 and matching Off Side Ottoman for $518. What was up at Knoll?

Getting to results like this is not a simple, one-step process. As Tom Geismar says, "We went back and forth a number of times."

[I spoke with the client, David Bright, at the Knoll Design Center in Manhattan's SoHo district.]

Q: A new corporate or brand identity often signifies change, a restructuring, or repositioning. What was the situation at the time Knoll began working with Chermayeff & Geismar?

A: Bright: From an identity point of view, it was a time of considerable chaos. There were four companies with four separate identities and corporate cultures, and we needed to fuse all those traditions, many of which were very strong, into a singular identity.

Once the strategic decision was made to create a new business based on the best aspects of all the players and to capitalize on the recognition factor of the Knoll brand name to leverage all their attributes in the marketplace, we embarked on the new identity program. Our goal was to reinvent or redefine many of the elements and messages that had existed in the past—without denigrating any of the work that had been done previously, especially by Massimo Vignelli, who had been responsible for the worldwide Knoll design and communications positioning.

It's widely acknowledged that the work Vignelli had done for Knoll was world-class in scope and execution. One might ask, why go somewhere else? On a less exalted level, readers might be wondering why they lost their last client . . . why that client went somewhere else.

How do clients think?

Clients will change designers when their communication needs change. Prepare yourself.

Bright: The company founded by Hans and Florence Knoll had transformed itself from one involved with furniture for executive offices, corporate boardrooms, and high-end residences to one primarily focused on office systems and ergonomic seating. The scale of the company had quadrupled in size overnight. Our graphic and communication demands became much greater, and the markets in which we were operating were very different. Office system products, such as ergonomic seating with adjustable features, required technical and planning guides that had to rely on text more than on beautiful visual elements.

We had a big job to do. It was an unparalleled opportunity to start at square one with identity issues, to strategically look at the situation, to decide how we were going to approach the problem, and then work out a written execution plan that would serve this company long-term. And there was the implementation of everything from business papers to truck graphics to plant signage to product literature formats.

Did you approach several firms that specialize in corporate identity? Was there a request for proposals and a competitive bidding situation?

Bright. We did not solicit bids, and we did not go through a protracted evaluation process. We initially contacted Tom Geismar based on a referral from a writer and consultant who recommended Tom as an excellent person to work out business and executional issues. We hired Chermayeff & Geismar on the basis of that referral and on the historic strength of their work and their ability to interact with a diverse group of people. Their experience in varied sectors of the economy was appealing, and they had proven themselves over the years by completing broad-based programs for large corporations. A second aspect of this decision was pure personality.

> **Will your design fly?**
>
> There's a much better chance if you're in a collaborative relationship with the client, and view arriving at the results as a process.

I found Tom to be pragmatic, sensitive, artistic, and concerned with the impact of his work on a client's business. Our senior managers developed a good rapport with Tom and Ivan. They're easygoing and have a nonconfrontational style that is appealing to an organization going through lots of change.

What was working on this project like on a day-to-day basis?

Bright: This was not a project in which we sent designers off with an assignment and asked them to make a presentation. It was a process, and as the client, we were embraced in it. Tom Geismar led the team, but all the partners at C&G have developed a practice that fosters collaboration and interaction. The presentations were more or less conversations, and as a result of those conversations, the work evolved. We had discussions and presentations with all the people in the room who needed to make a decision; we would think about it for a while, come to consensus, and move on. To establish a new identity in the marketplace, we needed to move exceptionally quickly. In some cases, our products had previously been sold by different sales forces in different showrooms.

So a chair that is now being sold under the Knoll name that might have been previously sold under a different name?

Bright: Correct. All of a sudden, we needed to have a singular brand identity, and we needed our salespeople to be out there right away selling hard against the competition. We compete in the general office market with Herman Miller, Steelcase, Haworth, Kimball, Allsteel, and a host of smaller manufacturers that are also represented by our dealerships. One of our biggest challenges was to get our dealer community behind us, understanding the commitment the corporation was making to support the Knoll brand.

Are you saying that a collaborative process can lead to better solutions because it doesn't foster situations in which the designer presents something and the client says, "We can't do that"? There is the traditional battleground in which the client pushes to make changes and the designer desperately tries to hold on to what he or she considers the integrity of the design.

Bright: Absolutely. Those types of confrontations don't happen here because they are adjudicated at a different level.

Since its early years, Knoll fostered the idea that graphic design is just as important as product design. We are totally involved in the design development process for our products and for the whole range of marketing materials we produce in-house. There's a common interest in design management and appreciation of design, especially as it relates to Modernism.

One of the things I most respect about Tom Geismar is that he never comes in and says, "Here is the solution." He certainly has personal preferences and he may have a preconceived notion of how he thinks something should be, but one of his strengths is to reveal a range of ideas. Unlike principals of other corporate identity firms that are more research-focused, it's not his style to write lots of decks and create reams of documentation, but he operates strategically rather than from a visual execution point of view.

Are you hearing what the client is saying?

It's important to spend more time listening to the client than to come in right away and proclaim, "Here is the solution."

Some people might characterize this work—the colors, the imagery—as a departure for Knoll. What was the reaction in the field?

Bright: The response was extraordinary. It was overwhelmingly positive from our salespeople—the folks who use the tools in the field every day. And it was overwhelmingly positive from the dealers—the individuals who are on the front lines of our business—as well as from the architects and interior designers and corporate facilities managers who specify our products. Every time something from Knoll comes across their desks, it just pops off the table. The materials are charismatic in a way that's not off-putting or unapproachable by a broad range of people. There is a visual sense that is exactly right for this company.

If another company would like to achieve identity standards and graphics of this quality, is there any rule of thumb you might offer as to what they should be proparod to opond?

Bright: Although implementation costs can add up, the relative cost of good design and corporate identity is minuscule compared to the total investment a company makes in undertaking a merger, upgrading manufacturing technology, building plants and showrooms.

I am constantly amazed by the responses of other corporate executives to the Knoll Group identity guidelines. They say things like "I've never seen anything done to this level of finish before," and "Wouldn't it be great if my company could take on this kind of program." My response is, in certain businesses you can't afford not to. If you believe your brand has a long-term value in the marketplace, building that brand among the people who work in the company and among the outside people with whom you do business is a key factor that will drive the success of the company.

There's also an investment here in quality photography, printing, paper, in good writing.

Bright: Knoll historically has recognized the value of those components in marketing communications. This is a company that was founded on the idea that graphic design and communications go hand in hand with product design. It's just one of the special things about Knoll. There's never a need to rationalize or justify those investments.

[Later, I spoke with Tom Geismar at Chermayeff & Geismar's art-filled offices overlooking Madison Square Park.]

Do you consider your work for Knoll a departure for Chermayeff & Geismar?

Geismar: No. People aren't aware of the range of things that we do. I see the Knoll work as an expansion or further expression of that range. It's all part of a continuum. We have been purposely trying to reestablish the Knoll tradition and play up some of the things that were done in the past that established the company as a leader in design. Knoll graphics have a great Modernist tradition, and it just seemed appropriate to us that it should be carried forward. The difference is that computers enabled us to do things with imagery that might not have been possible before, so there is more complexity. For example, to convey the basic attitude of Knoll—the idea of the intelligent workspace—we looked for imagery that would suggest that, and it ended up as photographic collages.

Can you describe how the images were created and how they were reproduced?

Geismar: We started out looking at something quite different—symbolic fish and animals—but eventually we decided to combine images that are more closely related to Knoll's business. And as the collages developed, they became more and more interesting as a visually exciting way to express the message of a company that sells design. We combined especially shot and stock photographs and manipulated the images to change the colors to a range we selected. We also changed the percentages of intensity, so certain layers became transparent.

What was the design brief? How was the scope of the project presented to you?

Geismar: Our original involvement was to look at the identity of the newly merged company, The Knoll Group, and its long-term business plan. We ultimately recommended that "The" and "Group" be dropped and that everything be marketed under "Knoll," which was so well known in the marketplace.

We went through a whole study and came up with a new design for the Knoll logo. But in the end, the decision was made to stay with the basic Knoll typography that had been in use since the late sixties. Our focus was on using the single word "Knoll" on everything.

Colors were standardized. We developed a system with interim guidelines, how to do the letterhead, and very basic guidelines for the dealers, who were encouraged to use the Knoll name but also shown how to use their own store names on stationery. We did the same with signage. There were a whole series of interim guidelines books, and a compilation of them became the identity manual—a relatively compact manual that codifies everything in one convenient place.

How did you present your ideas to the client? Did you ever have to go back and change things?

Geismar: No, never (laughs). Knoll has always been a very demanding client, and it's also a company in flux. There have been changes in direction, changes in people—all the things that make life complicated. Even though we have had presentations with everyone from the chairman down, all along we worked closely with David Bright, and that gave things stability. But, yes, things did go back and forth a number of times. The identity went into various directions, with agreements one way and then a shift. But these things are normal in these adverse times.

Young designers often wonder how firms like yours get projects like this—how you make proposals, how you price, how it all really works. There's kind of a fantasy that only five guys in the world really know how to do this—you're one of them—and that you work some kind of magic no one else can quite figure out.

Geismar: I don't know any secrets! Identity is difficult. It takes a lot of experience and clear thinking, because you're dealing with long-term issues.

Generally, graphic design is ephemeral; you're creating things that are seen, used, and done away with. There's a certain charm to that. But identity is different; if it works, it's going to be around for many years. At this office, we've always taken pride in the fact that most of what we've done is still around and doesn't look dated. We're not interested in what's in fashion. In fact, we try to avoid being fashionable, and attempt to think through the implications of what we're doing and how it will physically work in all its uses and ramifications.

We go to great lengths to never simply present a mark or logo, but always show it in context. As a way of evaluating it, we do mock-ups of the most-used and most-seen applications: the stationery, ads, trucks, brochures, and signs. And sometimes when we get to that point, we realize that the thing doesn't work and either throw it away and start again or change it. If you don't go through that process, you might fall in love with something and think it's really clever without ever objectively and properly evaluating it.

> **Take it from the expert, Tom Geismar:**
>
> Don't fall in love with your design without objectively evaluating it and how it will serve the client.

How different is what we're looking at today from your first presentation?

Geismar: It's only different in detail. In fact, the cover of the identity guidelines manual is one of the first things we showed: how we could break the logo into two parts and make it more decorative and abstract. There were certain concepts presented originally that have continued to form the basis of the ongoing program. One is to use the Knoll logo simply and boldly. You can see this on the trucks, on the catalogs, on the signs. Another concept is to use Bodoni Book as the major typeface. It provides a nice contrast with the bold logo. It's elegant and was already being used for Knoll product literature. Limiting the number of typefaces can often be a big help in terms of achieving a consistent look, and you can see Bodoni Book on everything from stationery to the newspaper ads. The third idea we originally presented is to use overlapping and transparent imagery, in a variety of forms, to convey ideas and feelings. The fourth basic concept is to use bold colors. I personally love bright colors. Sometimes it seems like Ivan and I are the only two people in existence who still do.

I wonder how many clients would automatically reject certain color combinations, saying things like, "Purple with green, that's too weird" or "We can't have an orange cover." Do you have to sell your ideas, to convince clients of their rightness, or do you find that a correct solution sells itself?

Geismar: Again, I think "appropriate" is the key word. In terms of "selling," we have a rationale for what we're doing, and explain it to the client. But the design itself has to be interesting and convincing.

> **Does the correct solution sell itself?**
>
> You've got to develop a rationale and explain it—and make sure the design is convincing, interesting, appropriate.

Where do you stand in the legibility versus visual excitement debate?

Geismar: Those things don't have to be mutually exclusive. Covers can suggest a brochure's contents in an evocative and attractive way, and the inside pages can be absolutely straightforward if they're intended to be used as functional tools.

There is a tremendous amount of self-indulgent design being done right now. I always consider what a piece is trying to convey, who's going to read it, who's going to understand it. The graphic design problems that most of us face every day can be a struggle. But if people would stop looking at design magazines so much and think more about what it is they're trying to say, it would expand the potential of what they're creating.

Here, we play ideas off each other and see if they work. We formed our office so that we could work in a collaborative way, and collaborating with each other and with our clients opens up more possibilities.

Many designers are reluctant to turn over their finely honed work to the client's in-house people. What's your reaction to the in-house work Knoll is doing?

Geismar: They're doing some very nice things. It has always been our attitude that certain things should absolutely be prescribed in an identity manual—labels and binder covers, catalog pages, and so forth—so people don't have to spend too much time making decisions. There has to be a commonality, so when you put everything together it won't look like a mess. But you don't want to restrict the creativity that goes into promotional pieces and posters, whether directed to the consumer or to the salespeople. You want to make those things lively and fun, be part of the interesting spirit of the company.

Although this client came about by referral, do you get into competitive bidding situations?

Geismar: All the time. In the case of Knoll, David Bright called me up and it was as simple as that, but it usually doesn't happen that way. This week we spent a lot of time writing a proposal for a very large project, and I have to do another one today. They are all competitive, absolutely.

Do you feel that at some point in a design firm's history, you ought to be able to say, "Our fee is $100,000, just to use a round number, and if you want to work with us, take it or leave it"?

Geismar: Well, I understand Paul Rand did something like that. But I don't think there is anyone in the world now who can get away with it. It would be great if that were the case. It is very much a competitive situation, and you're not judged just on your fee, it's your past work, your approach, and your fit for the particular problem.

You are known for going beyond traditional graphic design services: interior design, exhibitions, art consulting. Has that been the case with Knoll?

Geismar: We designed showroom environments, always looking to make them special, like a series of laser-cut aluminum silhouettes of people. Our office works on many museum exhibits and we also do a lot of work with architects, such as environmental graphics. People in corporations who are involved with identity and graphic design usually don't care about these areas. We do. One of my partners is an architect by training, and Ivan comes from a family of architects, and we continue to do these diverse things because we enjoy them, and they make our practice more interesting.

Do you see a competitive advantage in offering more services?

Geismar: I don't think so. But it does give us a slightly broader perspective on things, which is helpful.

Do you also get involved in the copy concepts? For example, here's a cover that reads, "Smell, touch, taste." Are these ideas, in which the copy is integrated with the visuals, generated by you, the client, or a writer?

Geismar: Actually, by a designer. This series was created for people who come to see the Knoll plants and tour the facilities, and includes nametags, menus for luncheons, notepads, and so forth. We had a lot of discussion about which words would be most appropriate.

Good to hear that. To you, what is it that most makes an identity successful? Do you think that companies generally undertake new identities when the going gets rough, when customer or investor confidence is low?

Geismar: They might, but management soon learns that it's not as simple as that. Graphics don't make a company successful or unsuccessful. The products, and the way they are sold and distributed, are at the heart of every company. In order to work, graphics have to reflect reality. ∎

The Publisher

Faber & Faber
AND Pentagram

Matthew Evans, chairman of EFG Private Bank and a member of the British House of Lords, was the longtime chairman of **Faber & Faber Ltd.**, the publishing group founded by Geoffrey Faber and T. S. Eliot in 1925. Best known for literary fiction by contemporary authors, as well as great British classics, the company also publishes poetry, plays, screenplays, and nonfiction books about architecture, current affairs, history, and music.

A partner in **Pentagram,** which has offices in New York, London, Berlin, San Francisco, and Austin, Texas, from 1974 to 2005, **John McConnell** is a board member of Faber & Faber — an unusual role for a designer. He was responsible for overseeing, in addition to various international identity programs, the design of nearly three hundred Faber book jackets a year. Co-author of Pentagram's books *Living by Design* and *Ideas on Design*, he has received many prestigious awards, including a London Design and Art Directors Award for outstanding contributions to design. McConnell now runs his own London studio.

The book jacket has become an artist's canvas—the illustrator's as well as the designer's. An exhibition of the latest trends in typographic design and visual imagery is as close as the "contemporary fiction" shelves of your nearest bookstore. Each cover of the more than 6,000 designed by Pentagram for Faber & Faber not only identifies the publisher—in the UK, book jackets are more a tribute to the publisher than to the author—and captures the spirit of the book, it is a pocket-sized exhibition of the best in illustration. That's not only due to the talents of John McConnell, it's the result of executive decisions by Lord Matthew Evans, a chairman who was not afraid to buck tradition—or start new ones. His strategy doesn't sound too complicated: hire the best design firm you can and let the designers do their job. Perhaps other firms could have developed an engaging design concept. But could they have kept the momentum going at the rate of three hundred jackets a year? It took developing a "house style," and a client and designer both determined to see the program succeed.

"There is inevitably resistance when you put change into any organization," says John McConnell. "The board was very brave. They supported me, finally the success started to happen, and all the criticisms went away."

[The conversation began with designer John McConnell at Pentagram's office in the London neighborhood of Notting Hill.]

Q: Can you provide a capsule history of book design at Faber & Faber?

A: McConnell: Faber is one of the few private publishers left, and they were one of the first to actually take on the responsibility of designing the interiors and covers of the book. Until the turn of the twentieth century, the publishing house simply brought a manuscript to the printer. There were classic printers who produced beautiful work, but it came from a craft tradition. Faber was the first to appoint a design director and had a small in-house team that commissioned illustrators. They used some very, very fine people: Eric Gill, William Morris. It was really quite a remarkable tradition. But it was not looked after properly for a long period. When Matthew Evans became chairman and managing director, he looked for someone to take on that mantle, and they experimented with a couple of people, both of whom failed. I was the third person asked to take on the job. The department had been left alone for such a long time, they resented anyone coming in and suggesting change, and so the production department saw off the first two candidates.

Saw off?

McConnell: Got rid of them, made them resign, made their lives so miserable they packed up and the programs they wanted never succeeded. So it was a fair challenge when we came on. We said, okay, we'll try again. That is partly why they asked me to join the board. The other people had been employees.

What was the first thing you had to do?

McConnell: There had been no budget for doing covers and doing design properly and there was no mechanism to manage it. There were no regular meetings. The first thing I had to do was find a way to manage these internal people, stop them, make sure nothing went wrong. Now, all the jackets are done here at Pentagram, 250 to 300 a year, that sort of mark. I set up a manager and a number of staff in Faber who do the interiors of the books.

And in terms of the design?

McConnell: In America and here in the UK, too, the current publishing technique is to suggest that every book jacket should be different. I went against that and argued that there is real benefit in having a house style. I said, "There is value in this book looking like that book, or looking like a brother or sister of that book." Because, as a reader, if I have good experience with this book, I then can assume that I will have a fairly good chance of having a good experience with the next book. And, therefore, goodwill builds up for the publisher's product.

That point of view will probably strike Americans as very strange.

McConnell: It is un-American, certainly more European. All the research said I was wrong. I'm sure if you were in a bookshop and I asked you, "What are you looking for?" you'd say that you were looking for a book on gardening or a novel or an author. But, I think, eventually you'd start to think about who it might have been published by. Penguin is a very famous brand, and people used to say, "I'm going to buy a Penguin." So the publisher is part of the purchase decision. The other terrific thing, of course, if there are six books in a bookshop window, and they look like brothers and sisters, you appear to have a greater presence.

But within the house style, you introduced a range of variations.

McConnell: I introduced a new look for each of the areas. A look for poetry, a style for fiction, and a style for nonfiction. What they had in common was the panel—a rectangular panel in which the author's name and book title appeared. We also put certain authors and illustrators together. The illustrator Pierre LeTan did all of the jackets for Garrison Keillor's books, so Keillor became absolutely associated with Pierre's drawings. It's nice because you can give an author a little personal style.

We ran with that scheme for ten to fifteen years. Three years or so ago, I revisited Faber and we instituted a whole new look.

I understand one reason for the new look was that other publishers followed suit to the first look you designed. Did they copy the designs outright?

McConnell: You couldn't tell the books apart.

If Faber enjoyed the reputation you describe, do you think the motivation to copy was to fool people, to get them to think that their book was published by Faber & Faber?

McConnell: No, I think they saw it as representing classy literature.

How would you describe the new look?

McConnell: It stands out by reversal. Every sales director wants to know if they can have the title bigger. So I say, "The book is only six inches wide, and you cannot get it any larger. I've blown it up as big as I can. I simply cannot get it any bigger." But what they really mean is, "Can you make my book stand out more in the shop?" Nothing stands out in American bookshops because they treat every book as a product in its

own right and they're all screaming so loudly. They have their volume knobs turned up full blast.

So when you look around, it's a blank-out. You see nothing. The trick is to go the other way.

And they listened to you . . .

McConnell: By being quiet, you actually get recognition. You have to remember that Faber & Faber has a very unique position. They are a specialist in high-quality fiction, not pulp romance fiction. They don't need the gold-embossed title and the lovely lady fainting in the arms of the handsome man.

What did the client see when the concept was presented?

You don't always have to shout. Sometimes, by being quiet you can get more recognition.

Faber's books on the whole are more difficult to read properly, so the small type says, "I'm a more serious book." People are attracted to a tranquil look, and quiet, centered type is a very English tradition. The illustration tends to come fairly low down on the book, and that gives the type space to breathe.

The titles and author's names don't appear to be any larger than 18 point. And within each group, they're all set in the same typeface. Was there any resistance to this extremely restrained approach?

McConnell: There is inevitably resistance when you put change into any organization. But it wasn't immense, and the board was very brave and said, "No, we're going to back John." They supported me, and finally the success started to happen and all the criticisms went away.

How much does being a partner in Pentagram help you overcome a client's initial resistance?

McConnell: It helps. No question. And of course, so does bringing other commercial experiences to bear. Most people in the book publishing business are amazingly uncommercial.

Can you describe the process by which the jackets get designed?

McConnell: When I first went into Faber, covers were designed in the corridor or they sort of just materialized out of ether. I set up a meeting routine every fortnight, every two weeks, in which the editor brings in a brief that describes the book, and that brief is discussed by the sales director, the overseas salesperson, some marketing staff, and me. Then I make the necessary design and bring it back a fortnight later.

The financial rewards for doing book jackets are not high, so you have to get very good at doing a lot of them very quickly. Every fortnight, I pick up twenty briefs and drop off twenty designs. Some of the meetings are funny and some are tense; there are good days and bad days

When you say, "Make the necessary design," does that mean one design, or does the client want to see a few alternatives?

McConnell: I have always done only one. I don't believe in the business of, "Here are six designs," because I don't know how you could do more than one properly. That's not to say that they all get through every time.

When they don't get through, what kind of criticisms do you hear?

McConnell: Usually it is, "You've missed the flavor of the book." In fiction, what you're trying to do is get a sense of the mood of the book and the atmosphere the book provokes. So the editor is much more likely to say, "You haven't gotten it yet," or "It's more surreal or less surreal than that" than, "I don't like that yellow."

I've heard that you don't read any of the books.

McConnell: I argue that if you read a book, and get enthralled by it, your emotions about it become too complex. You're trying to translate a five-hundred-page novel, which is an extremely elaborate, layered object, into one image. It gets dangerous if you get too close to it. People may resent me for this, but I find that by standing back, it's easier to get a sense of it.

The editors at Faber are extremely good at explaining an idea, a feeling, what it's "sort of like." They might say, "Do you remember such-and-such a book we did three years ago? It's sort of like that." The beauty of dealing with fiction is that it helps not to be too literal. You want to come in slightly obliquely, to give sufficient room for the reader to interpret the imagery. And if you make it too direct, the author might get upset because somehow you've turned an idea into hard reality by making a picture of it. If you depict a character in the book, it's dangerous because they didn't see it that way in their mind's eye.

Over all the years, you've done more than six thousand jackets. Is it still exciting and fun?

McConnell: Yes, absolutely.

I understand you are a director of the company. Isn't this an unusual role for a graphic designer?

McConnell: I was a board director of Clark's Shoes in America, so I've done it before. If you consider that the visual presentation is of commercial value, you really should have someone in authority managing it. All companies have personnel directors who manage people and financial directors who manage the money and probably a legal director. Why not a design director?

Designers must get out of the position of being typeface-choosers and must take the debate to senior management about the assets and value we can bring. If you think about it, they commission us to make their businesses better. The discussion is not about whether you should use Times Roman, but about how what we do can make an impact on how well the company does.

What is your opinion of design in which typographical forms are treated as purely decorative elements?

McConnell: Like bits of concrete poetry. I have a feeling that all of that is a backlash against clients who are too demanding and want you to work more for less money. It relates to the Victorian concept of the artist who starves for his art in his garret. The argument goes that being commercial is in poor taste; doing your own thing is the only thing worthwhile, and it's worth starving for. It's marvelously self-fulfilling, because you could be producing the worst stuff in the world. No one's buying it, but at least you're starving, so you must be doing something right. It's a lovely way out.

[Later that day, I met with Matthew Evans in Faber & Faber's offices in Bloomsbury, near the British Museum.]

John explained the strategy he presented to you at the outset: if a reader enjoys a book by a publisher, he or she will seek a similar experience from other books in the publisher's list, which are identifiable because of a house style of design. Was this a radical idea for you to accept?

Evans: In the sixties and seventies, Grove Press followed that kind of thinking. The City Lights bookshop imprint had a certain pulling power. Actually, it was a very easy idea for us to accept. Most of our books have a comparatively small audience, say, five to ten thousand people, so you can take that kind of approach. When you get into the mass market, we approach things a little differently.

How did you get started with John and Pentagram?

Evans: In 1982, I went to Australia and suddenly saw how dowdy and dull the Faber book covers looked in comparison to what was on the shelves there. I came back saying, "We must do something about this." It was a moment in Faber's history when a whole new generation had come into the firm. So, it seemed a good idea to use design to reinforce the idea that the firm was pointing in a different, more modern direction. Somebody here knew a partner in Pentagram, we started discussions with them, and they decided it would be good for them, too. They seemed incredibly grand for us. They were doing a lot of work for Swiss banks and Arab banks and perhaps feeling that they'd lost touch with their real constituency, which was publishing. They all loved designing covers.

The only reason we were able to afford Pentagram was because they wanted to do it and agreed to a rate we wouldn't have been comfortable with had they charged us full price. Once they came on board, they set up a way of running design, which has worked quite well.

> **Takeaway message:**
>
> Designers must get out of the position of being typeface-choosers and be able to communicate the assets and value we can bring.

And that way of running design is . . . ?

Evans: The first lesson we learned is that you can't design by committee. When Pentagram made its presentation to Faber, which was an all-embracing presentation about what our books looked like, our writing paper, the way our invoices looked coming off the computer, what our packing cases looked like in the warehouse, the only reason we were able to force it through was because I said, "This is going to happen." If I had asked everybody here, "What do you think?" the whole thing would have been watered down. Fortunately, I had the power base to do that.

A total corporate identity or branding program. What was the reaction?

Evans: At first, the marketplace hated the sudden switch from basically typographical covers to this modern look. Ever since T. S. Eliot, Faber poetry has been looked on with great interest. When a new book appeared in a bookshop, people said, "I must buy this because it will be interesting." All of a sudden, everybody was wondering what on earth had happened to Faber. The sales reps hated the new look. The poets hated it.

But we just kept going. Gradually, everybody's attitude changed. After a couple of years, it was something that everybody liked.

From everybody hated to everybody liked? What do you think caused that kind of change in attitude?

Evans: To look at a cover in isolation is very difficult. But soon things began to build up to a range of covers. So when you went into a bookshop, you began to see a whole row of our books, and that had a real impact. And because the new covers were perceived to be so attractive by the retailers, they used Faber books almost as design statements themselves. And so the windows would be filled with our books; they thought the design was so

All you need is love?

Allow time for a relationship between a client and a designer to develop. It takes a while for the partners to really appreciate each other.

attractive, it added value to the store. At the Frankfurt Book Fair, praise was heaped on the Faber stand. We started getting compliments from design markets that are much stronger than Britain: Italy, Germany, Sweden.

Are you saying that the relationship between the public and a new design is something like an arranged marriage, at least as they're depicted in literary fiction? It takes about two years for the partners to appreciate each other?

Evans: Absolutely. It's hard to describe the impact now because we've been doing this for such a long time. But all of a sudden, here was Faber demonstrating that design matters.

And your competitors followed suit?

Evans: Faber could not claim to be the first publisher to put titles in rectangular panels on covers. But certainly the idea was copied in the sense that a lot of publishers then went to design firms, some of which came up with a solution that wasn't a million miles away from the Pentagram work for Faber. There were one or two European publishers who just completely ripped off our look. I mean, it was like looking at a Faber catalog. That's when I asked John to take things in a new direction.

Can you tell me about your firm's design briefs?

Evans: The way you run design in a place like this is interesting because editors tend to be quite articulate and quite difficult. John's idea was to have a meeting every other Wednesday in which the editors present a brief for their books.

The idea of the brief is to describe the book, not to tell the designers how to design the book. After they describe the book, the editors can say, "I suggest this or that," but they can't say anything about the design, because that isn't their talent.

I understand that authors can be difficult, too, and can have veto power. What percentage of jackets are not approved?

Evans: Chances are that if we like them, the author will as well. It's a very small percentage. That's because we have a very dictatorial way of doing things around here. Me supporting John. It was wonderful in the early days.

It was very tough, there wasn't too much consensus, and there was a lot of tension. I think that a lot of good design came out of that tension.

We've all seen that some of the best design can happen when there's a visionary or two in a dictatorial position.

Evans: Everybody has an idea on design, which they don't have on the content of the book, or on how to sell the book. I'm amazed by how people don't respect the designer's position, because by saying, "I think this or that color ought to be altered," what they're really saying is, "You don't know how to do your job."

Why do you think people believe anyone can be a designer, but not a writer?

Evans: Design is all around us, and everyone has a view on it. Design is what sort of shoes you put on in the morning, what color tie. Everybody makes design decisions all the time, and nobody can evaluate how good they are at it. In moments of extreme anger, the sort of abuse that comes out of my mouth has to do with calling editors visually illiterate who say they want a color changed or something moved. You've got to be very tough. But we also get one hundred and twenty-five unsolicited manuscripts a week, all of which except the tiniest fraction of a percent are dreadful, so a lot of people do think they can be a writer.

> **The Design Brief**
>
> It is the client's responsibility to describe the situation, the needs, the desired results—in detail. And provide the budget and the schedule.
>
> It is the designer's responsibility to make the desired results happen.

After all these thousands of jackets, does Pentagram bring in designs that astonish and delight you?

Evans: Yes, absolutely. Ours is a creative relationship, but it's also a sort of sausage-machine relationship because we have to have two hundred and fifty to three hundred new designs every year.

A huge amount of that work is fantastic. This is the thing that keeps it all going and alive. ∎

9

The Financial Wizard

The Linc Group
AND Rick Valicenti

Martin E. Zimmerman is president of **LFC Capital**, a Chicago-based boutique investment bank that providies financing to healthcare providers and service companies. Previously, he was chairman and CEO of **LINC Capital,** an equipment leasing and financing company. Zimmerman earned a BS in electrical engineering from MIT and an MBA in finance from Columbia Graduate School of Business, where he was a Kennecott fellow and a McKinsey scholar, and is now on Columbia's board of overseers. A contemporary art collector, he is a trustee of the Museum of Contemporary Art in Chicago.

Rick Valicenti is the founder and design director of **Thirst**, a communication design collaborative "devoted to art, function and human presence." A member or AGI and an AIGA Chicago Chapter Fellow, his notable awards include the 2006 AIGA Medal and a 2011 National Design Award by The Cooper-Hewitt, National Design Museum. His works are included in permanent collections, including the Museum of Modern Art. He worked on the projects for Linc in conjunction with marketing consultant Todd Lief.

Marty Zimmerman is the consummate designer's client. Rick Valicenti calls him "brilliant." That's because he sees the big picture. He does not want a repetition of what his competitors are already doing. He's a guy who says, "In many companies, there tends to be a kind of committee approach to design. We are more forward thinking." Zimmerman sought a designer who would never give him the look favored by many financial services companies: the blue textured cover, the gold-stamped logo, the group shots of the partners. Instead, he chose someone who's known for pushing the edges of the envelope pretty hard. Zimmerman's ideas about proven concepts, industry expertise, and using experts illustrate how to respond when a client asks a difficult question—or asks you to design a carbon-copy of what the competition is doing. "Being able to translate someone else's success into something fresh and new to your industry is what separates successful businesspeople who don't make many mistakes from those who do," he says.

NEW CASH FROM OLD BRICKS, CREATIVE LEVERAGE TO CAPITALIZE NEW OPPORTUNITIES.

If you only read and absorb one chapter of this book—and pass the messages along to your clients to demonstrate the thinking of a client who knows how to get great work from designers—this is the one.

[The conversation began with a phone interview with Marty Zimmerman.]

Q: What are your objectives for your company's communications?

A: Zimmerman: I want to influence people's thinking about us. Our printed communications are a means for closing a sale at the second level after we've been recommended at the first level. It's common in selling to hospitals, for example, that you sell to the person you're initially in touch with, usually a technical or financial officer. Then there's a recommendation to a committee—maybe of two alternatives—and the committee or the administrator who is his superior will make a decision. You can't get at that second level directly. You have to get at it through advertising or printed materials.

Are you competing against big-name investment banks?

Zimmerman: We're competing against big-name commercial banks, big-name leasing companies, and in some cases, big-name investment banks. We call our business "lease investment banking" because it's more than leasing. But it's not typically long-term financing; it's typically medium-term. We're a smaller company competing with large institutional-type players. We have to be able to explain why it is an advantage for an institutional user to work with someone other than an institutional supplier.

> You can't do a good job as a designer unless you:
>
> Know who your client is competing against and familiarize yourself with the industry's issues and terminology.

Institutional clients—banks, accounting firms, other service companies—often request a design approach they think will appeal to their clients: a low-key, restrained look. What makes you more daring?

Zimmerman: In many companies, there tends to be a kind of committee approach to design. Our approach is more forward thinking, more on the leading edge. We sell the firm with this concept: we're more specialized, we've got all the experience, but we're not as large; along with our smaller size comes flexibility and responsiveness and more attention by senior people. The whole idea is to have a serious approach to solving problems, but one that is more creative.

How much direction did you give Rick Valicenti?

Zimmerman: Quite a bit. First of all, we voiced our philosophy. That took a series of meetings. We have content objectives that we need to accomplish with a given piece of collateral or advertising. A certain type of content or editorial approach suggests a certain type of design approach. But we don't want to be totally pinstriped, so I'll give a designer flexibility in terms of imagery. The whole idea is to create a feeling of success and sophistication. We want to be known as a creative-type financing source, where people can get new concepts for existing problems. There are lots of problems out there, but there are not too many fresh ideas on how to solve them. We're the guys people come to for the tough ones. With that reputation, I hope we'll be called on for the easier ones, too. The idea is to get on everybody's bid list and have a shot at getting new business, not simply by virtue of a low price, but by virtue of more value added.

You are the chairman of the company. I am impressed that you deal directly with designers.

Zimmerman: I don't like to work through someone else. I want the designer to be there, and he appreciates it because he can defend himself. I might comment on what I think is wrong or right. Then he'll say, "Here's what I've been trying to do," or "Here's why I did it." And sometimes I'll step back. I don't dictate to designers—ever—particularly if a designer feels strongly about something. Most designers are sensible enough to know that their client has a sense of what he wants to communicate; that he wants something fresh, attractive, and interesting; and that he wants to avoid the dull, repetitious stuff that bores him and, ultimately, bores the reader.

Do you ever criticize a detail, such as "Why do we need this little red line right here?"

Zimmerman: If I think something's extraneous, sometimes I'll ask why it's used, and sometimes I'll get an answer. I usually don't fight that kind of thing. I do pay a lot of attention to things like legibility of subheads—the layout from the point of view of the reading public. Sometimes, designers will devise a layout that's simply hard to read because they use reverse type or type that's not bold enough. For example, in our brochure the subheads have been screened back too far. Small matter, but it's something that impacts legibility. Now, when we reprint, we're not going to change much, but we'll make those heads darker. Ordinarily, though, I wouldn't say anything about little red lines. I want the designer to feel that it's his or her design, and that it hasn't been all gouged up by the client. I refrain from commenting on design issues that don't directly pertain to the communication of the copy.

What was the industry response to your publications?

Zimmerman: Quite positive, on the whole. Actually, our own people found them a little sophisticated at first, but they've gotten used to them. Have they changed the way our clients think about us? There's no doubt in my mind.

Do you view your brochures as an investment? Very often, to accomplish something this ambitious, designers have to do a huge selling job on the client, who might not be able to project the benefit of techniques like matte and gloss varnish to his business. Did you have to be sold?

Zimmerman: Well, I certainly looked at the pros and cons of those decisions. Ultimately, we look at something major like this brochure series as having at least a two-year life. We're dealing in an area where the difference of $5,000 or $10,000 in production costs can be made up for by just one sale. So if I can see something that might get me a sale over the course of a year or two years, it's much easier to justify.

Can you relate specific things like additional ink colors to making a sale? Or do you feel, instead, that high quality in general makes a subliminal sell to a prospective customer?

Zimmerman: Both. We want to make sure that our stuff looks as good as that of any bank or investment bank. I mean, you decide how you want to spend your money! A six- or seven-color job can be appropriate for an omnibus corporate brochure. We made it go further by using the imagery in the individual operating company pieces. When you spend a lot of money on getting original images, the cost can be amortized over many different pieces. And sometimes we do produce one- or two-color pieces. And then it's especially important that the design is striking and enhances the message.

If other clients wanted to educate themselves about using the available marketing tools and talent to impact their businesses in a positive way, how would you suggest they go about it?

Zimmerman: I think you learn a lot by interviewing the smartest, most successful practitioners around. I got my first designer by calling a houseware specialty retailer in Chicago, Crate & Barrel, that had—and still has—wonderful design. I knew Gordon Siegal a little bit, and I asked, "Gordon, who do you use for design? Who's terrific?" And he said, "Here's the guy."

That's how I got started, and from there it was just constant interviewing, constant talking to people, and constant looking at design work. Making sure that I kept up with some of the good stuff that's been done.

I'd like to discuss another issue, which is the line between industry expertise and perceived conflict of interest. First, industry expertise. Would it matter to you if your designer had never done a brochure for a company in the leasing business?

Zimmerman: It wouldn't matter a bit. In fact, I'd rather they had never done one. What concerns me is whether the designer had worked for companies that wanted to achieve the kinds of objectives we want to achieve. I'm concerned that the designer know the kind of look I identify with as an emerging growth-type company, trying to be leading edge in a conservative market. Being able to reflect that image is more important than knowing anything about the technical side of my business.

One designer I know submitted a proposal to one of the major airlines for a series of international tour brochures. Apparently, the airline was impressed with the proposal, but because the firm's portfolio didn't include another travel brochure exactly like what they were looking for, they chose another designer. What would you say to a client like that?

Zimmerman: I would tell a client that if you find exactly what you are looking for in a designer's portfolio you are setting yourself up to get a repetition of what somebody else—your competitor—has already used! The advantage of using someone who has done effective work in a similar opportunity or problem area, for another industry, is that you can translate someone else's success into something fresh and new to your industry.

That's a perfect answer. If the designer had said that, the client might not have believed it.

Zimmerman: That's what separates really successful businesspeople—who don't make many mistakes—from the people who do. Let me explain. The way of avoiding mistakes is to take a proven concept and use it in another industry. To come up with a concept that's never been used anywhere is risky, because you don't know whether it will work at all. But it's a lot less risky, for example, to introduce McDonald's in Uruguay when you know it has worked in Brazil and all over the US. That's what we do to minimize risks.

It's not always possible, but I've borrowed lots of ideas from computer leasing and from investment banking. I try to bring them into the context of health care finance and our other activities. Our corporate structure reflects the structure of one of the most successful computer manufacturers, an emerging growth company. Why? Because I've seen it work, and I'm close enough to what that company's done to know that it's a sensible corporate structure for us, even though I also know that there's no other corporate leasing company in the country that uses it. To me, it's been proven. I'm just applying it to a different industry.

When a prospective client says, "You've never done one for someone exactly like us before," I bet a lot of designers wish they could make an argument as articulate as yours. What should they say?

Zimmerman: If a person knows they might not be able to respond persuasively, the easiest thing to do is to refer to an expert.

Here are three ideas: One way—and this is not the solution for everyone—is to work with a marketing or communications consultant. Our consultant, Todd Lief, the interface between us and our designer, was formerly a principal at a couple of major Chicago boutique agencies. Designers are constantly faced with marketing issues that are difficult for them to respond to, and they just don't have the credibility of people with a full-scale marketing background. So it's helpful for a designer to have someone like that on board. Then the designer can say, "Look, it's worked here, and our marketing expert recommends it for your situation. Why don't you discuss it with him?"

The second thing the designer could do is tell the client directly that it's very effective to apply something that's been done for a company in a different industry. In reality, the problem's the same, but this approach will give the client something fresh and not a rehash of what his competition has done. The last thing we want is something another leasing company has done.

A third way to sell a concept is to ask the client in your initial conversation, "What company in another industry would you model yourself on?" It may be that someone would model his company on Federal Express. Then when you come back, you can make that comparison and say, "Federal Express has used this technique and this kind of a look to distinguish themselves, and we're suggesting that you use something a little bit like that, but updated." Comparative selling can work very well. It depends on the person you're trying to sell.

Need Help Selling Your Ideas?

1. Get a credible marketing expert on your team (even on a part-time or project basis).

2. Show the client how a similar idea worked successfully in a different industry.

3. Ask the client to tell you what organization they'd model themselves on. Demonstrate how that organization achieved success with the technique you're proposing.

You suggest working with a marketing person. Many clients I've spoken to are opposed to the kind of marketing person who sells design services. But you are talking about a different role: someone who is working on behalf of the client rather than selling for the designer.

Zimmerman: Yes, exactly. The marketing person we work with is an independent professional. He's on our team, so to speak, as well as on the designer's team. Together, the two of them provide many of the services of an agency. From Rick Valicenti's standpoint, I think, Todd not only writes the copy, he translates our objectives and sharpens the focus of the materials. Because of that, Rick doesn't waste time going down creative blind alleys; the work is on target.

How to market services is always a dilemma for the independent designer. An agency has its own people to market its services—the account managers, the senior guys, and design is provided within the context of the overall solution. But a more interesting issue is how an independent designer markets services, and does he or she use a marketing person? It can work if the marketing person is not just a salesperson, but an adviser to the client.

Let's talk a bit about the flip side of "You've never done it before," and that's, "You've done too much of it." Some clients, especially in the service and financial sectors, are worried about conflict of interest. The designer who didn't have specific travel experience went to see a large accounting firm, and the reaction was, "You work for our competitors. We can't use you." He couldn't win! It's seen as a potential problem: "You're going to let our secrets out."

Zimmerman: It's a problem shared by agencies, a complicated issue. Certain clients resign if their agency gets another client in the same industry.

How would you feel if your designer also worked for one of your competitors?

Zimmerman: I wouldn't want it if it were exactly the same direct market, with the same customers, with the same kind of product. If it were a different product, or a different market, I wouldn't have a problem. My thought would be that a designer, having worked closely with several competing firms, could see their differences clearly and would be better positioned to give them different looks, different approaches.

Does the concept of industry expertise have value for you?

Zimmerman: Yes, except I use a designer for ideas as well as for visuals. And I want to make sure that other people don't have access to those ideas. In terms of something like a stationery design, it really wouldn't be a problem. But I use a designer for considerably more, such as coming up with thoughts and observations, as well as reflections on marketing communications. I don't want to get thoughts that are reflective of what someone else is doing.

[I followed up with Rick Valicenti.]

When you started working with Marty Zimmerman, did you know anything about the technical side of his business?

Valicenti: No, and I probably still don't. But I know a lot about him. I was able to design ads and brochures about equipment investment banking because, in that situation, I had the luxury of working with Todd Lief, and he distilled the message in language I could understand and that Linc's audience—an enlightened and curious audience—could understand.

How would you describe Mr. Zimmerman as a client?

Valicenti: Not only is he brilliant at acquiring companies and creating new

Takeaway message:

Successful designers navigate the process so that in the finished product, the compromises are not apparent.

business models, he is a contemporary art collector. He started his collection with artifacts of contemporary architecture—architects' drawings and models. He has a particular interest in Chicago architecture—Louis Sullivan terracottas and Frank Lloyd Wright drawings and glass. There was new art in his office every time I visited. It could be Jenny Holzer, Andres Serrano, Cindy Sherman. The walls were painted by Sol LeWitt. I would ask him, "Marty, how do you have the radar? When you're collecting it, it's unknown, and a year or two later, it's at the forefront of the art world."

How does that relate to being a good client for a design firm?

It's his vision. He sees the world with clarity.

What took place during your initial conversations?

Valicenti: The first thing he said to me was, "What I admire about your portfolio is that you conceal compromise." He told me that he knew that every process has its compromises. He had evidently interviewed several designers in which the compromises were evident in their work. You know, when you're looking at a portfolio and the designer says, "The client made me do this or that." He recognized that it takes a good designer to navigate the entire process and have the compromises be transparent at the end.

How did you work through the details, such as the little red lines or slightly too-hard-to-read subheads he described?

Valicenti: I would make page compositions with greeked type and photo collages using stock images or pictures we would shoot to show what we were proposing. I would bring in a number of these collages or mock-ups, variations on a theme. In his office, I would move the pictures and the copy blocks around, and we would talk about them. That's a good way to get agreement from a busy person.

Are you working with Linc or LFC now?

Valicenti: In the last several years, we've moved away from financial services and other corporate clients to design clients. By that, I mean clients who are involved in "design" the process,"design" the noun. Our clients are architects, companies who are bringing designed objects to market. Inherently, this type of client understands a forward-thinking position.

You can pick and choose your clients so precisely?

Valicenti: We have a bit of that luxury, but we've consolidated our space and are working a little leaner, with nine people. This has always been a teaching environment. At least once every six weeks I visit a school—a design department at a college or university—and I give a lecture or a workshop. We always have an intern at the office, spending a year or two, learning.

What do you teach about how to best work with clients?

Valicenti: There's one word that sums it up. That word is "relationship." Good work only comes from a good relationship. And that means a relationship in which there can be a discourse. There's give and take. You build the relationship on that trust. It's not like you're presenting to Julius Caesar. Then when the client calls and says, "I'm in a pinch. I need something really good, but I don't have the budget," you can give of yourself, agree to a reduced fee. Down the road, he or she is going to remember you.

And your definition of discourse?

Valicenti: Being able to have a discourse means I am not seen as a vendor. I'm perceived as counsel. And I encourage everyone here to behave as counsel. That means being able to ask the client, "Are you sure?"

To the question, "Are you sure?" the client might say, "Yes, I'm sure. Now use this picture." What about being more direct and telling the client, "No, it's not a good idea to use that picture"?

Valicenti: "Are you sure?" is a question that encourages dialogue. It's less aggressive, less defensive than, "Don't use that picture." I don't like to give outright advice. That's not how I want to be spoken to. Another line I use is, "I want to go on the record [as recommending such-and-such]." It's a classic line. It buys time. It challenges the client to think about the issue. The next morning, he or she might call back and say, "I thought about that" or "Let's talk about it." Then you have another opportunity to build on your successes. ■

> **Are they hearing you?**
>
> Good work comes from a relationship where there is a discourse, where you are not seen as a vendor, but as counsel.

10 The Biotech Entrepreneur

Abiomed
AND Weymouth Design

Abiomed, Inc., is a Danvers, Massachusetts, manufacturer of cardiac-assist devices. With an initial public offering that raised $12 million, Abiomed became a public company in 1988, and since has led in the development of break-through technologies, including a heart pump that benefits patients during or after surgery, after a heart attack, or while waiting for a donor heart for transplant. **Dr. David M. Lederman** founded the company in 1981 and was its first chairman, president, and chief executive officer.

Graphic designer and photographer **Michael Weymouth** studied at New England School of Art and worked for ten years in the Boston design community prior to founding **Weymouth Design** in 1973. His firm, which has offices in Boston and San Francisco, specializes in identity design, web, print, and video, including annual reports and communications for many high-technology companies and start-ups. His firm's design work and his photography have repeatedly been honored by the Mead Annual Report Show, *Communication Arts*, *Print*, and *PhotoGraphis*.

Years before it would have any FDA-approved products to sell, Abiomed invested in top-quality photography, design, printing. It made sense; why not do things from the outset that communicate quality and get noticed by the investment community and the media? Dr. David Lederman, a leader in developing cardiac support technology, also proved himself a leader in how to find and work with a designer. He devised a test: "I asked designers whether they would do things in a particular way, intentionally giving them examples that exhibited very poor taste . . . they said okay; they'd do it." He wasn't impressed with anyone too willing to compromise. After choosing Mike Weymouth, he resisted, as he put it, the temptation to micromanage, saying, "If you demand mediocrity, I think a smart designer would drop you and your company as a client." The result: publications that, unlike some others for growing companies, don't look like low-budget, do-it-yourself solutions. Why doesn't everyone do things that way? I was pleased to have the opportunity to speak with Dr. Lederman and find out.

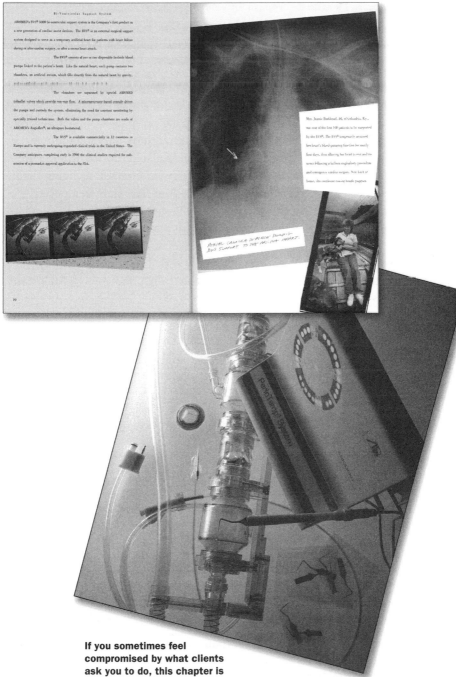

If you sometimes feel
compromised by what clients
ask you to do, this chapter is
intended to get you thinking
in a new direction.

[A phone interview with Dr. Lederman began the conversation.]

Q: Several years ago, *Business Week* ran a cover story, "Small Is Beautiful: America's Hot Growth Companies." I wrote to the companies for their annual reports and found out that even if the numbers were beautiful, with a few exceptions, the annual reports were anything but. You've done things differently than many CEOs of young companies, for whom extremely low-budget productions seem to be good enough. Why?

A: Lederman: Many young companies, start-ups, do not pay enough attention to the market. An annual report is a mechanism to tell the stockholders the status and prospects of their investments. But it is also a mechanism for the company to present itself to the world. If you think of yourself as being "beautiful," to use *Business Week*'s word—even if it's your first year as a public company—it is important to show exactly what is beautiful about you, and it is very important to find someone who can do that well. I have been told that the majority of people spend somewhere between seventeen and twenty seconds on a report before throwing it away, and that they only look at the chairman's letter and at the photographs, so the design becomes as important as the words.

Well, I've read they spend five minutes in a couple of studies by investor relations firms.

Lederman: I'm glad to hear that. I certainly spend more than five minutes on the companies I follow. Typically I ask, "Why did they decide to show that picture, that product, that person?" or "Why did they say this or that?"

What you think of yourself, your self-image, also applies to a company. Quite frankly, I don't think the issue of cost is the deciding element in the decision to go with a leading graphic designer. While cost consciousness is obviously a concern, when you break down the cost of making any publication, there may be a tendency to be penny-wise and pound-foolish. You may try to save on something, and in the long run, it costs you more. All smart companies realize that the marketing of the company is as important as the marketing of the products. Companies that think small are likely to stay small.

For many small, new companies—whether its an annual report or marketing materials or the website—budget is often the number-one consideration. If they went directly to a printer, for example, with pictures from the files or cheap stock photos and said, "Put these together with our financials and print 10,000 copies" maybe they would spend $20,000, just to use a round number. On the other hand, a graphic designer might propose, "You need original photography and a much higher level of quality." Perhaps the cost would then be five times that much. And to the client, that would be a significant amount of money that could be spent on something else. The thinking might be,"Our audience just want the facts and won't care about all this stuff." Is your feeling that they do care?

Lederman: Yes, but the spread you have given me could be narrower. One can spend more than $20,000 with a printer or get something very elegant for a lot less than $100,000.

Before we were a public company, we issued literature where we didn't hire a graphic designer—and it shows.

But all this is noise compared to the overall cost of going public, and the cost of maintaining a company in terms of legal, accounting, and other related expenses. You have to put everything in the right perspective. Think of the cost of doing business, and try to assess what percentage of that should be spent on projecting your message and informing the world and your stockholders of what you have done, are doing, and are planning to do. Again, very small companies tend not to be market driven. As they mature, companies become more market driven, so I would think that in most cases, the successful ones will change their minds. Am I right?

Yes, but by then there might be quite a lot of bad work that will need to be redone.

Lederman: Well, not for us. I am very happy we decided to go the way we did with our first annual report as a public company. And I have to tell you that our marketing staff is also happy because the book becomes more than just a financial report to stockholders. It serves numerous functions. It also becomes a marketing instrument for our products. It is also very important for recruiting. When interviewing prospective employees, especially during the phase of building the management team, the first document candidates ask for is the annual report; sometimes they won't even schedule an interview until they've seen it. It is to their benefit to read something that presents the company fairly and accurately, and the report pays for itself in that sense.

How did you meet Mike Weymouth and start to work with him?

Lederman: Since becoming a public company, we have used an outside consulting firm to help us set up an investor relations program. They introduced me to four different graphic designers. Each presented to me a representative assembly of work. I was simply and overwhelmingly more impressed with Mike's work. I have a lot of respect for good photography.

> **When you're negotiating, always remember:**
>
> What a company spends on design is "noise" compared to the costs of overhead, salaries, product development, and everything else.

Mike doesn't strike me as being the type of person who will do any project for any company; he apparently has to feel that there is something of real quality before he takes an assignment. There is a correspondence between the elegant kind of book he likes to do and the type of company that the book is about. It's not just a question of dollars and cents. Our mission is to save lives, and we derive a great sense of pride from our work.

Our company's success is not only measured by our ability to generate profit, but by our ability to develop medical technology that will save or improve human lives at a cost lower than comparable or existing therapies. Mike also gets a great deal of satisfaction and pride from his work. I asked him questions, and I asked the other graphic designers that I met—I won't reveal their names, of course—whether they would do certain things for me because I wanted them done a particular way. I intentionally gave them examples that, in my opinion, exhibited very poor taste. Imagine the layout or structure of a very ridiculous type of book. I said, "I would like something like this." They said okay; they'd do it.

Do you think that those who agreed weren't very good at what they did?

Lederman: Yes. It meant to me that it wasn't important to them how the piece was going to end up looking. If the designer doesn't have a strong feeling about his or her work, even if he or she disagrees with me, then I'm not very impressed.

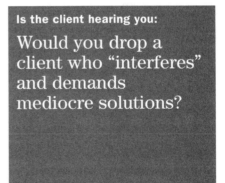

Is the client hearing you:
Would you drop a client who "interferes" and demands mediocre solutions?

You conducted something that delved much deeper than a portfolio review. You tested people to see if they were just going to be "yes" people and if your book was just going to be another job.

Lederman: Correct. To me, that was very important. If the others were as good as I am told—and I'm not saying they didn't do good work—they were not consistent. They were driven by the economics of their business.

They might also have been driven by being intimidated by past clients. The clients may have "made them do stuff" that they didn't feel was right, and they assumed that's the way these relationships had to be.

Lederman: That is precisely what they said to me! When I reviewed their work, I asked them how they could do work like that, and they said, that's how the client wanted it! That may be true. But if you look at the work of a designer of Mike's caliber—whether you like it or not—however diverse and different, he is consistent. Working with him, he voiced strong opinions, and I learned to respect him even more. His attitude is similar to and compatible with our corporate philosophy, our culture. I want to work with a person who seeks long-term relationships. After Mike thought about and discussed what he recommended as the focus of our first annual report, one can sort of project what the second one should be like, and what the third one, and so forth. I like that. I like the idea of long-term planning for annual reports and everything else. I would be curious to know how different I am from the others you have spoken with.

Several years ago, I surveyed a group of designers about what they found most rewarding and most problematic about client-designer relationships. To reflect on what you're saying, most designers told me that their biggest overall business problem was that clients seemed to want mediocre solutions. "Seemed to want" is too mild a term. They described clients who demanded mediocre solutions, who would say, "This is the picture I want for the cover; this is what we want on page three." How would you address clients like that? What advice would you offer?

Lederman: I consider myself to be very knowledgeable in my own field of medical device technology. I expect people whose expertise is in other areas of interest to recognize that, and acknowledge that I am better qualified to determine what is extraordinary or what is mediocre about medical-device products. If you have chosen the right graphic designer, he or she should also be considered an expert. I would say that once you have chosen someone you are comfortable with, the design should be driven more by what the designer feels than by what you feel.

Mike asked in the beginning, "What is it that you're trying to say?"And then he decided how to implement that. The client must offer the direction, but once the direction is given—if you have retained the right professional—you're not doing your job if you cannot delegate the creative decisions. If you interfere and demand mediocrity, I think a smart designer would drop you and your company as a client.

Here's an example: to my thinking, photography is one of the most important elements in a report. I am personally an enthusiastic photographer; I have my own darkroom and a collection of cameras. The temptation was high to get involved and try to micromanage. However, I pretty much left Mike alone. When the selection of photography came up, I asked some questions, and made some recommendations. But ultimately, the choices were the shots he selected, except for one photograph that I thought didn't look right and that we should reshoot. He agreed.

I don't think that we disagreed about anything; the book became largely what he recommended. This had never happened to me before. Very seldom have I been able to interact with someone from the outside in that way, and we do interact with a lot of outside professionals who provide us with various services. There are always disagreements. Maybe it's just personality compatibility, or maybe that's just how a relationship should be. But I do think the decision maker in a company must choose someone he can rely on to produce a high-quality product that represents the company well.

Sometimes those decisions are delegated to people who don't have the CEO's vision.

Lederman: That's a mistake. It's shortsighted. There are certain functions that are part of a CEO's job. You used the right word, "vision," which is one of the things you want to project in an annual report—and all other corporate communications. And that comes from the top. In this company, by the way, there were two people involved in the process—me and the person with the most marketing and sales experience in the company. He is a very important member of the management team and it is his charter and focus to sell our products. We didn't want to make a product catalog out of the report, but we did want to project the credibility of the company to our product customers, as well as to the stockholders. Our reports have done that very effectively.

[I followed up with Mike Weymouth.]

Many of your clients are high-technology and biomedical start-ups. What is unique about working in this market?

Weymouth: The majority of tech and biotech companies are headed by dynamic young scientists and management teams who embrace dynamic thinking in their graphic material. Unlike larger companies, where we often work with middle management, with start-ups we most often work directly with the CEO and can tap directly into his thought process. That's the magic formula for great design.

I was impressed when Dr. Lederman said that even though he's an amateur photographer and has his own darkroom, he resisted the temptation to micromanage. How rare is that?

Weymouth: Very rare. David is the quintessential great client in this respect. When you know your client has good taste, you raise our own creative bar. It's the best kind of challenge.

What do you think about his test for avoiding mediocrity, i.e., describing what he calls "a very ridiculous kind of book" and seeing if a designer would be willing to do it?

Weymouth: He's a sneaky guy. I am nothing but cautious in this respect. The process of feeling your way along in early meetings is tricky. I liken CEOs to supertankers. They have big, unwieldy egos, and they take a long time to turn around. Sometimes, as in the case with David, the tanker is going in the right direction under a full head of steam. With other CEOs, it's not so easy to detect their course. They may think the designer only cares about design principles. But in my case, I really do care about the CEO's objectives and less about my own, especially in first encounters. Also, if I'm talking to a potentially great client, I tend not to be unnecessarily opinionated. It's all part of the dance. David is just a lot smarter and intuitive when he plays it. And yes, many designers are willing to do ridiculous things, or at least things they aren't very happy about, in order to satisfy clients' wishes.

> **Will your idea fly:**
>
> For many designers, the magic formula for great results is working directly with the person at the top—and tapping into his or her thought process.

In general, how do you handle it when you're asked to do something you don't think is in the best interest of the client?

Weymouth: Clients who come to my firm tend to know they're going to get "new and different," and they actually listen to us, believe it or not. They ask us for our advice and, by and large, they take it. The dynamic you refer to happens mostly in the design review stage, in which the interview process weeds out uppity designers or those who do not fit the client's profile. I suspect we've lost out on lots of work at this stage because the clients didn't believe we would do what the CEO wanted and that we'd over-argue our own case. They probably looked at our design solutions and couldn't believe that a client actually agreed to them, when, in fact, the client was very happy with our work. It only points to the problem of dealing with middle management—when second-guessing the person at the top results in a safe, mediocre design firm getting hired. ∎

11

The Military-Industrial Complex

Northrop Corporation AND James Cross, Peter Harrison, Doug Oliver, and Mike Weymouth

Les Daly was with **Northrop Corporation**, Los Angeles, for thirty-three years as vice president for public affairs and chief communications officer. Prior to that he was based in Paris, where he directed Northrop's communications in Europe and the Middle East, taking a leave to become chief spokesman for the US Department of Energy.

Jim Cross, the designer of eighteen Northrop annual reports, started his career as Northrop's corporate design director. After three years there and a stint with Saul Bass, he founded Cross Associates, which became Siegel & Gale/Cross in 1988. A graduate of UCLA's College of Fine Arts and former director of the International Design Conference in Aspen, he is now a fine-art printmaker in Napa Valley, CA.

Peter Harrison studied at the London School of Printing and Graphic Arts and emigrated to New York, where he headed his own multidisciplinary practice until joining Pentagram as a partner in 1979. There, he designed the Northrop annual reports for 1991 and 1992.

Doug Oliver, an Art Center graduate, worked for James Cross and Robert Miles Runyan before founding his own Santa Monica consultancy, which designed the Northrop Grumman annual reports for 1996 and 1997.

Mike Weymouth, a photographer and design firm principal (see chapter 10), designed the Northrop annual reports for 1983, 1984, and 1987 through 1990.

The printed annual report, once the feather in every designer's cap, seems to be going the way of the dodo bird. SEC requirements for public companies—reporting of consolidated financial statements—stay the same, but most companies publish online. Many still realize the benefit of print communications, often a capabilities brochure with a pocket to hold the financials. Yet, all companies and designers would do well to study the example set by Northrop Corporation's history of extraordinary annual reports. Deceptively simple, elegant, and black-and-white, each book used museum-quality photography and printing to explain how massive aerospace-defense projects like fleets of fighter aircraft are designed, built, and tested. I was asking the questions when Les Daly, the Northrop executive who directed the annual report process, joined four of his longtime designers for a discussion that illuminates many of their secrets of success.

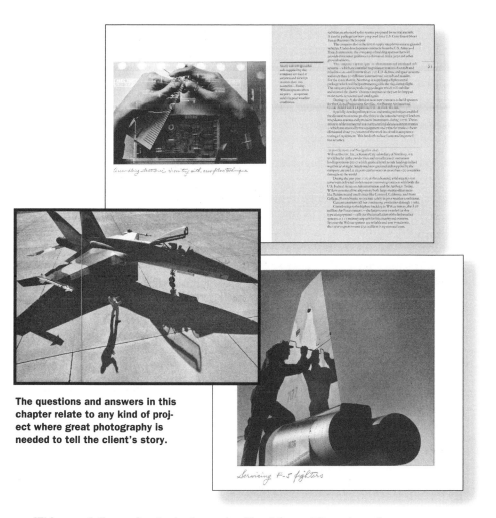

The questions and answers in this chapter relate to any kind of project where great photography is needed to tell the client's story.

[This panel discussion took place at a Mead Annual Report conference, chaired by Doug Oliver, in New York City.]

Q: Doug, why was it important to you to honor Northrop in this way today?

Oliver: Northrop was a touchstone of my career. After graduating from Art Center, I joined Jim Cross's office, and the 1978 book unfolded before my eyes, showing me the kind of work I wanted to do for the rest of my life. It had beautifully reproduced, dramatic, black-and-white photography framed by sensitively handled white space; elegant type that was correct down to the tiniest detail; paper chosen deliberately only after testing on press. I worked on quite a few reports with Jim, and over the years, I learned—among many other things—that you don't chase the Northrop annual report; they call you.

My call came when I was selected to design the 1996 Northrop Grumman report. I had visions of a long and rewarding run of books. But after we'd begun work on the next year's book, it was announced that Northrup Grumman and Lockheed Martin would merge. It looked like the company would disappear, and that my 1996 book would be the last of a tradition. I wanted to commemorate that tradition. As it turned out, the Department of Justice blocked the merger. But the genre is gone. The company is now a broad-based electronics supplier pursuing a new look and direction.

Les, you were responsible for selecting a stellar group of designers. What were your criteria?

Daly: We didn't want people to pick up our report and say, "That's a great design." We wanted them to say, "That's a great company." Good design, except to designers, is practically invisible. And good design doesn't cost any more than bad design. We wanted to sculpt everything down to perfect, functional design. And we needed solutions that were enduring, solutions with legs. We aimed at the core, not the edge: an absolutely perfect platinum sphere. We made our share of mistakes. But one thing we worked the hardest at—and that I'd advise other companies to do—was to create our own orchestra. By that I mean select the very best designer, photographer, printer. We formed a team, not a hierarchy with the designer in charge of everything. Then the designer could put every ounce of effort into designing and didn't have to worry about managing suppliers. The team would get together and everyone would contribute ideas and learn from each other. When we finished, everybody thought it was "their" book.

How did the process get started every year?

Daly: It started with the written word. What were we trying to say? Then we wanted to use photography to make it real. We wanted nothing faked or manipulated, no airplanes superimposed on backgrounds via retouching. The chairman's letter was real and the product descriptions were real and the numbers were real. The photos had to be real, too. If you fake an annual report in one place, it's not real in every place.

The direction remained remarkably consistent, didn't it?

Cross: It has, since the early sixties when I was Northrop's design director. I established the black-and-white medium because it was appropriate to the company's products and mission. It's not a colorful, glamorous type of business; it's a serious company involved in serious missions of national security. One year we might focus on the sculptural aspects of a guidance unit. Another year, it might be the people working on prototype fighter aircraft.

Do you think the best pictures come about through careful setting up, or are there

fortuitous accidents when something just happens or the light is perfect?

Harrison: The answer is both planning and magic. Sometimes the photographer will see something no one had planned.

Weymouth: Northrop had a natural instinct to let people go for it, to talk with their eyes, so to speak. There was a lot of control, but there was also a lot of respect and giving free reign, letting the designer and photographer do their thing. But always within the framework of the team.

Daly: If the photographer says, "I want to do something else," the corporate staff has to know whether it's appropriate to go off in that direction. Often the answer is, "Go get it. Shoot both. The picture we want and the one you want. Then we'll choose the right one."

Mike, were you the photographer on the reports you designed?

Weymouth: No. I don't think Northrop was aware of my photographer side when they hired me. I recommended that Northrop hire Bruce Davidson. We got the great photos and that's all that mattered. The fact that I was a photographer, though, made me a better designer. I knew the problems photographers faced. But I never went on shoots. Obviously, not every designer feels the same way, but maybe because I never wanted a designer hanging around when I was shooting, this was my chance to practice what I preach. And I was never disappointed with the results, although there are many factors besides aesthetics that go into the choice of a particular photo.

Daly: We were always looking for new talent. The idea today was to find the great young photographers who haven't been discovered yet—and to spend the time and work with them.

How many days of photography are required to accomplish results like this?

Harrison: Fifteen to twenty-five days. There's a lot of scouting and setting up.

And in fifteen to twenty-five days, how many pictures did you end up using?

Harrison: Eight to twelve.

I think that will surprise a lot of people.

Weymouth: Les used to say, "I want a photograph worthy of hanging in an art gallery." I never failed to be awed, entering Northrop headquarters, by the black-and-white photography on the walls.

Harrison: Because of that, Northrop owned black-and-white.

Isn't the process you're describing too costly for most clients to consider?

Cross: It can be worked out as part of the photographer's fee. The photographer has a vested interest, too, in taking the time to experiment. The best print for hanging in a gallery might not result in the best reproduction. We experimented: The first book was printed in rotogravure, a process using thick metal plates with deep incised dots, which gives you deeper tones. Another year, we worked with a chemically dulled ink.

Les said that good design doesn't cost any more than bad design. I want to give readers a sense of what a project of this magnitude does cost. What would a company need to budget to achieve this kind of quality?

Daly: We were all over the place, some years up, some years down.

Weymouth: It depends on the quantity.

Let me be more direct. What would you say if a company budgeted $100,000?

Harrison: Even if there were a budget of $250,000 for 150,000 copies, I would say it would be extremely difficult to achieve. Managing the photography takes a lot of planning and scouting, a lot of careful effort. It's enormously complicated. The best photographers are hard to find, and when you find them, they are almost impossible to book. And then, if possible, you have to budget to go on location with them.

Daly: This is where the staff is instrumental. I really want to make this point: designers tend to ignore the staffers' experience and creativity. They tend to think creativity walks in the room in the person of the designer or maybe the photographer. They say they want to deal directly with the CEO. If designers appreciated the talent inside the room, more learning would go on. The CEO probably knows zip about how to make any kind of publication. And if he's working on the annual report, somebody's not doing their job.

With all due respect, I can't tell you how many times designers have told me they worked with the communications staff, only to have the CEO tear the whole project apart at the last minute because he said it didn't reflect his vision.

Daly: That's why the CEO has people like me: so he doesn't have to think about the annual report and can concentrate on being CEO.

You are unique! If every communications manager were like you, the world would be a different place. This also relates to what you said about putting together your own orchestra. There's nothing that can sink a designer's heart faster than coming in and learning that the client has already picked the photographer and the printer. Most of us believe that those decisions should be the designer's, because the client may choose the wrong people for the wrong reasons.

Cross: You're right, Ellen. Ninety-nine percent of clients can't do it.

Harrison: Northrop is the exception, not the rule. It almost never works. The worst is when they try to hand you a box or file of photographs. In general, that's a lose-lose situation because there's no concept or strategy. Without focus, a project usually ends up as something of a dog's dinner.

Harrison: The important thing is that the design team has to operate high up on the client management food chain, preferably with access to the CEO. It's dealing with people several tiers down that can create a problem. Quite often, they're scared and don't have the authority to make real decisions. The worst results come about when you can't take appropriate risks. It has to be a passionate endeavor, and sometimes it's the designer's responsibility to push the client to take those risks.

Is the client hearing you?

When you present an idea, you have to be able to explain why it works. "I like it" isn't good enough.

Les, did you ever feel pushed? Or did any of you push beyond his comfort zone?

Cross: There was that book with the handwritten captions. We weren't totally in agreement, were we, Les? You weren't sure.

Daly: Right. I wasn't comfortable with it. Maybe I didn't understand it because I have terrible handwriting and this was beautiful handwriting, and it was supposed to be written by someone like me. I just had to get used to it.

Cross: And I had to sell it. A lot of designers aren't very articulate. When you present an idea, you have to be able to explain why it works. "I like it" isn't good enough.

Daly: Sometimes I had to push. Sometimes the designers did. And when they were doing the pushing, I needed to understand the reason for it. How does this advance where the company going? How will it help us get there?

In defense of designers, the designer needs an almost-scientific explanation to sell an idea. "I like it" is never good enough. You have to be able to say, "Ninety-seven percent of consumers responded positively . . . " But all the client has to say is "I don't like it," and the idea is killed.

Oliver: Unfortunately, it's sometimes part of our role to protect the client from himself. Sometimes what they ask for is not really what they need.

Cross: Don't listen to what a person is saying. Listen to what they mean.

Weymouth: It's all in the body language. At one point, I spent two or three nights on press, and the job still wasn't right. Les let me know how he felt with his body language.

What is it that causes a company like Northrop to change designers? Why are there four of you here?

Harrison: Isn't it amazing that we're all friends? ■

12

The Challenger

Revolution Foods
AND Addis Creson

Revolution Foods is an Oakland, California-based company founded in 2006 by CEO **Kristin Groos Richmond** and chief impact officer

Kirsten Saenz Tobey, who met at UC Berkeley's Haas School of Business. Their mission is to transform the way America eats by providing access to healthy, affordable meals at schools and food stores. Launched in 2006 with a pilot program serving lunches in five Oakland schools, the company delivers 200,000 meals a day to 1,000 schools around the country. They recently launched a rival product to Kraft's Lunchables.

Addis Creson is a Berkeley strategic design company with a twenty-five-year history of shaping brands to positively impact people's lives.

CEO **Steven Addis**, a graduate of Haas School of Business, is a brand expert who serves on the board of the UC Berkeley Art Museum.

Chief design and innovation officer **John Creson** has a BFA from Academy of Art University. He advises AIGA/San Francisco and the Sustainable Brands conference and mentors MBA students at California College of the Arts.

Can a fresh, colorful brand identity and packaging help a young company beat the entrenched leader? Let's cheer for the challenger in this underdog vs. giant story. In 1988, Kraft Foods' Oscar Mayer brand created "Lunchables" prepackaged meals for kids, and has owned the $1.35 billion niche category ever since. Now they've got competition. With the help of a Berkeley, CA, strategic design firm, a healthier alternative was developed by two Bay Area moms, the founders of Revolution Foods, a company that serves fresh meals at a growing number of K–12 schools across the country. Their slogan is "Real Food for All," and after a year of testing, Revolution Foods Meal Kits are now sold at Target Stores and at many Safeway and Whole Foods markets—and new retail outlets seem to be added daily. With no ad agency or television presence (except for segments on the news), they're taking on a giant conglomerate by using design to transmit the message of less fat and sugar and no artificial ingredients. And, it's hoped, help parents raise a generation of healthier kids.

Clean, colorful design presents kid favorites like PB&J, ham and cheddar, and cheese pizza as "grab & go meal kits with nothing but the good stuff." The package was designed to act as a billboard at shelf level.

Addis Creson transformed the company's previous apple symbol into a stylized graphic icon. In conversation, the word "Revolution" is often shortened to "Rev," so "olution" is grayed back to support the name "Rev Foods."

A fifty-five-page Revolution Foods identity guidelines book visualizes potential touchpoints with consumers, including billboards, T-shirts, and trucks.

In addition to logo standards, color palettes, and typography, the guidelines demonstrate photographic style and a "plate system" that extends the circle from the Revolution Foods icon to a system of circles that can be used in many applications.

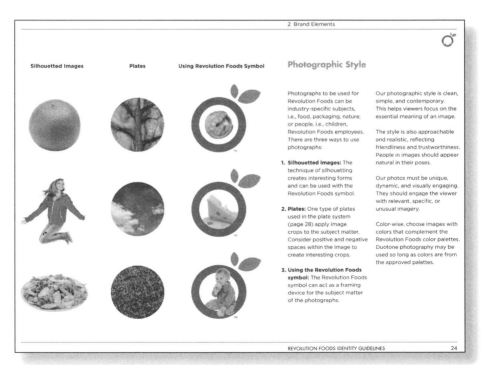

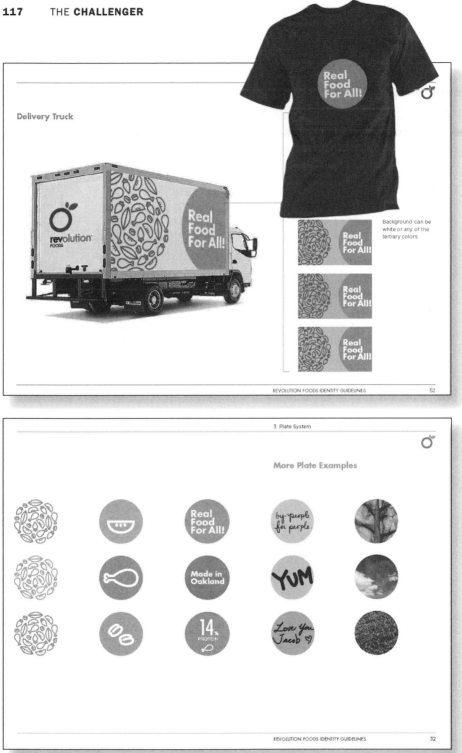

Delivery Truck

Real Food For All!

revolution
FOODS

Real
Food
For All!

Background can be
white or any of the
tertiary colors

Real Food For All!
Real Food For All!
Real Food For All!

3 Plate System

More Plate Examples

Real Food For All!

Made in Oakland

14%
PROTEIN

by-people for people.

YUM

Love you Jacob ♡

[The conversation began with questions for Steven Addis and John Creson.]

Q: Steven, I understand that you have a business degree. What inspired you to start a design firm?

A: Addis: After graduating from UC Berkeley and getting my degree from the Haas School of Business, I was in brand management at The Clorox Company. I felt that the creative agencies Clorox used had little to no ability to get into the heads of consumers. The people at those agencies had trouble getting away from their own biases. They would create advertising that seemed to be designed to motivate themselves to buy something. But my audience was doing seven loads of laundry a week and had nothing in common with a twenty-something creative director in San Francisco or New York.

As strategists and designers, we have the responsibility to move beyond "the focus group of one" and deeply empathize with people who are unlike us in every way. Without the ability to empathize, it's impossible to do what we do. So in 1987, I left Clorox and joined a small, three-year-old design studio and helped transform it into a firm that marries strategy and design. I later bought out the founder, and since then have managed the firm though the ups and downs of the industry.

I'm proud to say that today it's the kind of agency that I would want to work with as a client—one that's collaborative and conscientious, and that can tell a great story.

What has most contributed to the longevity of your firm?

Addis: Through nearly thirty years in business, we've had different chapters of business life and different teams. I'm proud to say that today we are an exceptional group of strategists and designers. One thing that has never changed is a philosophy that everyone contributes to our assignments. A strategist can sketch an idea and a designer can help develop a positioning. It's a supportive group that listens to each other and builds on everyone's ideas.

Creson: Our independence has also allowed us to be nimble and adept.

John, when did you join the firm, become partner?

Creson: I began my career at the San Francisco office of Addison, which specializes in brand strategy. In school, I'd learned about concept and craft. At Addison, I had the good fortune to work under Phil Seefeld, an integrated thinker who introduced me to the idea that design was beyond aesthetic. I carefully reviewed all the decks he created for clients, trying to understand how to develop strategic insight and create avenues for opportunity. That relationship had a big impact on how I approach design and brand development. I joined Addis in 1999 and became a partner in 2006.

Why Berkeley?

Addis: Berkeley provides us with a great quality of life. The weather is better than across the bay in San Francisco, there's wonderful food, and it's easy to get to and from any part of the Bay Area. It also fits our positioning of creating positive change in the world. We seek clients who are passionate about what they bring to the market, as well as their values and ethos. Berkeley combines everything we love, especially the diversity of thought.

You say that you seek clients. Do you reach out to certain industries, for example, speaking at conferences that potential clients attend?

Addis: We focus on brands that create positive change. We love working with a diversity of industries, and we seek clients that are trying to change the game for the better. If it's food, we like to work on healthier food, for example, for eleven years as Kashi's branding firm. In technology, we created the processor identities for Intel from 1992 to 2005. Now we're working with brands like Revolution Foods and Audi. Both are redefining how things are done in their industries.

Between work and our families, it's hard to find the time to speak at conferences. John is an advisor for and has spoken at the Sustainable Brands Conference, and I never miss going to TED, and spoke there once. But we do need to raise the awareness of our boutique firm and get out there more often.

Whom does your work speak to?

Successful designers keep their focus on the needs of the audience—the people out in the world buying or using their clients' products and services. And they never underestimate the intelligence of that audience.

To you, how important are design awards? Do you think the kind of clients who are looking for firms like yours read design magazines or awards show annuals?

Addis: These days, we enter very few competitions. Frankly, awards have little to do with attracting clients. They're more about giving recognition to the team involved.

Creson: There are so many award shows these days, so we try to be selective about the ones we enter. I would agree that we don't enter to try to attract clients, but we've been fortunate and have attracted clients because of our award-winning work.

Did Revolution Foods find you, or did you identify them as the right kind of client?

Addis: Revolution Foods did their homework and contacted a short list of firms that they felt would be a good fit. Then they met with each firm. There's no substitute for chemistry and shared passions. For us, we had an instant connection and just hoped they felt the same. Luckily, they did.

How was the assignment presented to you? At what stage of development were they? For example, did they bring you any packaging prototypes?

Creson: When we started with Revolution Foods, it was immediately clear that they are special. Not only are they the kind of people you'd want to work with, it is a company driven by a clear sense of mission. Our challenge was to help them evolve their brand and products while maintaining the goodness that already existed. They already had a few products at retail, but had shifted their approach on how and what they would market to consumers. The previous packaging was not considered as part of our development.

Specifically, the project was to develop a new brand identity and package design. Early on, they expressed a desire to refresh the brand in a different way: different in both the process we followed and the results that would differentiate them from the competition. They wanted to be creative and collaborative. Their desire suited our approach, and we began by developing many different ideas and stories that positioned and expressed the brand.

What is the thinking behind the logo? For example, what is the significance of outlining the *O* of the apple symbol?

Creson: We create brand identity systems versus engaging simply in logo exercises. MeaniOg that each mark is shown within a larger ecosystem of elements that include strategy, story, and experience. The symbols we create are markers of meaning within the overall brand narrative.

Throughout our process, the idea that Revolution Foods was leading a movement to provide real food for all was critical. We believe the company will become one of the rarefied few, iconic brands. The new symbol conveys the idea of simplicity of ingredients. More important, it conveys that a single ripple can start a profound transformation for a healthier future.

The new logo is a modern evolution from their previous mark, which was a cartoonish apple appropriate for another time in the business lifecycle. After developing a variety of options, it became clear that maintaining the equity of the red apple was essential. A further goal was to create a look that would appeal to both kids and adults. The new mark struck that balance and could be playful or formal depending on the audience and message.

And the choice of lower-case Futura type with 'rev' in black and 'olution' in gray?

Creson: In conversation, the word "Revolution" was often shortened to "Rev." In the wordmark, "olution" was grayed back to support this. A special version of Futura was created in which the weight and several letterforms were modified to enhance the look and readability.

Is your office divided into teams that serve certain accounts, or does everyone contribute design concepts?

Creson: It varies. For some accounts, we tend to have a core team that works with that client day-to-day and brings others in to stretch or freshen the thinking. On projects, who is chosen to work on a specific assignment depends on factors like expertise required, relevant experience, and passion. For projects of a certain size, we also like to bring in outside contributors. We find that this nourishes us and is beneficial to the work we do for clients.

In general, do you feel like you have to 'sell' or rationalize the best idea to the client, or is it usually clear to everyone around the table that "this is the one"?

Creson: Working with clients who are founders is different than working with other types of companies. I've learned that it requires an ability to really listen. Understandably, there is no separation from who they are and what their brand reflects. When you're progressing the brand it, becomes a very personal process. I've found that allowing them space to consider and discuss helps to build the best outcomes.

I'd like to believe great work speaks for itself, but find that to be rare.

On your website, you show process photos of what appears to be a brainstorming session in a cabin in the woods. It looks like the evolution of a package design and post-its with reasons parents might want to buy healthy meal kits for their kids. Can you describe the concept development process you go through: is it collaborative with the client, or do you do the work internally and then present a recommended direction?

Creson: The client was interested in developing the brand in creative ways. The photo is of Gunther Lie, director of brand experience at Revolution Foods at the RevFoods Summit that took place over several days at an inn on Mt. Tamalpais. About fifteen of us from various backgrounds went into the woods to ideate, debate, and develop the next revolution.

Internally, we go through a process of design thinking to develop customer empathy and opportunity for the brand. It's a great way for every-one to contribute unique perspectives. We do workshops with clients and do this internally as part of our process.

Focusing on the Meal Kits that were featured in the newspapers and on morning talk shows, can you describe the process of designing the package?

Creson: The package design happened quickly after the identity system was developed and tightly defined. Initially, we showed a number of different options for consideration. Each option explored something different (e.g., food as hero, bold communication) for consideration.

The package serves as the primary advertising medium and needed to stand out in a meaningful way. The four circles implied the idea of balance and created a very strong billboard at shelf. This was also a place where a unique tone of voice could be showcased. No focus groups, just a lot of excitement and conviction. We are very proud of the work and believe great work comes from great partnership.

Is the client hearing you?

A key concept to consistently communicate is that it pays for brands with small budgets to invest in design.

To you, how important is design to the success of products in the marketplace? Can design really make a difference in differentiating products of equal quality? In this case, you have a higher quality product but, I assume, tiny marketing and advertising budgets compared to the established brand leader?

Addis: Design can be a great equalizer. Every consumer of your brand sees the package. A fraction of them see the advertising. Brands with small budgets should consider this as a competitive advantage and invest in shelf presence. That's where the purchase decision is made.

It's been shown for sixty years that the manner in which something is packaged changes the perceived performance of the product. Wine tastes better in a better package, food tastes better, and pain relievers work faster. Skim over package design at your own peril.

I'm remembering a piece I did about Primo Angeli's redesign of Treesweet orange juice. Juice that came out of the same vat, reconstituted concentrate, a commodity product, was tested in the existing carton vs. Primo's new carton, which had a luscious painting of just-picked oranges. The testers thought the juice in the new cartons was fresher and more delicious.

Getting back to the specific expressions illustrated in the brand guidelines . . . Are you recommending that all photos be original or that stock photos might be OK for images like an orange, a leaf, a wedge of cheese? What about a person? Is it important to use images that aren't available to everyone else?

Creson: For inspiration purposes, we used stock photos to illustrate the many ways you can incorporate the symbol with photography. Preferably, we do photo shoots so clients have relevant, unique assets for communication. In this case, we styled and shot the food for use on the packages.

On another page, you show a poster/billboard for Revolution Foods that looks like it's on a city street. I understand they aren't doing any paid advertising—outdoor or TV. Is it part of your practice to do prototypes and recommend media buys or other sales strategies to clients?

Creson: That is an example of how we develop brand identities. We consider a broad number of potentially relevant touchpoints that could benefit the brand. Even if not specific to the assignment, we try and design holistically.

There are production shots on your site, checking press sheets of the packages. Do most clients want you to be involved at that level of detail?

Addis: We pride ourselves in the value we add in production. Our production team is incredible and, yes, we still go on press checks. The clients who appreciate that quality has to be maintained all the way through printing, and those who devote the resources to getting it right are the ones with the best shelf presence.

Tell me about the production. Are the packaging materials and manufacturing processes environmentally friendly?

Creson: The Meal Kits packages are printed on board that is 100% recycled with 65% coming from postconsumer waste. Inks are veg-based. Early on, we discussed more ambitious forms and materials, but costs were prohibitive.

Like many clients, Revolution Foods is doing implementation in-house following your guidelines; for example, the trucks that deliver to schools. How do you ensure that client relationships endure beyond the launch and that the quality is kept up?

Addis: We hope they trust us for our expertise and rely on us to help them protect our shared vision.

> [I followed up with Kirsten Saenz Tobey, co-founder and chief impact officer of Revolution Foods.]

You are making big news these days: *Bloomberg Businessweek*, *Forbes'* "40 Under 40" list. Congratulations. It seems like just about everybody these days wants to be an entrepreneur and come up with a new product or service that makes it big. In your opinion, what is it that makes certain ideas—like yours—really worthwhile and successful, while others fall by the wayside?

Some of the most successful entrepreneurial ideas are addressing the most obvious problems, only in a way that no one has ever thought of. I call these the palm-to-the-forehead ideas—the ones that make you put your hand on your forehead and ask, "Why didn't I think of that?"

How did the first Revolution Foods Meal Kits prototypes get made and tested? In the home kitchens of the "two moms"—you and cofounder Kristin Richmond—and at your kids' schools?

We developed this idea based on our own insights as moms, as well as by listening to a broad group of parents and students across the country. We've been listening to feedback and ideas from kids and parents from our school communities for the past seven years, and one thing we heard over and over again was, "It's great you're feeding my kid high-quality food at school, but how can I access that food for other occasions, at home, on the weekends? That sparked us to create the concept of the Meal Kit—a concept that balances great-tasting food, convenience, and high-quality ingredients, all in a format that works in traditional retail grocery channels to ensure they would be accessible to all.

I managed to raise my kid without ever buying a Lunchable, but so few American parents can't. I have the set of Time-Life "Foods of the World" books, and one photo that stands out in my mind is a picnic in "The Cooking of Provincial France" where the children are enjoying roast chicken and salad, cheese and fruit along with their family. What is it about American kids that makes them such fussy eaters that they have to have special kid food? Or is this a global phenomenon?

I think we spend too much time in America giving kids "kid food." Once they have teeth, there's no reason why kids can't eat all the same kinds of foods as adults. But America has an obsession with the notion of the picky eater, which I believe is a self-fulfilling prophecy. If we offer kids a variety of fresh and nutritious foods, without too much added sugar and salt, kids will become accustomed to eating these foods. I think the amount of sugar in kids' food is a major problem, as it trains kids' palates to prefer sugary foods, and to reject the more savory tastes of things like vegetables. I am a firm believer in the theory that parents must decide what and when their kids should eat, and kids decide how much.

There was a segment on the news last night about school lunches in New York. Apparently, they are dropping some of the healthier whole grain and veggie offerings because kids won't eat them and they end up in the garbage. How is your product line going to be successful in this environment?

We have always focused first and foremost on listening to kids and creating food that is relevant to them. We refer to it as being "kid-inspired" in all that we do. This has helped us to increase participation in school meals in our largest school district, San Francisco Unified, by 15 percent. We also believe that starting kids into healthy routines early in life helps set them on the right track, develops their palate, and builds healthy habits. Kindergartners today will graduate in the high school class of 2027. Imagine if those kids were exposed only to high quality, healthy foods every day for the next twelve years at school—they wouldn't know that another, unhealthier option exists. Change takes time, and habits take time to form.

Based on solid evidence we and others have seen, the hype about schools quitting the national school lunch program is really exaggerated and overblown. For example, Dr. Janey Thornton, US Deputy Undersecretary for Food, Nutrition, and Consumer Services, reported recently that the vast majority of schools across the country are meeting the USDA's updated meal standards, including delivering healthier options and appropriate portion sizes, and that participation is increasing as students and parents become accustomed to healthier options.

How did you know you had a hit?

We tested our Meal Kits with kids from across the country—from Texas to New York to Colorado and California. We worked with groups of kids all over the country on developing and refining this product for more than twelve months.

According a recent article in the business section of the *New York Times*, "In 2011, Kraft introduced "Lunchables With Fruit" that featured a fruit cup (instead of, I assume, a cookie) with a $20 million advertising campaign. How do you compete with that?

> **Will your idea fly?**
>
> You are invited to use these interviews to demonstrate to clients the transformative value of design: it can be a major factor in their success stories.

We have focused our efforts on creating a product that has high quality ingredients, is great tasting, and is convenient. That's what we heard from parents and kids alike that they are looking for.

It sounds like you are saying that consumers will seek out what they're looking for on store shelves without seeing television advertising for it. I hope so. Did you kid-test the package design as well as the product?

The feedback is that a lot of kids love the circles on our package, and they are attracted to the apple logo on our brand. Kids recognize shapes and colors easily, so this is actually a familiar design to them in many ways.

To me, there is no contest between your packaging and Lunchables. I would buy based on design alone. But graphic designers are not your average shoppers. Do you think design is entering the hearts and minds of the typical mom and dad?

Most people are not actively thinking about design, but they notice good design when they see it. They may not even be able to identify it as good design; they may just say, "That's appealing to me" or "It looks good." We think good design is essential, but the design should serve to make the product look great and appealing and to tell the product story.

Were other design firms considered or interviewed before you chose Addis Creson?

We did look at other firms, but Addis Creson really stood out to us. The combination of their fantastic talent, their passion for our mission, their experience with food packaging, and their location right down the street made it a really easy decision to work with them.

Was their work for other food companies like Kashi and for children's products part of the deciding factor?

We were definitely looking for a design firm that could demonstrate familiarity with both the food sector and appeal to kids and parents. Our relationship with Addis Creson began with a complete logo and brand identity redesign. And we involved them in the food concept development work. John Creson was an important player in our brainstorming process.

How much of the look and feel—primary colors, bold shapes, white background— did you know you wanted, or was it completely open?

We knew we wanted to keep the apple motif, and vibrant colors were important to us. We were open-minded about the packaging design, and they came up with more than ten concept directions for the packaging. We all gravitated very quickly toward this one.

How do you know when a design is right? Do you test with focus groups?

A combination of instinct and, yes, external feedback.

What about plans for the future? Baby food? Adult fast meals? Drive-throughs?

At this point, the future is wide open. We are exploring many different avenues for increasing access to real food. We have a lot of ideas, but none that we can share yet.

If you were advising young designers who'd love to get a client like Revolution Foods, what would you say?

Just do great work and be great people. And show that you really care about the company's brand and product. ∎

Retail and Entertainment Clients

Every retail environment and entertainment property is a brand and a consumer experience. And all brands require a graphic identity, a website, interior design, packaging, direct mail, and print and interactive advertising that connect with their audiences.

In your work, is the client seeing concepts that will create positive consumer experiences and brand loyalty?

13

The Megastore

Barnes & Noble
AND Farago + Partners

Leonard Riggio is the founder and executive chairman of **Barnes & Noble, Inc.**, parent company of BN.com, Nook Media LLC, and Barnes & Noble College Bookstores LLC. Traded on the New York Stock Exchange (symbol: BKS), with $6.8 billion in annual sales and 700 retail bookstores in fifty states, Barnes & Noble, Inc. is a Fortune 500 company and the leading retailer of content, digital media, and educational products. Active in many civic, public art, and philanthropic endeavors, Riggio was awarded an honorary doctorate from Baruch College, City University of New York.

Peter Farago is president of Farago + Partners, a boutique New York City advertising and marketing agency. Farago was previously an art director at Jordan McGrath Case & Taylor, J. Walter Thompson, and Geer DuBois, where, working on the IBM account, he developed a passion for bringing the benefits of information technology to the creative process. Farago + Partners creates advertising and marketing communications for clients, including Pantone Inc., Dow Jones, Brown & Williamson, and Prudential Securities.

When I met with Leonard Riggio, he had been taking a beating in the press, accused of not only putting small booksellers out of business, but forcing publishers to change their jacket designs. Yet all of a sudden, perhaps with Barnes & Noble's online bookstore coming on strong and the success of its private-label publishing venture, he was being called "the smartest guy in town" on the business pages. As you'll see, he knows how to manage an interview. At one point, when asked about the demise of small booksellers, I was afraid he was going to throw me out of his office. "I thought this was going to be about design," he asserted. It was. His agency, Farago + Partners, was producing nearly ten thousand ads a year and was responsible for branding the consumer's entire experience, from shopping bags to coffee bars. In Peter Farago's words: We, Barnes & Noble, are not what you think we are. We are not a huge, impersonal chain. We are a champion of literature and a large version of the family bookstore or clubby library. Let's find out what he meant.

No matter how you choose to buy books, this chapter is intended to be good reading— the story of how illustrations by Mark Summers presented authors as icons of the brand and how store interiors were designed to feel like home.

[I met with Peter Farago in his agency's office on Fifth Avenue in New York's Flatiron District.]

Q: Peter, how did your agency's relationship with Barnes & Noble get started?

A: Farago: Len Riggio and I go back many years to when Barnes & Noble had one store and Geer DuBois was its agency. I was a twenty-nine-year-old art director there. Steve Olderman, who headed up the business, came to me and said, "Lenny wants a shopping bag." I'd just seen an illustration show and had fallen in love with R.O. Bleckman's work, that squiggly style, and did a comp I wanted Bleckman to illustrate. It was a skyline of Manhattan, but instead of skyscrapers I drew books—"bookscrapers." I did it to impress the account executive, Jeri Bag, who was my girlfriend, soon to be my wife. Apparently Len flipped out, he really liked it. I said, "Okay, let's get Bleckman." Jeri said, "Len wants to use the drawing just the way it is." I said, "You don't understand, this is a comp." They printed my layout anyway, coerced me into doing it. Embarrassingly, I'd signed it like Milton Glaser, with my name, Farago, in a little lozenge shape. Eventually there were millions of those shopping bags around town and it made me crazy to see them. After a few years—I wasn't at Geer DuBois any more—I decided to sue Len for copyright infringement.

Didn't you get paid for the work while you were at Geer DuBois?

Farago: It was done on the side, as they say. That's how it goes in some agencies: the account executive, in this case Jeri, placates the art director with gift certificates for doing extra work for the client. I'd gotten paid $75 in gift certificates and it was my understanding that the use was for one year. After several years, I felt entitled to more money. The whole thing was unclear, fuzzy, on both sides. I got cranky that this thing was a huge hit and all I'd gotten was $75. Actually, I had no right to sue. I was a naive kid trying to make my way in a world I didn't understand. Len just kind of shrugged it off, laughed, and asked me if I wanted to do more work for him.

Already he sounds like an unusual guy.

Farago: He's the son of a prizefighter from Brooklyn. He doesn't think like anybody else, especially people in literature and publishing. I made a deal with him. I had friends at Apple and Adobe and had spent the past five years learning about computers. I'd developed a total electronic environment for manufacturing ads. Len saw me walking up the street with some equipment and asked what I was doing. I told him I was opening an agency that would create ads on computers. It was revolutionary at the time. I said, "You're paying $12,000 an ad to Geer DuBois. I'll make you a deal." I showed him how to manufacture his existing ads for a quarter the price. We made up to nine thousand ads a year for him.

Was it only the equipment that was revolutionary?

Farago: The way agencies used to work, a copywriter would write a headline and four days later the art director would come back with a layout. The AD's job was to decorate the words, make everything fit. We were the first agency at which copywriters and art directors could work together in real time. Our agency developed the system by which everyone shared the same set of tools. The enthusiasm bonded them together. When the copywriter could see his or her words set in type on the screen minutes later, it would crank up the process another notch and the project could evolve. You could see your layout with an image and change a word to make it work better. Or you could change your image to make your words work better.

More important, when the copywriter and I went out with the ads under our arms, we were wildly enthusiastic about the work because it was so fresh. That enthusiasm couldn't help but be transmitted to the client. Clients can sense that. They know when you believe in something or you're just trying to shuffle off some half-baked idea.

What was your thinking behind the initial presentation?

Farago: I knew that Len wanted to be loved by the literary community. So Steve Olderman and I—Steve was by then recruited by Len and working for Barnes & Noble—helped him create a brand that said, in essence: "We support the important works of great literature." I recruited Mark Summers, who was known for his author portraits in the *New York Times Book Review*, and we bought drawings of five dead authors for $500 apiece: Shakespeare, Virginia Woolf, Oscar Wilde, Isak Dinesen, and Theodore Dreiser, everybody's favorites. We showed the world how to take the high ground in bookstore advertising: Let the authors sell the books. It was an instant hit. After the dead authors appeared, we were able to convince Kurt Vonnegut to let us use his likeness. Then everybody wanted in. Authors and publishers.

> **What is the client seeing in your work?**
>
> Transmit your enthusiasm to the client. They can tell right away when you believe in something (and when you don't).

How did you choose which author gets to play center stage in an ad? Is it related to the book that's being promoted most vigorously?

Farago: In the beginning, it was related to who we could get. But once it started to go, the concept went like a house on fire. Every publisher wanted their people in our ads. Soon, it seemed to be almost as important to have

your picture in a Barnes & Noble ad than to get a good review or to get on the best-seller list. You would be handsomely presented as one of the icons of literature: Stephen King is in the company of Shakespeare; Mary Higgins Clark is like Virginia Woolf. For the first time, publishers fell in love with and came to support a co-op campaign; they didn't have to be coerced.

Let's see if I understand the co-op concept. Let's say a page in a newspaper costs $40,000. There are ten books featured on it. So each publisher pays $4,000 for the space?

Farago: Right, and typically there's a little margin in there. That's where we do some branding. We chose to give people a brand reason and an emotional reason to shop at Barnes & Noble. That's another way our ads are different from typical co-op ads, like those old "Nobody Beats The Wiz" [an East Coast electronics chain] ads. The Wiz was so hungry they chockablocked every ad, engineered them to get in as many products as they could fit. The director of co-op has only one master: the bottom line. That puts you in a commodity business. There's no reason to shop at stores that advertise like the Wiz did except for selection, selection, selection, price, price, price.

Len Riggio has a passion, a desire to create something of value. That's where the authors come in. For Nike, it's the athletes. For us, it's the authors. That's the people we represent. We give you the works of great authors, so you can be smarter. A visit to a Barnes & Noble is a visit to a place where I can get my act together: With these self-help books, my life will be better. With these books about health, my body will be better. With these classics, my mind will be better. If I read this author, my social life will be better. I will have something to talk about. Hell, I might even meet someone in the store.

Your involvement with Barnes & Noble goes far beyond advertising, doesn't it?

Farago: We are a combination of advertising people and designers. You can't sell pure design any more because it doesn't work fast enough. The average duration of a brand manager is eighteen months, and he has to show increased sales. Farago + Partners is responsible for what we call "deep branding." It's a combination of design and sales messages, down to the fax paper and coffee cups. Deep branding means applying the brand identity to every object you see as a consumer. We've done five different trucks. Twenty coffee cups. In-store design. T-shirts. Ads are only 20 percent of the communications. Do people come into a new store because of an ad? No. They come in because of a sign they saw in a parking lot. Every year we continued with Barnes & Noble, their brand equity grew. Our job is twofold: to move books and build brand. Move books, build brand. Sell. Brand. At every opportunity. Right down to the bookmarks. It shows in sales. You can extend the brand into every portion of your business. Or, to put it another way, if you are in business today, and miss any opportunity to brand, you're missing an enormous opportunity.

How about the research side of the agency business? How does that fit into the mix?

Farago: Instead of formal focus groups, I go into stores and ask people, "What does this store feel like? Does it feel like home?" What we're trying to do is make an experience that people will really love. You want to find out why people come back to one store and not another. You can buy the same books in other stores, but people used to say, for example, that Borders looked like their college library. Barnes & Noble looks and feels like home. They say, "It's quiet like my home. It's comfortable like my home. I meet friends here. We come for coffee." The answers to those questions help Barnes & Noble decide, what do I put more of where? More books? More furniture? More coffee?

> **Takeaway message:**
> Do not miss any opportunity to brand. That goes for your own design business, too.

Were you also involved in the store design?

Farago: It started with Steve Olderman walking over here with some William Morris wallpaper, and we'd sit down at the computer and work out William Morris interiors with dark green accents. Of course, Steve worked with architectural firms, too. But he worked out the look and feel with me.

Do you have a background in interior design?

Farago: I'd just have to close my eyes and remember what my parents' home looked like. My parents bought their home in Lake Forest, Illinois, a suburb of Chicago, from the Scribners, the late publishing family, for a song. My father was a doctor and one of his elderly patients, Mildred Fitzhew, one of the last of the Scribner family, said to my dad, "You take the estate and I'll live in the guest house. Just make sure I'm well taken care of." It was a Victorian country mansion with suits of armor, libraries, mahogany paneling everywhere, thick, rich, cushioned furniture. There were paintings of great authors all over the place. As a kid, I had no appreciation for any of this, but it's amazing to realize how much it's influenced my life. There were lots of other people who contributed to Barnes & Noble store design, too, but I never had to do any research. I'd lived with the classics and knew how to apply them.

What was the process of working with Len Riggio like, especially in the beginning?

Farago: We sat in a room, Lenny, Steve Olderman, and I. No minyan, no shareholders, no committee. Steve and I played writer/art director and Len played impresario. Lenny loved getting involved. He's a great collector of art as well as a lover of books. He put everyone in a room and let the sparks fly. Everything emanated from him. Nothing got in the way. It was absolutely joyous. Nobody asked middle-manager-mentality questions like, "Doesn't this compromise the author's relationship with other booksellers?" Or, "It looks like he or she is endorsing Barnes & Noble and not the others."

How much time did you spend on the account?

Farago: Every day. Every day. As the business grew, we continually reinforced this message: We, Barnes & Noble, are not what you think we are. We are not a huge impersonal chain, a giant conglomerate. We are a champion of literature and a large version of the family bookstore. Hence the easy chairs, places to sit and read, cafés.

Tell me about the book about your agency's work for Barnes & Noble [*Deep Branding: A Case History*] and the other books you've shown me. Are these one-of-a-kind? How do you make them?

Farago: Agencies typically don't have good, current information. No potential client wants to read sixty pages of account-exec dogma. It simply won't work. We make these books ourselves. We have a skilled bookbinder who wears little white gloves and puts them together in our studio. We make them from 600-dpi color photocopies. How? It's our secret. But they typically take about four hours to make. It's our intention to simply show pieces of work that relate directly to a client's business, and let them and the consultants who recommend agencies to clients decide for themselves.

[As we continued to talk, Peter Farago steered me across the street to meet with Leonard Riggio at Barnes & Noble's executive offices.]

Mr. Riggio, were there a real Mr. Barnes and Mr. Noble, booksellers since 1873?

Riggio: There were such people in the nineteenth century. Unfortunately, the history and lore of the origins of the company have been lost. The modern-day predecessor of this company moved in around 1920.

When did you enter the picture?

Riggio: The company formerly known as Barnes & Noble was bought by a conglomerate in the 1960s, when conglomerates were buying up all kinds of unrelated companies, whether they had synergy or not. Essentially, they failed. The once-proud, fifteen-store chain had shrunk to one, that store being the one right under where we are sitting right now. I bought the flagship store and the rights to use the name.

What had you been involved in up to that time?

Riggio: I was in the business of college bookstores. SBX—Student Book Exchange. We have 600 college bookstores in addition to the 700 Barnes & Noble retail stores all over the country.

How much of Barnes & Noble's growth do you attribute to Peter Farago?

Riggio: Peter and I go back a lot of years. When we met, he was an art director for Geer DuBois, a hot, hip agency that prided itself on having a few exceptional clients. That's what attracted me to them. Most of the clients had a fairly high profile, including a division of IBM for which they were doing great work. They created "Who's Behind the Foster Grants?" a very memorable campaign, as well as "Dry Dock Country," an endearing campaign. Their specialty was image creation through advertising. With Peter as an art director, we created many memorable, award-winning campaigns, including the first TV campaign for any bookseller in history. During those years, Peter had designed a shopping bag. I'd been shown a sample of it. It was kind of a prototype, almost a sketch. I said, "Why don't we just print it?" They said, "You don't understand, that's not the finished art." But I knew what I wanted. I was the client. The customers loved it. It was the best bag we ever created.

Peter told me he rekindled his relationship with you by suing you over it.

Riggio: He'd left Geer DuBois by that time and was starting his own agency. I got a letter saying he intended to sue us for using the artwork. I'd obviously thought I had good title to it, that I owned the bag. When he threatened to sue, instead of being angry I was amused and asked him to come in and talk to me. I asked him, "Why don't you make a proposal?" I had always thought Peter was one of the most brilliant people I'd ever met.

So in that way he wrested the account away?

Riggio: Geer DuBois was in the process of going away anyway. They did eventually fold. When I started with them, they were a cottage company, about a $15 million agency. The agency went out of business at $250 million. All that growth doesn't necessarily help. By getting Peter, I could again have a relationship with a smaller-size agency. I like having a direct creative relationship with the owners.

What did you think of Peter's presentation?

Riggio: Most good advertising is the result of a collaborative effort. In the best work, you see the account executive, copywriter, art director, and client all taking credit. As a client, I had a lot to do with it, as did Steve Olderman. He came from Geer DuBois to work for us. It was just a great collaboration. I wanted our advertising to be distinguished by the richness of the graphic images and the look and feel of our ads—more so than by the copy. Advertisers spend far too much time talking to people and get far too cutesy. We don't do enough about letting the customer decide for himself. Peter's job or mission was to create a look for Barnes & Noble that was both very hip and produced in impeccable detail and quality. His agency had to create a new ad every day—either for the *New York Times* or someplace else in the country. Production costs had to be in proportion to our budget for each ad. Peter was and still is on the cutting edge of computers and technology. He did it. It was kind of marvelous that he was able to turn out that kind of quality so inexpensively.

> **Why choose you?**
>
> Many smart clients like to deal directly with the "creatives" whose names are on the door.

I'd like to turn to an item from the news. Here's a front-page story from the *New York Times* titled "Book Chains' New Role: Soothsayers for Publishers" that reports that publishers are using Barnes & Noble to tell them which jacket designs will sell better, even which book titles. Readers who design book jackets will be interested in knowing whether their clients are ultimately the store chains, not the author or publisher.

Riggio: It just doesn't happen! We buy more than 50,000 titles a year. Once in a while, a publisher's sales rep may ask us what we think of one jacket over another. The whole story was a complete fabrication.

And the accusations of putting small neighborhood bookstores out of business? Is that because you can buy in volume more cheaply?

Riggio: We pay the same price as they do. The real question should be, why do independent booksellers charge so much? People in the world of literature tend to look down on people who make a profit.

You were quoted in the *New Yorker* as saying you envision online stores as a supplement to, not a replacement for, the store environment. In an age when

books—and so much other merchandise—are sold without real estate and inventory, tell me about your commitment to the store.

Riggio: The store transmits our biggest message, the message that's central to our ad campaigns, which are rooted in the store experience: A home away from home. A place with lots of books and crannies. Bright, cheerful, warm, promising, full of energy. We try to create an emotional environment, to make a public space. When you walk into a typical store and a salesperson says, "Can I help you?" that is a form of, "What are you doing here?" We want to make our stores an extension of people's lives, to give them a feeling of ownership. When it's welcoming, they spend more time. We provide easy chairs, rest rooms, baby-changing stations. Children's sections don't make money, but they make future readers. Families spend time together in our stores. Peter Farago was intimately involved in prototype store design, with the emphasis on lighting and messaging graphics.

Typically, a client's ad agency and architectural or interior design firm would have little to do with each other. What's behind your thinking on overlapping these disciplines?

Riggio: If you think of an agency to just do ad campaigns you're missing the full potential of what an agency can do. Your primary marketing vehicle is your retail environment. Our mission is to make the store the most pleasurable shopping experience possible. You want the brightest minds designing it.

[I recently followed up with Peter Farago.]

You were not the agency of record for a while. What happened?

Farago: When Tibor Kalman, who'd gotten his start at Barnes & Noble, came back from editing *Colors* magazine in Italy, he became Lenny's impresario again, and they held agency reviews. We were in review, along with several others. The mandate was: "It's time for a change. Jettison the authors; they're old hat." We refused to do that. We did what we thought was right. We said that *Rolling Stone* would never walk away from the rock stars on the cover. We would never walk away from the authors.

And the business went to . . . ?

Farago: To TBWA/Chiat Day and then to Steve Olderman's group at Digitas. They ran through a few other agencies and then came back to us. Things may be in flux again. Did you read today's paper?

Hmmm. And what about the store experience? Is it still valid? Do you, personally, still want to shop for books in that homey living room of a 25,000-square-foot store when you can do it on your laptop or your phone—or your B&N Nook?

Farago: No comment. ◼

14 The Counterculture CEO

The Nature Company
AND Kit Hinrichs

Tom Wrubel and his wife Priscilla opened the first **Nature Company** shop, which sold products related to the observation and understanding of the natural world, in Berkeley, CA, in 1973. Two years later, **Kathy Tierney** joined as executive vice president—responsible for all store operations, store design, and marketing. The Nature Company became a nationwide chain of 114 stores and a mail order operation with a circulation of six million catalogs, employing eight hundred people. In 1996, it was purchased by The Discovery Channel for $40 million.

After twenty-three years as a partner in Pentagram, **Kit Hinrichs** established Studio Hinrichs, an independent design firm, in San Francisco. A native of Los Angeles and Art Center graduate, he was a partner in Jonson, Pedersen, Hinrichs & Shakery, which became Pentagram's San Francisco office in 1986. Hinrichs has received numerous prestigious awards, including Gold Medals from the New York and Los Angeles Art Directors Clubs. The author of three books, including *Type-Wise*, published by North Light books, he was awarded the profession's highest honor, the AIGA Medal, in 2004.

Sixties counterculture guru Tom Wrubel's quest was to sell quality products in an environment in which employees could take personal responsibility for sales success, which was closely linked to design. Leafy spaces with waterfalls and natural wood beams, the Nature Company stores were designed as places to experience (and buy) field guides and binoculars; wind chimes and sculptures, fossils and crystals, jewelry and scarves with fish and bird motifs. Graphic design was as important as environmental design. Catalogs brought that experience to the printed page and the mailboxes of millions of shoppers across the country. The relationship between Tom Wrubel and Kit Hinrichs, a Pentagram partner at the time, went much deeper than a business plan or a square-inch analysis of catalog sales. Every entrepreneur wants to sell his or her company for millions of dollars. But not every entrepreneur is as invested in design as a component of that success. As these interviews show, Wrubel and Hinrichs spent time together, visited stores, and talked about life—and about design.

The Nature Company's stated mission was "to make customers feel good about themselves and the natural world in which they live." Kit Hinrichs had major responsibility for transforming those words into a visual brand.

[After visiting the Nature Company Store at New York's South Street Seaport, I spoke with Cathy Tierney.]

Q: How did the Nature Company concept begin?

A: Tierney: Tom Wrubel had been in the original Kennedy Peace Corps in Liberia and in Africa on a Fullbright. He and Priscilla didn't start out as merchants or retailers; they were idealists and naturalists. Tom was trained as an architect: he was fascinated by design; he had an incredible respect for it. He was back, teaching at Mills College, and simply wanted to turn people on to nature. He thought it would be great to open a store in Berkeley where people could buy tools that would enhance the experience of being outside.

The Nature Company is just one company—others are Esprit, Banana Republic, Smith & Hawken—that grew out of the Bay Area in the sixties. Tom didn't start out to make a lot of money and have a big company. He wanted to sell high-quality products, to express his love of good design, and do things in unconventional ways. He thought that paraphernalia for the naturalist— things like field glasses—didn't have to be sold in musty old stores, but could gain a larger audience in a new kind of environment. Priscilla focused on products for kids—toys and books that would teach children about nature.

In addition to Berkeley in the sixties, I also sense the presence of the human-potential movement of the seventies, specifically in language in your materials like "taking responsibility" for success. Did anything like the "est" training also influence the concept?

Tierney: Yes. We did all that stuff. And Tom really believed in all those movement ideals, and applied them to business. For example, we never use the term "customer service." Instead, we encourage our staff to share their love of nature. It really is a humanistic approach to retail. We choose the right people and let them be themselves, be sincere and honest. None of that phony, "How can I help you?" stuff. Tom was fond of saying to our staff, "You have this wonderful opportunity to greet and talk to strangers."

There is a lighthearted approach in many of your products. But aren't there also some serious ideas behind The Nature Company?

Tierney: We don't just dress up things with pictures of animals; we're committed to certain principles. For example, no killing living things, no trophy collecting. We follow Thoreau's words, "Go out and leave only your footprints." We won't sell butterfly collections, or even seashells found on the beach if that would mean disturbing the hermit crabs that live in those shells. The sixties were a time of heavy political and environmental organization, and Tom could have easily jumped on that bandwagon. But he wanted The Nature Company to be a place where everyone would feel welcome. As soon as you take a political stand, you polarize and alienate people. So we'll never show pictures of whales being slaughtered; we show the beauty rather than the wrongs. People learn by opening their minds, not by being intimidated.

You are a company in both retail and catalog. Can you explain the difference in approach?

Tierney: Working women make up the largest percentage of catalog customers. Part of it has to do with not having time to shop. But it's really a lifestyle choice. There's a mystique about catalogs. Some people really enjoy getting a gift in the mail that they've ordered for themselves. And when you think about it, it's a tremendous leap of faith: seeing a picture, giving your credit card number over the phone, trusting the system that you'll get what you've ordered and like what you get.

Tell me about the evolution of the catalog.

Tierney: It started out as a homegrown kind of thing. There were sketches of products, and Tom, who was a pretty good photographer, took some of the pictures himself. Those early catalogs were folksy and earthy. We outgrew that and wanted a much finer design. When Tom and Priscilla wanted to expand nationwide, CML, the conglomerate that by that time owned the company, gave the okay to work with Kit Hinrichs. We finally had the financial stability.

Was money an issue?

Tierney: It's definitely a commitment to find the best designer. And as a business, you have to see that it's repaid in terms of profits. Our success is measured in sales. The unconventional side to The Nature Company, though, goes beyond sales and means being a leader.

Can you describe how being a leader translates into catalog design?

Tierney: Most cataloguers take all their products and say to the designer, "This is where I want this and that. Here's what goes on the cover, what should be biggest on each page. And when I get my sales figures, I'll do a square-inch analysis to figure out what's selling best, what to feature next time." We threw all that out the window. Kit took something like a $14 fish potholder and made it four times bigger on the page than a sculpture costing many times more. We're never boring because we never do the expected or the mundane.

I can buy a potholder at Kmart for a dollar. Are you saying that an page layout or an experience will make me pay $13 more?

Tierney: We're definitely not a discounter, but we give people the best, the most value. It's worth what you pay for it. Instead of potholders, let's talk about toys and gifts for children, an area in which there's so much junk. We really do select and edit, find the highest quality, the toys with the most educational value. There's a loyalty and trust in what we're doing.

And would you say the retail customer is the one who has to feel and touch things?

Tierney: Yes, and to have the experience of being in the store. Tom was driven by the desire to continually evolve and do things better. Every time we opened a store, we had the opportunity to refine the concept. The original stores were primarily about books and tools. With every store, we added another department, keeping a mixture of fun and serious, inexpensive and expensive. It creates a feeling people love. As you've discovered, we don't sell things you need. We sell an experience and appreciation of the natural world—in an environment of dappled light, streams, waterfalls—that makes people feel good. So they want to buy a piece of the feeling.

Some strong voices in the design community have said that designers have sold out to the capitalist system. That instead of using our talents to create better products, we have become mere decorators in the service of big business, making things appear as they aren't. Some designers are saying that we ought to be "bad" and say "no" to our clients.

Tierney: I agree. You should. But that's not the way things are at The Nature Company. We're not asking anybody to make anything look better than it is, to make it into something that it's not. Just put it in the right environment. As we grew and evolved, we needed someone like Kit Hinrichs.

How would you characterize Kit's role?

Tierney: To lead us to the next plateau in design. To be on the leading edge of catalogs. We spend time together and talk about these things, to get that tension going. We disagree all the time, in a very healthy way. As I said, many clients will say to their designer, "You will feature the product with the most profit potential." Kit will see a $19.95 rubber reptile and say to us, "What a wonderful design element! Look at the way the tail curves!" And he'll use it across two pages.

He makes the photo selections himself? He's that personally involved?

Tierney: He spends the time on it. Kit and The Nature Company go back eight years. And we can still call him up and say, "We're concerned about this," or, "We don't like the way that is working." He'll listen. And he can be the same way with us.

So often clients complain that the only time they see the design firm principals is when they're selling or presenting work.

Tierney: Sure, Kit has assistants and a photo stylist we work with. But we won't have a meeting without him.

I'm impressed by the level of detail given to visual merchandising. Is this unique to The Nature Company?

Tierney. All retailers who are doing a good job have defined how they want their stores to look. Because of our variety of merchandise, we had to get very organized. And we must be doing it right because we're getting knocked off all the time. People even come in and measure our fixtures.

Pentagram also consults in architecture, interior design, and product design. Have you worked with them in those areas?

Tierney: Kit has designed many products for us, mostly T-shirts and posters, that are excellent sellers. He's gone far beyond catalog design and into packaging, which has become very, very important to us.

How do you determine when something's right?

Tierney: When Tom Wrubel died in 1989, it left a huge hole in the company. We relied on Kit to keep up the creativity. At one time, he served on a committee to review graphic identity, packaging, posters, T-shirts, wrapping paper. From that have come all kinds of ideas and themes. As our needs have changed, Kit's role has contracted and expanded. For example, because we couldn't pass along to our customers the costs of doing all the design work outside, we put together a strong internal creative department. Instead of being threatened by this, Kit helped us set it up and find and interview the people. What's right is the pace Kit set: warm, friendly, whimsical, lively. When you turn the page or go around a corner, you're never quite sure what you'll see. We're always experimenting, always trying something new and different. And Kit's right there with us.

[Later, I spoke with Kit Hinrichs.]

Kit, do all your clients value you as much as the Nature Company does?

Hinrichs: (Laughs). It isn't always roses. There are always times when each side needs to test the other. It's important for me to test the edges, to take the client somewhere they haven't been before, to get them to do something they hadn't thought about. As designers, we have to constantly challenge ourselves; that's why we're in business. Tom Wrubel liked to test the edges. He was a counterculture guy with an entrepreneurial attitude. He knew that businesses must continue to grow or they die. The Nature Company would have grown and been successful without us, but probably not as well or as quickly.

I'm especially interested in Kathy's statement: "We won't have a meeting without him." Is that much client dedication and contact typical for you?

Hinrichs: I sure like to think so. It's not unique to The Nature Company. Tom and I spent a lot of time together. I was on retainer as a consultant, and we used to drive around to the stores together and spend hours talking. You can always do better work if you know the top person well. And, sure, you can be dedicated to more than one client. It varies. Some clients want to be "your clients." Others want you to do a special project or consult for a specific period of time.

> **Kit's advice:**
>
> Start with earning the client's trust. Prove that you are the right person for the job. Then take them, designwise, someplace they've never been before.

At a conference last year, I opened my presentation by talking about how the best and best-known designers get and keep clients. Someone got up and said, "I don't want to hear about those superstars! I want to know how I can do it." There was a general feeling in the audience that "ordinary" designers have nothing in common with people like Kit Hinrichs. **What can readers learn from what you do?**

Hinrichs: Well, we can start with how to earn trust. Designers make thousands of judgments on behalf of clients, from the choice of typeface and photographer to how a store is sold to someone who's never been there. Someone may get a catalog for five years in a place like Kansas City, and then a store opens up and you have a pre-sold customer. Over the years, we've been able to prove that we are the right people to make the right decisions to accomplish something like that, whether it's a two-color job or a World's Fair exhibition. If I lose a client—which happens to everyone—it's because in some way that trust was broken. The Nature Company must have gone through ten designers, one a year, some very good ones, before they talked to us. For some reason—perhaps because we were able to visualize Tom Wrubel's philosophy—that trust was able to take root and grow.

According to Kathy Tierney, few designers are given the freedom to choose the scale and location of items in a catalog. Is this something you were involved with from the beginning?

Hinrichs: When Tom selected items for his stores, he liked the way they looked or felt. It was intuitive. And he just said to me, "Do what you do." At the time, we had no experience doing catalogs, so we drew upon our editorial experience with annual reports, magazines, and books, trying to bring in wit and a sense of humor.

What about the photography? I'd imagine that your approach cost many times more than what they were spending.

Hinrichs: They used to pick up the manufacturers' supplied photos. We initially showed comps that demonstrated the value of establishing a photographic look and creating a visual tone of voice for all the photos.

The ideal client-designer relationship?

Drive around town together, check out the competition, and talk about life.

Was all new photography a difficult sell?

Hinrichs: We explained that what they were responding to so favorably in the comps was the quality of the photography. And in terms of sales, the costs all come back, many times over. A cataloguer is already spending heavily for paper, printing, postage—whether the recipient looks at the catalog or throws it in the garbage. The difference between keeping it and throwing it away is often good design and good photography. And the impact on the budget is usually less than 5 percent. Without good design, you may be wasting all your money. Luckily, a catalog has direct feedback. With most projects, it's the chairman or president who has to like it, and that's as much as you know. A catalog goes out and the phone starts to ring. You know right away if it's successful.

Tell me about the Nature Company products you designed.

Hinrichs: All the products are collaborative and initiated by the client. They may come to us and say, "We'd like some T-shirts, and frogs are really big this year." Or they'll buy the rights to an idea that needs some work. For example, someone owned the rights to a list of all the multiples of animals, like "gaggle of geese" and "ostentation of peacocks." We thought it was a great idea, and designed a typographic poster and T-shirt.

Is it fair to say that you give them product ideas—but consult from a much broader perspective?

Sometimes I don't agree with everything they do; something may not look right, it may not look like it's from The Nature Company, so I make recommendations, help them stay within the family of design we developed. We do agree with them that making money and doing good work are not contradictory activities. ■

15

The Tycoon

Grand Union Supermarkets AND Milton Glaser

London-based financier Sir James Goldsmith purchased the **Grand Union Company,** a US supermarket chain headquartered in Wayne, New Jersey, in 1978. After Milton Glaser's $500 million redesign, Grand Union became the nation's fifteenth largest supermarket chain: a $3 billion company with 20,000 employees and 300 stores in eight states. The company was sold three times since then. **William A. Louttit**, who had joined as a part-time clerk, was executive vice president and chief operating officer during the redesign.

Milton Glaser, a founder of Pushpin Studios, opened Milton Glaser, Inc. in 1974 to work in interiors, exhibitions, identity, and restaurant design. Combining innovative lettering with his own illustrations, he created an influential and distinctively American graphic style. His firm's work for Grand Union brought together Glaser's personal interests in food, marketing, social issues, and town planning—and helped revolutionize the way supermarkets are designed.

David Freedman managed the Grand Union project as senior designer at Milton Glaser, Inc. for fourteen years.

For the late Sir James Goldsmith, buying and selling companies on the world market—oil companies and industrial companies—was all in a day's work. When he bought an American supermarket chain, the object was to redefine the category. "Why don't you just invent a new supermarket for me?" he asked Milton Glaser, who answered, "I know nothing about supermarkets." Goldsmith said, "Good. When can you begin?" Thus began an odyssey that took Goldsmith and Glaser to the food halls of London and Berlin and the open-air markets of Italy—and became one of the most remarkable stories in design history. "Our concept was to present food in a different, engaging way," says Glaser, "to break the up-and-down-the-aisles traffic pattern with piazza-like spaces, to take the customer on a voyage." Soon, Grand Union markets sprouted new signage and specialty departments and nifty packages for everything from jam to cat food. I was delighted to have the opportunity to meet with Glaser and lead project designer David Freedman to find out how all this came about.

If your supermarket has a cheese section, a bakery, and fresh fish and herbs, thank Milton Glaser. His $500 million redesign for Grand Union did not last forever, but the innovations did.

[I met with Milton Glaser and lead project designer David Freedman in Glaser's Murray Hill brownstone office.]

Q: When I moved about fifteen miles north of New York City, one of the thrills of our new neighborhood was the full-blown Grand Union with its imported cheese selection, fresh seafood, quality produce, even excellent breads. Tell me, how did all this come about?

A: Glaser: It all started in 1978 shortly before *New York* magazine, which I'd founded with Clay Felker, was sold to Rupert Murdoch. Clay and I were not happy about Murdoch and attempted to find another buyer. At a dinner party, we were introduced to Sir James Goldsmith, who unfortunately wasn't interested in buying *New York*. But six months later, he called me out of the blue to redesign *L'Express*, the leading news magazine in France. I redesigned it, and the relaunch was a big success. Then he asked me, "Do you know anything about supermarkets? I have this chain . . . why don't you invent a new supermarket for me?" I answered, "I know absolutely nothing about supermarkets." He said, "Good. When can you begin?"

Absolutely nothing isn't exactly true, is it, at least about food? There was "The Underground Gourmet" (a column in *New York* magazine and guidebooks describing inexpensive New York restaurants, coauthored by Glaser and artist/ food critic Jerome Snyder), *The Cook's Catalog*, your kitchen featured in various interior design publications . . .

Glaser: . . . and ventures with Burt Wolf and James Beard and Joe Baum. Well, over the next three months, we did a series of sketches, insights, of what we thought a supermarket should be like. We started with a New Jersey store— an existing space. Within a year, we went from concept to fully realized store. In three months sketches were done, another three months for detailed drawings, three months for construction. It was an enormous success. Our concepts were to open up and use the space generously and to present food in a different, engaging way; to break the monotonous up-and-down-the-aisles traffic pattern with piazza-like spaces. In other words, to keep the customer interested throughout the voyage, making shopping a kind of adventure, not unlike an editorial journey through a magazine.

What was working with Sir James like?

Glaser: We wouldn't have lasted a week without him. At the back of his mind was revolutionary change in all the assumptions of the supermarket business. I haven't met anyone like Jimmy before or since. He was the consummate marketer, a gambler; he risked everything at the roll of the dice. He wanted to see how far he could push it, and was involved in every detail. This was especially interesting because, at the time, he owned Diamond International and several oil companies; Grand Union was less than 10 percent of his holdings.

I would have never done the project without him and my personal enjoyment of the relationship. It was marvelously satisfying. I loved seeing him charm and muscle his way through the world. He raged against "industrial filth," his term for processed food, against pseudo-bread, fake dairy products.

Freedman. He was incensed that there was no fresh bread and fish in the supermarket, but that a bakery and a fish market could be located right next door in a strip mall.

Glaser: When the experts said, "You can't do it," he flew into a rage. Suddenly there was fresh fish, and not necessarily because the store managers or the corporate planning department wanted it. Our relationship with Jimmy was unprecedented in my professional career. Generally, we were encouraged to suggest everything we wanted. The corporate structure that kept things from happening was aborted. People disappeared who were unwilling or incapable of getting behind the new plan; everyone who remained got behind it with enthusiasm. Although Jimmy was open-minded, he didn't always agree with every detail we suggested. But he wholeheartedly embraced our philosophy: that the store must be on the customer's side, not on management's side.

What kind of presentations did you show?

Glaser: We put together a marvelous industrial design staff under Murry Gelberg and Larry Porcelli. For several years, fifteen to twenty people—about 60 percent of our staff—were working full-time on the project. Every day was a Grand Union day. After fourteen years, we wound down. But first you do an ideal model, plug in all the things you'd like. Then you deal with real constraints, like the number of running feet of shelf space for cheese.

Freedman: We created six prototypes, elements of which were applied to several dozen stores, that demonstrated ideas like fresh herb bars, fresh-squeezed juice bars, a ripening shelf that indicates which fruits and vegetables are ready to eat, custom lighting. The lighting was tricky because it had to illuminate the meat, fish, and produce without speeding up spoilage.

Glaser: We knew that consumers were interested in nutrition, freshness, and whole grains, and that supermarkets weren't there yet. This gave Grand Union an opportunity to respond to a market that was not being appropriately serviced. Getting in sync with the consumer required rethinking of a form. Food retailing is a conservative business, and margins are so small that a small mistake can mean enormous losses. The entire business operates by stealing tiny ideas from each other. All executives constantly tour the competition. One store puts up a candy stand; within days, all the others know that $1,800 worth of candy was sold.

You're Americans, shoppers, food lovers, designers. It makes sense. Who else could intuitively predict what the public would go for?

Glaser: If it hadn't worked, Goldsmith is the person who would have suffered. We might have gotten a slight dent in our reputation; he could have lost it all. And we weren't always perfectly on target.

Freedman: Most of the prototypes were successful. A few bombed. Sir James said that if we didn't fail some of the time, we weren't trying hard enough.

Glaser: They hired a research firm to find out what customers were looking for. Grand Union started out at the bottom of the category called "Best Liked." I was intrigued by the "Best Liked" characteristics, and found out that in that category consumers shopped at your store more often and bought more when they were there. Grand Union, however, started off at the top of "Most Convenient." They'd been making their living off good locations because they'd simply gotten there first. So my thinking was if we could move them to the top of "Best Liked," they'd have everything.

What did you have to do to get them there?

Glaser: All our design judgments grew out of answering that question. We changed the lighting. We gave shoppers nutrition information. We changed the spaces so people weren't forced to go up and down endless aisles in a proscribed direction. Quite simply, we tried to make shoppers feel good. It was shocking that these things were not at the top of management's or retailers' consideration.

Let's take as an example the Grand Union in my former neighborhood, La Guardia Place, which serves Greenwich Village and SoHo. Unfortunately, even after its renovation—which helped a lot—shopping there could be an unpleasant experience. It had to do with the piles of boxes in the aisles, the dented cans, the endless checkout lines, the surly employees.

Glaser: You're talking about commitment to training and the attitudes of personnel. It's a morale problem, a labor problem. Early on, almost before anything else had been done, I came up with a button for the checkers to wear: "Ask Me. I'm Here to Help." This is an example of benign social engineering that encourages people to be responsive.

And was Sir James happy that his designer got involved in social issues?

Glaser: Yes. At a regular presentation meeting, I showed a mock-up of the "Ask Me" button, and he said, "Let's do this." Other things were more difficult. It took two years to get the signs off the windows. You know how the windows of most supermarkets are papered over by "sale" posters, "Two for $1.39." The first thing you learn about retailing is to provide visual access. I said, "Your customers have already come to the bloody place to shop. It makes no sense to cover up the windows."

You really talked to management like that?

Glaser: Yeah. The nice thing was that we felt we were dealing with peers. On the other hand, we could be a real pain in the butt.

But they did it.

Glaser: They did it. Grand Union became arguably the best supermarket chain in America. This came about through tremendous investment. Millions of dollars went into retrofitting old stores, new fittings and fixtures, plus opening brand new stores. No other supermarket chain has made this kind of capital or development expenditure.

How did you approach the packaging?

Glaser: Like all things in this office, we're not merely interested in the decorative side. The traditional idea of private labeling was to provide low-cost alternatives to national brands; for example, slightly smaller kidney beans at 20 percent less cost. Our new position was to have the best, most competitive product. The slogan, "As good or better than national brands at a better price" went into the company manuals.

So they changed the quality of the products, not just the labels.

Glaser: Yes. If you bought Grand Union cream cheese and thought it was rotten, you'd think all Grand Union products were rotten. You can't deceive the public. The quality was improved, and we designed within categories to compare with the brand leaders.

As I understand it, the concept of "trade dress" is that a distinctive combination of lettering style, color scheme, and imagery associated in the public mind with a particular brand is protectable under trademark law. When do you get too close?

Freedman: At times, we were instructed to include a reference to the brand leader. For example, a cola label or can has to be red, blue, silver, white or cola brown. Our packaging is not knockoff; it just tries to make it very clear which product category it's in.

Glaser: All Grand Union packages, while true to their genre, are recognizable within the company design system. They look good. They don't look cheap.

Freedman: We brought together staples like flour and sugar with an identity within an identity, kind of a homey Pennsylvania-Dutch look. All the baking materials that people keep out on their counters—spices, salt, chocolate chips—were within this group. And perceptions have changed. People know you can get really good stuff under private label.

How much of our perceptions are based on advertising? I wonder if in the choice of something like catsup—and it's Del Monte versus Heinz—we're more swayed by the commercials than the package? But then when the shopper sees the great-looking, private-label catsup with its big red tomato costing significantly less than either of them, that's the one to choose, right?

Glaser: There's no doubt that television gives an advantage to the brands. Packaging is only a way of identifying what you've already received many messages about. Private labels can sit next to the brand leaders and say, "We, too, promise you quality."

[Later, I spoke with Bill Louttit.]

When Sir James Goldsmith took over, was it a scenario out of *Other People's Money*, the off-Broadway show that lampooned hostile takeovers?

Louttit: Not at all. He was a third party who bought the controlling interest in the company before he had a high public profile, and we really didn't know much about him. Many of us in management didn't have a strong opinion one way or the other, but waited to see what changes would take place.

In your view, what was he trying to accomplish?

Louttit: Goldsmith looked at food retailing in Europe and the United States and recognized that there was a big void in the fresh food area, that the American supermarket was pretty much a manufacturer's outlet for packaged product. Most US supermarkets were simple buildings with no warmth whatsoever, fluorescent lighting, maybe walls painted with red and blue stripes. He wanted to change all that. With Milton, he led us to the first phase of the revolution in style and decor. The next phase was the products themselves. Then we took another look at the stores and said, "This is all wonderful, but we still aren't offering clearly superior perishable products to the customer." Milton got very involved in that, also. We took big steps forward in terms of quality and had phenomenal improvements in both sales and profit.

As I understand it, the capital investment was unprecedented in the food retailing industry.

Louttit: It was unprecedented in the industry in terms of the amount of money spent in proportion to the total sales of the company. We spent $125 million in one year, which was more than 4 percent of sales. That was twice our cash flow, an infusion of capital into the company from Goldsmith. It was both his identification of the opportunity and his support of the capital program.

If the resistance wasn't a money problem, was it a worry that the public wasn't going to appreciate all these changes, that only a few gourmets are interested in fresh fish and pretty packaging and so forth?

Louttit: We had approximately eight hundred stores at the time in the New York tri-state area, plus the Carolinas, Florida, Texas, and Washington, DC, some in not-so-affluent neighborhoods.

So you questioned whether one design concept was going to serve everybody?

Louttit: Right. Question number one was, "Is this going to be equally effective everywhere?" Question two was, "How do we get from our old format to this new format?" And then there was the, "All of these things have been tried before and haven't worked" mentality. Yet, if you examine Goldsmith's concepts, many of them aren't profitable in and of themselves, but they add tremendous appeal to a store and attract customers who buy other items.

What was the consumer reaction to the redesign?

Louttit: The reaction was outstanding. We got lots of letters. We have a very thorough method of evaluating our customer comments and we break them down into all different categories, compliments, and complaints. But the financials are the true measure of success. We saw that the business in a single store could double when it went from a standard supermarket to the new-paradigm food market. In the upper-income areas, it was better than that, even during the recession.

> **Is the client hearing what you're saying:**
>
> If you really believe in something (and know what you're doing), don't back off. The client may come around.

Were you present at Glaser's presentations?

Louttit: Milton came to most of our store planning committee meetings, and he's just a wonderful person to work with. He combines artistic ability with fundamental common sense and a realistic approach to practical business matters. He doesn't have his head in the clouds and isn't daydreaming about what could be; he talks about what we can do and how it will work. In the early days, I had no idea what his skills or reputation were, and I was just amazed how well an individual with so much artistic ability was able to fit in and work with an old-line organization like ours.

Well, he used the phrase "pain in the butt" to describe himself, in terms of making suggestions some executives were not all that keen on.

Louttit: Some people characterized him as worse than that. But I thought he was progressive, clear-thinking, and not only one of the best graphic communicators I've ever met, but also one of the clearest verbal communicators. In meetings, there was plenty of give-and-take, and he didn't back off if he believed he was on the right track. Some people thought he came up with crazy ideas, but that's what we expected. He worked with us as a member of our team, not as an outsider, and helped us improve things we were doing as well as put new propositions on the table. In the beginning, there was some resistance to a few things like the pet food packaging (using half a cat's face each on two packages that line up on the shelf), but we got everybody out of the way and let Milton do his stuff, and it was great for us.

Some people in our profession think graphic designers are valuable enough to be paid as much as major league ballplayers. Others are sure we'll always be undervalued and our work thought of as decoration. When you talk about sales doubling, I wonder if the former isn't true more often than we're given credit for.

Louttit: Grand Union has enjoyed two major benefits. We not only attract more customers, the customers who come into our stores buy more product.

And your private label products often look more appealing than the nationally advertised brands.

Louttit: That's what can happen. Our objective in private label is to match the national brand quality, and if we can't find a supplier who can do that on a particular item, we just won't carry that item. For example, we renamed our cola Penguin Cola because we didn't want our name on something that wasn't clearly equal to the national brand. This is something that Milton proposed and has been very involved in, not just from a design point of view, but from an actual strategic direction. And the package designs are all his firm's, with very little input from anybody here.

No matter how good a designer might be, clients sometimes behave in ways characterized by designers as nit-picking: "We don't like this typeface. Isn't that color a little too bright? Aren't there too many polka dots per square inch?" What would you say to management in other industries? How would you describe the most successful way to work with a designer?

Louttit: I'd say, to the greatest degree possible, make the design part of the internal processes. Retail companies have many processes by which they oper-ate—meetings, internal communications. The designer needs to understand the mechanics of the organization in order to become effective within it. He also needs to get to know the people. The more people in Grand Union Milton knew, the better he was able to function. When he was kind of an outsider in the first few years, there was resistance.

We got him heavily involved in the organization, in the processes, and got him working with the people. He could see when they had a valid reason for objecting to something, and they could see the real beauty of his ideas.

[After the sale of the company, I followed up with Milton Glaser.]

I watched with dismay as Grand Union stores returned to the standard configuration of long aisles, and innovations like the herb bars and cheese shops disappeared. Grand Union declared bankruptcy and its stores were sold to other supermarket chains. What happened?

Glaser: They went through a series of leveraged buyouts after Goldsmith, the

> **Takeaway message:**
> If you design something revolutionary, it will not only serve your client well, it can change the way people shop, behave, or think.

guiding force, decided to cash out all of his businesses and become an ecologist. He owned forests. He was worth a billion bucks.

What would you say to people who, noting the return to the old paradigms and ultimately the bankruptcy, would call the Grand Union redesign a failure?

Glaser: We managed to move the company from the bottom of consumer preferences to second. Everything was working. Goldsmith intelligently sold it all at the top of its form. Then there was a series of purchases, new owners. None of the new owners were interested in investing, so the company got weaker and weaker and lost its vitality and its customers. Eventually, there was a financial collapse.

Which had nothing to do with the design program . . .

Glaser: Everything we did caught on across the entire supermarket industry! Everything we introduced that worked was immediately replicated. A new generation of supermarket owners moved in our direction. They brought in fresh fish, fresh herbs. They're doing it now at the Food Emporiums, the A&Ps. This isn't the story of the demise of Grand Union! It brought about a change in the whole supermarket industry.

Do you have any advice for young designers who would like to develop working relationships with their clients along the lines of yours with Goldsmith?

Glaser: Generalities are nonsense. These are very individual occurrences. Goldsmith and I liked each other. There was personal chemistry. With every client, you have to accommodate yourself. What is it that you want? What is it that the client wants? Your concepts should address the client's concerns, but ultimately, you should do what's pleasing to you and that is of high quality. ∎

16

The Retailer

Brooks Brothers
AND **Desgrippes Gobé**

As president and CEO, **Joseph R. Gromek** orchestrated **Brooks Brothers'** metamorphosis from a traditional haberdasher to a lifestyle brand for men and women. He previously held management positions at Ann Taylor Stores, Lord & Taylor, Bonwit Teller, Saks Fifth Avenue, and The Limited. With 210 stores in seventy countries, Brooks Brothers was a subsidiary of Marks & Spencer PLC, the UK department store, until the chain was purchased in 2001 by Retail Brand Alliance.

Marc Gobé is creative director of Emotional Branding Alliance, which focuses on consumers' emotions as the ultimate power in branding strategies. A graduate of Ecole Superiéure de Design in Paris, Gobé was previously CEO of Desgrippes Gobé, which created identities, packaging, and architectural interiors for clients including Adidas, Air France, Coca-Cola, and fashion retailers, including Brooks Brothers.

Design consultant **Peter Levine**, now head of Brand Communications Studio, was responsible for strategic planning and direction on the Brooks Brothers project.

Step inside the Brooks Brothers flagship store on Madison Avenue and Forty-Fourth Street in Manhattan and you might be greeted by a display of hot-pink, checked dress shirts. And then there are the mint green and deep blue shirts paired with iridescent purple ties. And you haven't even gotten to the sweaters and sport jackets. Clearly, this is not your grandfather's Brooks Brothers. Yes, the oxford button-downs are there, and so are the navy blue blazers with gold buttons. But it's a younger, hipper Brooks (not that The Clash will be shopping there any time soon). The store interiors are brightened, and the traditional graphics on the shopping bags are done in turquoise-on-navy. You are experiencing the revival of a dowager brand and, in the end, it all looks so easy. As this story demonstrates, it's anything but elementary. It requires the expertise of a design firm that specializes in consumer experiences, that undertakes rigorous research, and that can communicate its findings and recommendations using a methodology that gets all layers of management on board.

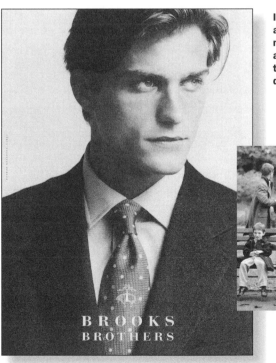

If you or your clients need any evidence why a $99 logo might not be good enough, absorb the information about the rebranding process described in this chapter.

[The conversation opened in the New York offices of Desgrippes Gobé.]

Q: How did your firm and Brooks Brothers get together?

A: Levine: Joe Gromek had been general merchandising manager at Ann Taylor when we helped them reposition their brand and refocus on their core customers, career women. We sent Joe a "congratulations on your new position" letter when he became CEO of Brooks Brothers.

Client nurturing:

This relationship was rekindled with a "congratulations on your new position" letter. How will you kindle your next client relationship?

I'm glad to hear that those things work. What was the situation at the time?

Levine: The typical Brooks Brothers customer was over fifty and nothing was being done to pass the brand along. The image didn't communicate that Brooks Brothers was about fashion. The customers they had were very vocal, even crotchety. They were complaining, but not shopping. They might come in twice a year and stock up on white shirts and underwear, maybe buy a blue suit or a gray suit. The rest of the wardrobe was up to the wife or girlfriend—gifts. Brooks Brothers needed to attract a younger customer, a more casual dresser, someone who says, "I can wear a colored shirt, a more interesting tie, spruce up that blue or gray suit." They needed to leverage socks, bathing suits, other kinds of purchases.

Do you consider yourselves fashion specialists?

Gobé: We like to specialize with clients that have a very high level of emotion.

Can you describe what you mean by emotion?

Gobé: Clients who reach customers with messages that make them respond emotionally. We are better at beauty and fashion than we are at industrial products. For example, a fragrance is nothing without a package that makes people respond. On an emotional level, a fragrance is a ten; cereal is a five. We also have Coca-Cola and IBM as accounts and they came to us because they want to be more sensorial.

"Sensorial"?

Gobé: "Sensorial" refers to all the senses: appealing to the eye, the sense of touch, smell. All the senses trigger emotions. That is part of shopping, too. The act of shopping needs to be a total experience for the consumer. When you design an identity for a store from packaging to interiors, you try to create an experience. You connect all the senses. Retailers have a unique opportunity to build branded experiences.

How did the assignment unfold?

Gobé: Joe explained to us his understanding of the business. Then we met with people who were responsible for store architecture, interiors, visual merchandising. It's critically important to line up everyone who might have a piece of the truth. Nobody has the whole truth. It's the same way in most companies. In order to create a really strong, focused visual identity, you have to get everyone together. We call this process, "BrandFocus." It's a proprietary technique we developed, an incredible tool to get people together. We get top management in one room and have them respond to visual stimuli, which are identified and classified in different categories.

Can you give readers an example of a category?

Gobé: A flower. We show pictures of six different flowers. We ask, "Which is a Brooks Brothers flower?" We want your first, visceral, response. Then pictures of cars. "Which is a Brooks Brothers car?" Then people, situations, accessories. There are thirty or forty categories. Then we have conversation, dialogue. Someone writes down every single word. The session is videotaped. Some words and phrases come up over and over again.

Levine: They are the core cues. At the end of an intensive one-day workshop, you have a mosaic, which becomes the vision of the brand pillars. And the advantage is that the people are all in sync—they are part of its creation.

Gobé: Then we start working on the basic expression. It takes two to three months to develop. We generally come in with one strong recommendation and show the steps, how it evolved.

What was the thinking behind the decision to keep the logo?

Levine: The Brooks Brothers golden fleece has a heritage as the mark of an American luxury brand, a destination, like Henry Bendel and Tiffany. It is a status symbol of America for Asians and Europeans. There is an expectation to see that logo. We cleaned it up, made it

> To make sure you understand what they're saying:
>
> When you're dealing with a committee or with layers of management, it's critically important to line up everybody who might have a piece of the truth.

more energetic, introduced the repp-tie pattern—an angled stripe in navy and bright turquoise blue—as a symbol icon for the shopping bags and other

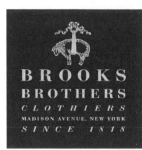

collateral. Just like Hermès orange, it is a distinctive characteristic. We developed a typographic vocabulary, the stacked, booklike type that also communicates the heritage. We then undertook a huge labeling program for garments, internal labels for suits, and external labels for casual weekend wear.

Here is the Brooks Brothers insert in a current issue of *Vanity Fair.* **How would you distinguish this expression, this look, from, say, Banana Republic? Prosperous-looking twenty-somethings, khakis, white polo shirts . . .**

Gobé: Banana Republic is very European in nature. More put together, predictable. They dictate how an outfit should be put together. There is something inherent in the Brooks Brothers brand that makes it an American icon. It has more heritage. Here the shirt is out. There are bare feet. It's energetic, highly personal, relaxed. This has appeal not only to Americans, but worldwide. Brooks Brothers has a great opportunity to grab that niche, to own it.

What's happened to the man with the blue blazer and repp tie?

Gobé: He is still here, but today he is more of an individual. On the weekend, he wears loafers, no socks. The American attitude is personal, eclectic, not dictated. It's something felt. It spans generations. The father can be wearing his blue blazer with gray flannels. But the son wears his with chinos and a different combination of tie and shirt. The tie will be slightly open.

How long did the design process take, up to the point that Brooks Brothers was ready to begin implementation?

Levine: A year, with a team of seven: Marc and myself as creative directors, a design director, a marketing director, two graphic designers, and a retail architect. We had a lot of group meetings; Joe is very team-oriented. They were trying to figure out how far they could go.

Do you ever push clients to go farther than they think they want to?

Levine: We never surprise clients with radical departures. That's not how we work. We collaborate. The client is focused on changing merchandise with the seasons, changing windows. Sometimes they lose the big picture. That's when we can help rebuild that visual portrait and regain the core cues of the brand.

You are very brave for describing all this, because now your firm may have a rash of imitators. "Is this flower the—name any client—flower?" How did you learn how to do this?

Gobé: My family has always been in the retail business. My grandfather had an operation in France that included clothing, millinery, a restaurant. We always talked about retailing. On our staff, we have graphic designers, product designers, architects. On the client management side, we have planners, headed by Peter. We are constantly looking to create useful tools for building brands. The people who head companies are the true visionaries, though. They don't necessarily have the time to think of their business in visual terms, in the creative sense. They think in numbers. But when you put them in a room and ask them to respond creatively, it's totally amazing how brilliantly they can respond and focus on their brand.

[A few days later, I met with Joseph Gromek in his office above the Brooks Brothers store on Madison Avenue and Forty-Fourth Street.]

What was Brooks Brothers facing when you took over the leadership role?

Gromek: It had stopped evolving. Once any business stops changing, it finds it's in grave trouble. Brooks Brothers was suffering from ten years of negative store growth. We needed to move forward without alienating the existing customer. Actually, we needed more than to move forward. We needed to be shocked. This was not a remedy for a cold. The patient would have been terminal without what we did and without the support of our parent company.

What were your first steps?

Gromek: A new store design. We changed from dark, clubby mahogany to cherry. We made the stores open and inviting. We took the merchandise out of cabinets and put it on tables. We took dress shirts out of cellophane bags so the consumer could touch and feel them. I'd much rather have a few shirts get dirty than have all of them under glass. We developed programs for the sales staff to help them be more friendly and engaging.

How would you describe the difference between your positioning and that of Banana Republic or J. Crew?

Gromek: We're all vying for the same customer. But our campaign is one of family values—a father and son story. We show happy, smiling faces, and that's not true for the other brands. We are less about style and more about relevance. We're not cutting-edge fashion; we are upscale Middle America.

How does the lavender tie with the mint-green shirt fit into this?

Gromek: Brooks Brothers was always about color. A fifteen-year-old red-and-blue striped tie was colorful for its time. That's one thing that made the business successful for 180 years. We are authoritative about color; that's part of the heritage and history of the brand.

You are the inventors of the button-down shirt, are you not?

Gromek: One of the original Brooks brothers originated it. John Brooks was at a polo match in the UK where everybody's collars were flapping around. He said, "I can solve that problem." We are also the innovators of the seersucker suit and the repp tie.

The book *Cheap Chic*, by Catherine Milinaire and Carol Troy, recommends that women who want to be fabulously dressed for little money shop in the Brooks Brothers boys' department. The authors devote a spread to what they call "The Ivy League Look" and illustrate Brooks Brothers shirts, sweaters, Bermuda shorts, and white bucks. Did that book affect your sales?

Gromek: Yes, and then the Condé Nast editors discovered us. They're next door and would come in to buy boys' suits and polo shirts.

How did the reengineering and redesign process work?

Gromek: On the product side, we hired a fashion designer with twelve years experience with classic contemporary clothing at Fenn Wright and Mason to be senior vice president, design director. He did all the right stuff. We hired Derek Ungless, who had been at *Rolling Stone*, as creative director, executive vice president for in-house advertising and promotion. We keep tweaking it. The product is the same in 90 percent of our stores, but we tweak the store design by climate zone. In one city, we may add more wood to the walls, in another, more limestone to the floors. Of course, we focus more on suits in business locations and on casual wear in suburban malls. We also changed our windows. There's a new color story in our windows. Now we appeal emotionally, rather than to filling needs.

And behind all of this was Desgrippes Gobé?

Gromek: They consulted on window presentations, merchandise presentation, in-store graphics, logo, and packaging.

That you kept the logo may surprise some people.

Gromek: The golden fleece denotes the finest quality in wool. It was originally the mark of the British wool makers, a guild sign that I think originated in ancient Greece.

What was the process like that ended with the updated golden fleece and the new shopping bag?

Gromek: It took months. Desgrippes Gobé came in with a range of options, from solutions with the highest degree of drama to those that were very conservative. It was a work-in-progress situation.

One of the legends in the design business is about how Paul Rand presented the NEXT logo to Steven Jobs. Rand came in with one solution and a little book demonstrating how he arrived at it. How would you have reacted to that kind of presentation?

Gromek: That isn't how we like to work around here! We like to look at different solutions and ask each other, "What do you think about this?" Does it reflect our heritage in a way that is newer and fresher? That's very important. We felt comfortable with the process all along and ultimately got to a point when we said, "That's it." They pushed us, but they made compromises along the way.

And everything emanated from the BrandFocus session?

Gromek: Let me show you . . . [Mr. Gromek led me into a conference room where framed boards with collages of "swipe" photos from magazine editorial and ads lined the walls] . . . the Brooks Brothers customer [pointing to the first of seven boards] is distinctively correct, casually elegant, genuinely eclectic, smart, and sexy. He's in his late twenties or early thirties, very active. He's social and athletic. He spends time with friends, day into evening. He's action-oriented.

Working styles: Some clients appreciate getting one well-thought-out solution; others want to be part of a collaborative effort. Some want to follow a tried-and-true process; others are keen on something proprietary like Gobé's BrandFocus. Figure out what will work for each of your client relationships. They are all different.

In his work environment, he's got a more relaxed attitude. He's not a stuffy banker. He's a father. He's a son. He may have young children. He drives an Audi or BMW.

And he likes Michelle Pfeiffer, BV Cabernet Sauvignon, and Rolex watches.

Gromek: You're getting it, and his home is an open, airy environment.

Hmm, from the looks of that house, he's quite wealthy.

Gromek: You have to remember, this is aspirational. He's affluent, but not stuffy. He likes to have fun. He's healthy. He works out. He reads. This is all about wardrobing. We want to dress this guy from head to toe. We can supply his business and weekend attire, his tux, his tennis clothes. The details are important: the buttons, the correct shoe, the right briefcase. It's all American traditional. All this is in place in this country now, and we're going through the whole revamping process in Japan. Europe and Latin America will be next. Desgrippes Gobé did a brilliant job. ∎

17 The Great Designer Himself

Joseph Abboud
AND Tyler Smith

Former Louis, Boston clothing buyer **Joseph Abboud** was associate director of menswear design at Polo/Ralph Lauren before forming a company under his own label, J.A. Apparel, a joint venture with Gruppo GFT. It grew into a $50 million fashion empire with men's, women's, and accessories lines. The company was acquired by a private equity firm for $72 million. The author of the exposé *Threads: My Life Behind the Seams in the High-Stakes World of Fashion,* Abboud is a two-time winner of the Council of Fashion Designers of America's "Designer of the Year for Menswear" Award.

Tyler Smith founded his shop, Tyler Smith Creative Direction, in 1976 with one client after leaving the Providence, Rhode Island, branch of a New York advertising agency owned by George Lois. He soon began his relationship with Louis, Boston, which established him as a specialist in menswear. He has remained in Providence as an independent creative director, providing branding and marketing communications for an increasingly international clientele in the fashion industry.

To some graphic designers, a fashion designer who challenges himself to win top industry awards might be a dream client. Others, who like to take control and take credit for the work, might not be contented working with someone who views the results as the outcome of the meeting of two creative minds. Joseph Abboud gives his colleagues—fellow fashion entrepreneurs—excellent advice: "Great art direction, great logos, great coloration, it all captures people's attention. If you are small, do a little bit, but do it well. If you grow, do a little bit more, and make it consistent. And you do have to spend some money." He puts his company's money where his mouth is. In Abboud's New York showroom, the look and feel of the identity—the logo sandblasted on fruitwood cabinetry—resonates perfectly with the earthy colorations and textures of the suits and ties, shirts and jackets. The shopping bags, ads, and hangtags are elegant and consistent—and the work of a single individual, Tyler Smith, who proves that you don't have to be a big design firm to do work with a big impact.

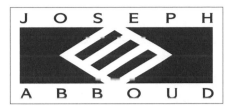

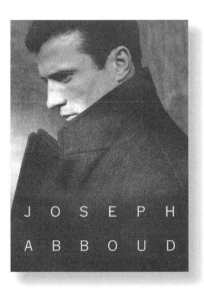

The Joseph Abboud story proves that you don't need to be a large firm to work with a company that wants to be a big brand. A talented solo practitioner can pull it off, too.

[I met with Joseph Abboud in his New York showroom.]

Q: Is it fair to say that you have joined the top tier of elite menswear designers, which includes Calvin Klein, Ralph Lauren, and Georgio Armani? And that graphic design had something to do with that success?

What does the client see when you present your work?

Abboud: "When I see something I like, I know I like it."

A: Abboud: Yes, but I didn't go to somebody and say, "Give me an image." I already had an image, and I asked Tyler to embellish it. I asked him to help me look like myself.

Generally speaking, a client who hires a graphic designer is not an expert in design. You are a client who is a designer himself. How did the relationship with Tyler Smith get started, and how does it work?

Abboud: I met Tyler at the Louis, Boston, clothing store fifteen or sixteen years ago, and I always knew I wanted to work with him. I have a great, energetic relationship with Tyler. We enjoy each other's company. It's really two creatives working together. I love the creative process, working together and within boundaries. By boundaries I mean consistency. Consistency for me is two complete clothing collections a year, the merchandise, the advertising, the shops. It's all one vision. I've gotten where I am today by following a singular path. Some companies have one look in their advertising one season and another, completely different look or campaign the next. I don't agree with that.

Do you ever have any conflicts about how things should look?

Tyler is on my wavelength. We always see eye to eye. He doesn't need to convince me of anything, and I don't need to convince him. When he shows me something I like, I know I like it. Working with him is fun. This business can be tough sometimes, but I still want it to be fun.

Can we back up a little bit? Where did you go to school? How did you get started?

Abboud: I went to U Mass and have a degree in English and French comparative literature. I spent my junior year in Paris at the Sorbonne. I don't have a design degree. You could say that I got my design education at a clothing store, Louis, Boston. As a buyer there, I would coordinate clients' wardrobes. I would use things that were in the store, things I was able to buy for them, and things I designed myself. When I had a thought, a design idea for an article of clothing, I was able to get it made, put it in the window, and put it on my clients' backs. I spent twelve years doing that.

What inspired you to go into business for yourself?

Abboud: It's the old Peter Principle. I wanted to see how far I could go before I couldn't go any further. For example, I always wanted to win the Designer of the Year for Menswear Award, and I won it twice. I always felt strongly about my own point of view: that there have to be a lot of men out there who want to dress the way I do.

Can you describe that way of dressing?

Abboud: My image is an American image, but sexier than the old American image. We started a look that is softer, looser. No more uptight, button-down guys. It's the American international look. Kind of restrained passion, restrained sexuality or sensuality. If you put Ralph Lauren—the wholesome American preppy look—on the right, and Georgio Armani on the left, I would fall right in the middle where those two circles overlap. Our look is one that people are chasing. A lot of other people have gotten on the bandwagon. Here's another thing I feel strongly about. I hate plagiarists. There are so many uncreative people out there. But our look is original; it's about sophistication, about people being themselves.

How does that translate into your marketing communications?

Abboud: It's simple. Show people and the clothes. I don't like copy. I like images. I want to get an idea from a picture. The pictures we use do it all. Sometimes we have to use copy, like on the last page of the image brochures. Other than that, it's show, not tell.

And the interiors, the showrooms, the shops?

Abboud: From the color of the metal on the door hinges, to the way the fabric swatches are shown to buyers, to the shopping bags and carpets and uphol-stered furniture, the whole company is design driven.

And you've done this all with one designer, a solo practitioner?

Abboud: I get calls all the time from slick salesmen representing supposedly the hottest marketing companies in town. They say, "Why don't you try some-one else, try us?" I say, "No, I don't want to." I don't want to change. The hottest new look is not for me. This company may be relatively new, but it's rooted in tradition, and I need someone who understands that tradition.

Do you think it's essential to work with someone who specializes in your industry?

Abboud: No. Someone with absolutely no experience in menswear can do a good job for a menswear company. Although almost everyone in my business knows Tyler, people who are good can catch on very quickly and come up with original ideas.

A colleague told me she got a call from a friend in the sportswear business, who asked, "I need a logo and hangtag design for a new line. How much?" She answered, "About $5,000," which to me sounds reasonable. He apparently said, "That's crazy, I was planning to spend about $500" and practically hung up on her. Is there a Seventh Avenue mentality that means cheap, cheap?

Abboud: A lot of people don't believe in advertising. In my opinion, they are not going to succeed in today's market. So much, psychologically, depends on it. Great art direction, great logos, great coloration, it all captures people's attention. If you are small, do a little bit, but do it well. If you grow, do a little bit more, and make it consistent. No matter how much you do, make it all consistent. And you do have to spend some money. My partner, the Italian company Gruppo GFT, which is also behind Armani and Valentino, understands marketing and strategy. The Italians seem to have design in their blood.

True or false: A company makes a product, a bicycle, a teapot, whatever, that functions just like its competitors' products. But the company's investment in design—the product's appearance as well as the design of logo, the collateral, the packaging, the sales promotion—will distinguish that product in the marketplace and cause it to be perceived as the best?

Abboud: If two products are equal, graphics can make one win over the other. But you can't fool the public and try to cover up a bad product with a good logo. A few companies have tried that, and it doesn't work. I think most companies with good logos usually make good products; they are committed to quality all around.

Tell me how the Joseph Abboud logo evolved?

Abboud: Tyler and I were playing around with some things in a coffee shop in Providence.

And the colors?

Abboud: We played around with those, too. I like warm colors. When we got around to where we wanted to be, we stopped.

What kind of presentation did Tyler make?

Abboud: None. The first thing we said was, let's get a photographer and take some pictures. Then we knew we had something beautiful. We tried not to create a logo that would mess things up.

How do you work together?

Abboud: When we're working on something, he sends me a sketch with a note, "Do you like this or that?" We cut through all the bureaucracy. I call him all the time and ask him things, "What do you want to do about this invitation? Is there any new paper I ought to see?" We talk all the time.

When it's all together, the products, the logo, the showroom, the shops, the advertising, what is it that actually moves the clothing off the racks and into customers' shopping bags? What makes a man think to himself not "I'm going to buy a new suit today," but "I'm going to buy a Joseph Abboud suit"?

Be happy when a client says:

This business can be tough sometimes, but I still want it to be fun.

Abboud: It's a complicated process. It starts with the trade press reviewing runway shows at market week. In January, there are two shows, in New York and Milan, the fall collections. At the same time retailers—department stores, Saks, Bergdorfs —are being contacted by the sales staff. In August and September, we run ads in consumer magazines like *GQ* and *Esquire*. At the same time, the retailers are featuring merchandise in newspaper ads. There are shows and personal appearances. I've been on *Donahue*, *Attitudes*, *Today*, all of them. Bryant Gumbel wore my clothes at the Olympics and gave us an on-air credit. He looked terrific. If everything goes right, the clothing is featured in magazine editorial spreads, showing the magazine's interpretation of the collection.

But remember that the designer name, the label, means nothing without the product. Some people try to put a product behind a name. That doesn't work. The product has to come first. If it's good, people remember the name.

The sense I got by stepping into the showroom was that your product would be special. When I looked at the women's line especially, I was reminded of great Chanel suits of the forties—not the lines, which are quite different—but the quality of the fabrics and workmanship.

Abboud: Correct. It's hard to find people today who make things like this. Everything we do is handmade in Italy by incredible tailors. It costs money. A lot of money. Of course, we think it's worth it, that these things will become collectors' items.

[Later that day, I spoke with Tyler Smith.]

Tyler, if typical agency people and graphic designers were characterizing their average client, it's likely that they would describe someone who rejects their best ideas and asks for what the competition is doing. Will readers of this book be able to relate to your dream client, Joseph Abboud?

Smith: Joe is admittedly the extreme. Sometimes he knows more than I do. That in itself can be a challenge.

What is the biggest challenge for you?

Smith: He expects new and stimulating ideas without me doing a stunt, without doing things that are ridiculous and decorative. They have to make sense. For example, the way the type on the image brochure covers works, the picture is swimming through the letters. Some clients might say, "This doesn't look right. I've never seen anything like this before." Or, "You can't read it, it's illegible." Instead, Joe says, "That's great, it's a whole new way to look at logos, now the logo is part of the photography." Or I might show him the idea of printing a page on vellum, and he asks, "Can we do the whole book on vellum?" And I have to pull him back, to explain why not, why it wouldn't work.

> **"Educating" the client:**
>
> Sometimes you have to explain to the client why something he or she wants won't work. Successful designers are able to do this and don't end up making too many compromises.

Have any of your ideas been rejected?

Smith: I get more static from Joe's people than from him. For example, the texture in the pictures. There's kind of a woven texture in every photograph. Joe does very unslick things, nothing shiny, everything earth-toned and textural. So we photographed fabric, hopsacking, and I put a weave right into the pictures with Photoshop. Sort of like a living logo that goes though all the images. A lot of people in his company did not like that, but Joe appreciated it right away.

Not every client is willing or able to override the naysayers in his or her company. What has the design process been like?

Smith: A real collaboration. Joe really understands the idea of a label and how it can create an image. The logo is a traditional American look, repp stripes, burgundy and green, and it was actually created to work, first and foremost, on a woven label. We didn't go about it in the usual way. It was mostly done on the phone, sending sketches back and forth. I started with a "JA" and got totally away from it. But don't think of the label alone as "the logo." In this case, the entire company look is the logo, the corporate signature. It's the Copperplate Gothic typography and the type arrangement, the way the letters line up. I put an awful lot of thought into that, and got lucky, the same number of letters is in Joe's first and last names.

A brand is not just a logo. It's the paper and the colors and the textures and the models we pick, the way they look, and especially the photography. Fabrizio Ferri, our photographer, is a big part of all this. We want our brochures to be like films, with no copy interrupting them; we wanted them to be the real visual experiences of the clothing. Choosing the right photographer is very important, and Joe picked Fabrizio. Joe wanted an American art director but an Italian "eye." Fabrizio's eye expresses a certain sensibility, a European sense of style.

Let's take a moment to talk about the material aspects of the relationship.

Smith: I have no contract with Joe. It's all done on a handshake.

Was there a proposal or a written estimate?

Smith: No.

Do costs matter to him?

Smith: Everybody wants to know the approximate amount of money. I work on a retainer-fee basis. You have to have a certain faith in what you're doing, what it's worth. I work out different arrangements with people. For example, my fee sounded too high to one client, a law firm; I wasn't going to compromise, but I said, "You can pay it out over twelve months." They said, "Okay."

As you know, so-called industry expertise can be a problem for graphic designers. If you've worked for other companies in the same industry, potential clients cite possible conflict of interest. If you have no experience in that field, then they might not hire you either, saying they have to see something in your portfolio that's exactly like what they're looking for. As a specialist in menswear, how do you deal with this?

Smith: When I started my little agency in Providence, I got a call from a writer in Boston, asking, "Do you want to work on a store called Louis?" Since then, other clothing stores and manufacturers have just called; I've never had to go out and hustle. After a while—if you do great stuff—everyone in that universe knows about you. There's not that many of them. So I've carved out a little niche and become a specialist.

But I have to be very, very careful and really dig and figure out what each one is about. And express that distinctive personality. Today, some designers give the same look to every client. I can't stand that stuff. I give a different look to every client. ∎

18

The Producer

Chicago, The Musical, AND SpotCo

Barry Weissler is president of Namco, National Artists' Marketing Company, producers of *Chicago, The Musical,* which has been running on Broadway and around the world since 1996. Namco, founded by Weissler and his wife, Fran, has been producing professional theater since 1982. Broadway productions also include *Pippin, La Cage aux Folles, Seussical,* and the revival of *Cabaret.*

Drew Hodges is founder and creative director of **SpotCo**, a full-service, New York-based advertising agency that specializes in creative strategy, media planning, direct marketing, and print, radio, TV, and interactive campaigns for the live entertainment and media industries. Clients, in addition to Broadway producers like Namco, are cultural institutions, film studios, and broadcast and cable TV networks, including Dreamworks, Bravo, and Nickelodeon. Now a subsidiary of R4e, a UK entertainment promotion company, SpotCo placed more than $100 million in media in the past two years. An SVA graduate, Hodges began his career with Paula Scher at Koppel & Scher and freelanced before opening Spot Design in 1987.

Until *Rent*—with its hardware-store-stencil logo and solarized, tinted, taped, scratched, photographic portraits of angst-ridden young performers—most stage productions were advertised with a kind of metaphorical, illustrative symbol (the *Phantom* mask, the *Les Miserables* little bearer of the French flag). Drew Hodges created a new paradigm: sell a Broadway show based on the talent of the performers, on how the audience is going to feel, not on the plot line. It worked. On the first day a *Rent* ad ran in the *New York Times,* half a million dollars worth of tickets were sold. *Chicago, The Musical* was his next big challenge. Thanks in part to the campaign, it became the longest-running American musical on Broadway and an international hit. Soon Hodges had an agency with a client list filled with Broadway producers. But that could mean a whole roomful of egos: the director, the playwright, the backers, as well as the producer himself. The son of a minister, Hodges has a sixth sense of how to work with show-business clients so that all psyches, as well as the box office, are satisfied.

This campaign, and the show itself, has been a hit for almost two decades. But, according to Drew Hodges, half a dozen other approaches could have worked, too. "I always want to see a bunch of ideas," he says. "So do my clients."

A campaign with legs, literally and figuratively. Says the client about developing a winning concept: "Drew wants his staff to love it. I want my marketing team to march to it."

[I met with Drew Hodges at SpotCo's offices in a former
bank building in Times Square.]

**Q: The first time I met you, to talk about *Rent*, you were working at your kitchen
table. Now you're in the middle of Times Square.**

A: Hodges: We're moving into a new office on West 41st Street that is our
largest yet, 23,000 square feet. It kinda looks like a Chelsea gallery, very white
and sleek.

**You told me in 1996 that when you came in to present the concept for *Rent*, the
attitude of the people in the meeting was, "And you are?" Obviously, a lot has
happened.**

Hodges: Well, we've worked in the field of entertainment, and more specifically live entertainment, for almost twenty years. We have worked on seven
Pulitzer Prize winning plays. We worked on the Tony Award winner for Best
Musical for the last six years in a row. The other day, we figured that we've
sold more than $250 million worth of tickets.

At this point, we are eighty-five people. We do media planning and
buying, account services, talent payments, copywriting, design, and anima-
tion. And we produce print, outdoor, transit, digital, social media, television,
radio, and longer-form content for the web.

Most of our clients are Broadway, but we also do the advertising and
promotion for Radio City Christmas Show, Cirque du Soleil, the Tony Awards,
and other live events, as well as a bit of television work like *Smash*.

**And you still have that a bit of that aw-shucks, this-can't-be-happening-to-me
attitude.**

Hodges: Yeah, at the time my studio was called Spot Design. We built SpotCo,
an entertainment and arts ad agency, because it was obvious with *Rent* and
then with *Chicago* that the agencies placing the ads were the ones making
the money. I think on the first *Chicago* campaign, Spot Design billed $40,000
and the agency placed $1 million of media. Now we're a subsidiary of R4e,
Reach4Entertainment Enterprises PLC, the London-based parent company of
four entertainment promotion and brand-building companies, including us
and Dewynters, a similar agency in London. But it really hasn't changed
anything.

What is it like to have Broadway producers as clients?

Hodges: They're all different. One is not like the other. A lot of different kinds
of people do this. Some of them worked their way up in the theater; they'd
always loved Broadway. Some of them are former marketing people from TV
or film. Some of them made a lot of money in other industries. For example,
the woman who founded the first biotech temp agency is now a producer.

There are a few heiresses who always wanted to be involved with the theater. All you need is money. You can buy your way in. Let's say you have $5 million. You can say, "Give me a theater. Give me a press agent. Give me a casting agent. Give me a writer." Some of them have a philanthropic bent; they're doing something useful with their money. You could give your money to the Cancer Society or you could produce a show, in which case you might get to stand up with David Mamet and get a Tony on national television. You can enjoy the community, the glamour, the challenge. Few of them have any sense of working with an agency or a designer. Maybe their closest experience was working with an architect.

And the producers of *Chicago*?

Hodges: Barry Weissler worked his way up in the business, from running touring companies, to *Grease*, to being one of the top theatrical producers in the world.

There are a lot of people involved in a show and in making decisions, but the producer is the one who pays your bills, right?

Hodges: Right. Everyone works for the producer. A show is like a start-up corporation. There are the legal papers, the business plan, the team of people who don't know each other very well. The producer hires the playwright, the set designer, the costume designer. Every show is a brand-new palette with brand-new imagery. Even if it's a revival, like *Chicago*—especially if it's a revival—they don't want to use old imagery. We, the designers, the agency, are just one more piece in the mix. All producers are total entrepreneurs of some kind, even the ones who come from a media background. Some of them enjoy the marketing aspects, the making of the advertising. The trick is to completely get to know each of them and what they need.

> **Do your clients understand what you're saying?**
>
> Some clients want you to tell them what to do. Others want to tell you what they want. The trick is to be able to figure it out.

How did you learn how to do that?

Hodges: My father is a minister. I was brought up in a church—the Methodist church in Hyde Park, New York, near the FDR mansion. As a minister's son, you learn how to talk to people, how to intuit what they want. It's all about personal relations. Some clients want you to tell them what to do. Some clients want to tell you what they want. Some clients want a collaboration, a group thing.

To get to know them, do you spend a lot of time entertaining, taking them to lunch or dinner?

Hodges: Nobody has the time for me to take them to lunch or dinner. Maybe I'd be more successful if I did more of that. We're here working all the time. Broadway is a way of living your life—morning, noon, and night. I see clients at opening nights. Every show has an opening night. That's where I see new clients, old clients, successful clients, not-so-successful clients. If the show you're associated with wins Tony awards, everybody is aware of your work. Every year, one of our clients is up for "best play" at the Tonys. The fact that we did the poster might make the producer of another play call us to design theirs. The success of a show rubs off on everything associated with it. And when we get a new client, they all want to imagine that we don't have another client, that we're 100 percent committed to them and their production.

What's your biggest challenge?

Hodges: Broadway is always fighting to stay relevant—important and relevant—especially in the face of film, which has the sense that there's no other type of entertainment. Every show is a defining moment for the producer, personally and professionally. Is it a hit or a flop? Their whole life is about this show until it succeeds or fails.

Can you describe how your company combines the role of ad agency and design firm?

Hodges: We plan the campaign. Who is the audience? When will the ads break? Will there be a TV campaign? What are the buying patterns? *Harlem Song* on 125th Street is very different from Albee's *The Goat*. We do a written statement for each show, ending with a mission statement that's two or three sentences. This is what we want it to feel like. Each one is different. We did the *Annie Get Your Gun* revival and it needed a sense of nostalgia, nostalgia for an old-fashioned musical western. To do this, you need experience in tactics. We develop a strategy—what the show needs to sound like, feel like, walk and talk like. You keep half your head in design: is it stunning, beautiful, surprising? You keep half your head in results. How many tickets did it sell? Our strategy is calibrated to produce very specific results. We have to sell eight thousand tickets a week per show. When that's not happening, we look at the reasons.

For example, after 9-11, Barry Weissler and I worked with the whole community to revive Broadway with the stars singing in Times Square commercials. At other times, we might change tactics: we'll try a price discount, we'll do a direct-mail piece, run an insert or another ad; we might do an e-mail campaign to a list of former ticket buyers. Sometimes you look for something new to promote, the cast changing, a new star. For three months, Michael C. Hall of *Six Feet Under* and *Dexter* fame starred as the male lead in *Chicago*. His then-new wife in real life, Amy Spanger, played Roxie. Here's the ad [the headline is "To Die For"].

I love it. It's hard to imagine the pressure of having to sell eight thousand tickets a week, though. How often do you get the numbers?

Hodges: Every day. The general manager of the show sends them every afternoon.

> When designing *anything*, keep these criteria in mind:
>
> What does it need to sound like, to feel like, to walk and talk like? Keep half your head in design, half your head in results.

We evaluate design and advertising based on its real-world effect. This is all about investors getting their money back. It takes a long time. *Lion King*, one of the most successful shows ever, didn't make a dime for five years.

How did you get started with *Chicago*?

Hodges: We had just done *Rent*, and Barry and Fran Weissler of Namco called, saying that they wanted to meet. *Chicago* had just had a short, successful run with Bebe Newirth and Ann Reinking at Encores at City Center, which does short-run revivals of classic shows. The Weisslers wanted to move it to Broadway just as it was. A concert. They needed positioning, a logo, media, TV, radio.

What drove your design concept?

Hodges: I had a real concern—no, make that fear—that it was going to be hard to charge Broadway ticket prices for a stripped-down version. According to union rules, in the Encores setting, the show couldn't have sets. Sometimes the performers had to have scripts in their hands. It was an almost-bare stage—no helicopters, no swinging chandeliers. The story was based on a real-live crime of the 1920s; the original show opened in 1975, with full sets, and it was not a hit. It was considered too dark at the time, and *Chorus Line* was the only show that people were paying attention to that season. But we often try to support a show's weak points.

This was my thinking: This is about two women who kill their husbands; about press, fame, corruption, injustice. It exists in the general sense of time, which makes it more modern. What did we want the show to feel like? Well, we had to find a way to own the minimalism. How could we give the minimalism form and style? Let's make it look as if we always wanted it that way. Let's use black-and-white. Let's use fashion photography in which minimalism is an asset. We picked Max Vadukal, who was known for his editorial spreads in *Vogue*. We comped up the campaign using his existing photographs. This is one of the hardest things to do, to get a client to understand what it will look like with the star in it. For the logo we used wood type from the Rob Roy Kelly book. But it was more about the pictures than about the logo.

How many concepts did you present?

Hodges: I always want to see a bunch of ideas. So do my clients. They want to have a role in it. They want to be choosy. I always say, "I think this is the one," but I show at least half a dozen concepts, each with variations. There are always different ways to solve something. Four or five different ad campaigns could be equally successful. The decision is based on answering the question, what do we want the show to feel like? Sometimes the porridge is too hot, sometimes too cold. Here's a funny concept. Here's a sexy one. Here's a classic one. Ah, this one is just right. *Chicago* needed to be sexy. Dangerous, modern, minimalist, and sexy. It needed to own black and white. When Barry saw the comps, he said, "I love it!"

Your agency has big enough budgets to develop that many concepts and variations. How would you advise the young designer just starting out? For example, do you think that the tried-and-true formula of showing three concepts—one a bit daring, one safe, one in the middle—can work in most cases?

> **Is showing one concept enough?**
>
> If you have a client who needs to be choosy, show a range. Here's a funny concept. Here's a serious one. Ah, this one is just right.

Hodges: Sure it can. But every designer has to work out who they are and how they present. I have always admired Paula Scher and her three- and sometimes even one-concept approach. But she is a master at telling you what you need to do to get on-course, and she sells her work as if you are very lucky to have her there to fix your problem.

I am about being a consensus-builder. I have to be. My clients come in big clusters and most likely haven't worked together before. It takes more options to bring that kind of group together. The longer I do this, though, the more I believe that selling the best idea from the beginning yields stronger work.

[Later, I spoke with Barry Weissler]

When you saw the ads for *Rent*, did you know that Spot was the creative team you wanted for *Chicago*?

Weissler: Drew came in to see me before he had his agency, when he was an art director on his own. I didn't even know he'd done *Rent*. I'm usually suspicious of people coming in to market services. But when I met him I knew right away he was my man. He thinks the way I do. We march to the same drummer. We have the same feelings about advertising and marketing and how to communicate with the public.

What's the most fun about being a producer?

Weissler: We've produced some of the great Broadway shows: *Othello* with James Earl Jones and Christopher Plummer in 1982, which won a Tony. There was *Zorba* with Anthony Quinn, *Cabaret* with Joel Grey. The most fun is when you have a success, and you transport thousands of people each night to a magical place. That's what's really exciting about what I do. When you have a failure, it's like being in an inferno.

You work with lighting designers, set designers, costume designers. Is there anything all designers have in common?

Weissler: Their creativity. Each one is different. Each one applies him or herself differently. All the good ones are passionate about what they do.

How many design concepts do you remember seeing for *Chicago*? What was it about the one you chose that made you say, "I love it"?

Weissler: I know that Drew presents several ideas to some of his clients, but that's not how he works with me. We begin alone. We talk to each other. He always begins by asking me what I think and what I feel. We work together like partners. After we come up with the idea, we show it to our people. He wants his staff to love it. I want my marketing team to march to it.

Drew said that one of the most difficult things for an agency to sell is a concept using existing photography, because the real pictures of the show, with the stars, haven't been taken. What's your experience with that?

Weissler: It was Drew's brilliant choice of photographer that made this campaign what it has been and is. I'd never heard of Max Vadukal and didn't know his work. I said I wanted high fashion, sex, and danger. This campaign began with six narrow vertical shots of the women, spliced together, black-and-white, with red type. That succeeded perfectly. I didn't need to be sold.

Do you really hold the agency responsible for selling eight thousand tickets a week? Aren't there other factors at play beyond advertising and promotion?

Weissler: Of course. There is word of mouth. That's as important as advertising and promotion. I have my own marketing division. We join hands with Drew's agency. If sales are down, we talk about what's going on and what we can do. Shall we try this or that? Should be put a wrapper around the whole *New York Times* on Thanksgiving and own that space for the weekend?

How important is a great website for a show?

Weissler: It's tremendously important, vital. Most people shop on the web, so it's a portal to ticket sales. Sales from the site account for one-third of the total. People may visit the site because they're curious. The site can turn them from merely curious to committed buyers. They buy tickets before leaving their hometowns, without leaving their chairs, without dealing with a ticket agent. Fans go to the site for updates on the show. We get emails every day with questions like, "How long is such-and-such a star going to be in the show?"

> **Takeaway message:**
>
> The client wants to take credit for "your" idea. Nothing should make you happier (except getting the check).

Drew told me that after 9/11, you and he came up with the idea of the TV commercials with the Broadway stars singing in Times Square. Do you think the American public would have rallied behind New York and Broadway anyway?

Weissler: That idea was born when I was sitting in my summer home trying to think of what we could do. I gave Drew the idea and he made it better. In the execution, you have a commodity that's as valuable as the idea itself.

When you begin producing a new property, do you consider different creative talents, different agencies, pick the one that's right for the show?

Weissler: No. Spot's my organization. Drew's my man. He's the best in the industry. There's no reason to go anywhere else. He gets me to delve more fully into my creative psyche; I come up with better ideas because of him.

[After that conversation, I had another question for Drew.]

Barry Weissler kept saying things like "Drew's my man." Now that eighty-five people work at SpotCo, you can't be everyone's man. Or can you? How do you divide up responsibilities so that clients feel they are getting top talent when you're not always in the room with them?

It would be disingenuous to say that this isn't a constant issue. Probably with Barry more than any other client, although others may wish for that one-to-one relationship. My best answer is that I focus on the big ideas, the execution. In some ways, not being in every detail gives me the vantage point to see the larger strategy. The work I do is a long way from design. I challenge my staff with the positioning, and it's up to them to solve the design. I edit, but a long time ago I left style behind and spend my time on message and strategy. The Tony awards are my favorite time of year, because everything we do is pure strategy, hopefully followed by brilliant creative from my team. ■

part  **IV**

Institutional Clients

They are schools, colleges, and universities, religious organizations, government agencies, foundations, hospitals, museums, and charities. Raising funds and recruiting constituents require increasingly sophisticated skills.

The work that really makes a difference touches the hearts of the audience and moves them to support your client's cause.

19

The Institution of Higher Education

Harvard AND Michael McPherson;
MIT AND Denise Korn;
Northeastern AND Robert Davison

As **Harvard University**'s director for alumni affairs and development, Andrew Tiedemann, now vice president for communications at Emerson College, headed the team responsible for all Harvard College publications and for developing the University's alumni affairs website.

Partner at brand strategy and design firm Corey McPherson Nash for twenty-five years, AIGA Boston fellow **Michael McPherson** has been creative director for many key projects for Harvard. Before cofounding his firm, he was design director at Northeastern.

Writer and communications consultant **Martha Eddison** is special assistant to the president of **MIT**. Former speechwriter for New York Governor Mario Cuomo, she was lead consultant to MIT's multi-billion-dollar fundraising effort.

Denise Korn heads Korn Design, with offices in Boston and New York, which provides branding, strategic positioning, and design services to corporate and nonprofit clients. The firm worked closely with Martha Eddison on strategy and design for MIT's capital campaign.

After directing communications for undergraduate admissions at colleges, including Northeastern University, for six years, **Caroline Jorgensen** joined Bally-whoSocial, where she helps clients manage their social media platforms.

Robert Davison was at **Northeastern University** for nine years, heading the team responsible for defining and maintaining the University's visual brand. He is now creative director at MathWorks, a Boston-based branding consultancy.

Of all the things graphic design does—sell products, change opinions, give people positive experiences—recruiting students and raising funds are two of the most significant. Colleges and universities are in increasing competition for the right students and ever-rarer donor dollars. As every parent of a seventeen-year-old with decent SAT scores knows, it's highly competitive. Every year, the need is greater and the stakes are higher. Producing materials for this market is an art and a science. Whether you're an in-house designer or an outside consultant, you can often feel pressured to satisfy too many constituents, in too short a time frame, with an inadequate budget. At a panel sponsored by CASE, the Council for Advancement and Support of Education, three top Boston-area university clients and designers revealed how they use the power of design to produce work that achieves mutual goals.

"I've felt at home at Harvard."

CALCULATED RISKS
CREATIVE
REVOLUTIONS

CAMPAIGN FOR
MIT

[In a Cambridge event space during a CASE Design Institute sponsored by the Washington, DC-based Council for Advancement and Support of Education, I moderated a "clients and designers" panel of Boston-area university communications professionals.]

Q: Harvard and Corey McPherson Nash have enjoyed a nine-year relationship. Andy, you and Michael have worked on many projects together. Harvard also has an in-house design staff. When and how do you choose a design firm, and when do you use your in-house people?

A: Tiedemann: The choice usually isn't very difficult. We're a small shop, five writers and two designers. We're responsible for communicating with more than 300,000 Harvard alumni and producing all the publications for Harvard College. Generally, we have twice as much work as we can do in a year. We meet with our in-house designers every three to six months to look at the projects coming up. They decide which ones they want to work on. The remaining ones go into the competitive bidding process.

I think that might be a surprise to many in-house designers who think that the really good projects go to outside firms, who get all the opportunities to do the great work and win the awards.

Tiedemann: It doesn't work that way for us. Our group will get together to brainstorm about whether a particular project is something we want to take on. What are the chances for success? Or that it will get into a political quagmire? If it looks like it might become politically difficult, we might call a freelancer or a firm like Michael's.

When you call an outside firm, do you invite people to come in, present their capabilities, and tell you why they're the right choice for the project?

Tiedemann: We have a small retainer with a few firms we work with quite a bit. Every year so we try to work through that retainer. Then there are situations in which we will entertain bids. But we try not to waste designers' time. If we're leaning toward a particular firm, we're not going to invite twelve firms if each only has a one-in-twelve chance of getting the job.

Is that chance based on price? Or do you evaluate other criteria?

Tiedemann: Price is part of it. But if we've had a good experience with a firm, if we know they can deliver, even if the cost is higher, we'll go with a firm we know is going to come through for us.

Can you describe your team structure?

Tiedemann: We have a kickoff meeting in which we define the audience and marketing problem the project is intended to solve. There will be me as creative director, the project manager, the writer, the designer from the firm we've selected, and our internal client, plus the person who will have the final say on the project. This could be the president of the university, the dean of a school, the vice president for fundraising or for alumni. I also include one of my in-house designers, even if we're using an outside firm. We talk about what the deliverables will be, the delivery date, whether a particular event or university happening is driving that date. We talk about past projects that are related to that piece. After that, meetings will involve the creative team only, and we'll brainstorm about design approaches, like whether we're using an illustrator or a photographer, and if so, who.

Good news:

If clients have a good experience with you, if they know you can deliver, there's a good chance they'll work with you again—even if your price is higher.

I'd like to talk about a piece you did with Michael's firm: "Twenty-Five Years: a Celebration of Women at Harvard." Here's a striking image of a fully dressed woman sitting on a diving board, her sweater color-coordinated with the pool lane markers. How did this image come about; who chose the photographer, the set?

Tiedemann: We chose the twenty-fifth anniversary of women moving into the freshman dorms as the occasion to do a major piece that profiled twenty-five Harvard women. We knew that some women felt that Harvard ignored them and that they felt they didn't have a place here. Some of the women pictured are students, some are graduates, some faculty. Each gave a short statement about her relationship to Harvard. We took some risks, which was not characteristic. So there are statements like, "I was the only black woman here and it wasn't fun." Corey McPherson Nash brought in photographers' portfolios. We decided on Tony Rinaldo. Tony has an unbelievable eye. The way he frames situations is unique. He shot in three cities for us.

One thing that strikes me is the luxurious use of space. Half of the spreads are bleed photos with no type on them, which is very unusual for a university publication. I critiqued brochures and magazines at the CASE Design Institute this morning, and it's evident many college designers are forced into fitting ten or fifteen or more pictures—people at events or smiling at the camera and shaking hands—on a page. How do you rationalize your use of space?

McPherson: This is a one-in-a-thousand project. When we proposed devoting a whole spread to each person, Andy and the client agreed. I looked at them and said, "Wow." We are often in the position of having to put ten photos on a page, too, and you just do your best. This piece needed to have impact. We made it oversized, and not look like another piece of Harvard propaganda.

As I understand it, there is no Harvard identity manual that suggests typography, page grids, how images should be used. As a communications consultant, do you wish there were more of a Harvard look?

McPherson: Yes. At one point, we had five different clients at Harvard—the School of Public Health, the School of Education, the Divinity School, the School of Art and Architecture, Admissions—and none of the projects were related to each other.

Does that give you a lot of freedom to do the most effective thing on each project?

McPherson: Well, most clients here start a meeting by saying, "We want this piece not to look like Harvard," which means no serif type and not a lot of crimson. There is a kind of mindset or cliché of what a Harvard piece looks like. And we're always working against that. The cliché piece would be black and crimson—and no one can agree what that crimson is, no Pantone color is quite right—on cream stock. It would have shields on it, small serif type. It might be quite beautiful. You have to remember that we are in a unique position. We have 17,000 applications for a few thousand positions. We are trying to maintain a certain level of selectivity and diversity.

To reflect on what you're saying, a few years ago I wrote an article entitled "Rating the Art and Design School Catalogs" for *Print* magazine. We received lavish viewbooks and catalogs from RISD, CalArts, Parsons, Art Center, all filled with dazzling color photography and all kinds of design tricks. Yale submitted a simple six-by-nine booklet on cream stock. It had a little Yale shield on the cover, serif type set in a single justified column, no pictures. I put together an informal panel of prospective students and parents to judge the books, and almost everybody said they thought that Yale was the best design school. A lot of what drives the choice is reputation, correct?

Tiedemann: Yes. But we need to make sure that each marketing problem is solved on its own and that we don't rely on the reputation or the cliché.

Michael, you also have corporate clients and have been an in-house college and university designer yourself. For you, what are the special rewards of doing institutional work?

McPherson: Designing for clients in education aligns with my beliefs about what's really important. Like all designers, I love to learn new things, and that's what schools are about. Colleges and universities create experiences for young people. We work hard to identify and understand the different cultures of schools. Superficially, some schools may seem very similar to one another. But they're not. For example, two fine small liberal arts colleges will be completely different once you get inside them: the texture, the attitudes, the kind of student.

As consultants, we try to discern the differences and speak with an authentic voice so each piece reflects a deep understanding of each institution and its culture. By deep, I mean that every decision, style, typeface, paper stock, photograph, has to feel like it's speaking from that school. And that requires a certain investment. Institutions don't have deep pockets, and some don't understand the necessity for designers to do an in-depth exploration, a discovery process, up-front. They want you to come in and start working on the brochure, but that's not going to yield the best results.

Andy, when you say that in-house designers get first choice, do you believe that they do have a certain advantage, that deep understanding Michael is talking about, without having to go through a briefing process?

Tiedemann: Definitely. They know the client, they have an innate sense of the client's hopes and desires. That's the reason we have one of our in-house designers on every creative team, whether or not they're the one doing the designing. They guide the consultants that are working with us. It's a balancing act. One of the advantages of using outside consultants is they're less afraid to take risks. We often involve outside firms on the projects we've collectively decided we want to take some risks on; we want some new thinking; we want someone to think out of the box and take the risk, politically.

Martha, as an independent consultant, what can you do for an institutional client that no one in-house can do?

Eddison: My job is to get you, the reader, to fall in love with the institution, as I have. And that can be a difficult task for people who are there every day. I can come in and spend six weeks interviewing forty faculty members and can communicate what's going on in a way someone in-house never could.

What was the situation at the time you started your engagement?

Eddison: MIT was gearing up for a capital campaign that was twice as big as anything they'd ever done before. They were doing this within an institutional culture that did not value graphic design; everything pretty much looked like an engineer typed it. Case statements—brochures that use words, numbers, and images to build the case for making a major donation—in the past had been viewed as necessary evils. You've got to have one if someone asks for it, but frankly, most were in boxes acting as doorstops around campus. The administration knew they had to produce one, but weren't sure how to go about it. There are no in-house designers at MIT, so MIT always goes outside. MIT has an in-house team of print brokers who try to help internal clients understand the value of design, the value of working with professional writers. The in-house team started by hunting around for a firm that could give them the kind of writing and design they wanted. They couldn't find one firm, so they decided to make a team of a design firm and me. Bringing in Denise helped MIT to learn the strategic value of design.

I'm intrigued by your statement that the culture at MIT doesn't value design. Has there been a big change? In his textbook, *The History of Graphic Design*, Philip B. Meggs singled out the high level of quality and imagination in the MIT design program, which he called a paradigm of the International Typographic Style in America. He referred both to the posters designed by Jacqueline Casey in the seventies and to the MIT design program that enabled all members of the university community to get free, professional design assistance. The MIT Media Lab is known as an incubator of design technologies. Faculty members like John Maeda speak at conferences on topics like the future of design.

Eddison: The designers and programs you're talking about were not anything that came up through the capital campaign design process. The MIT group that helps internal clients find good outside designers certainly took an interest in what we were doing, but they didn't play a role.

Denise, you have called your relationship with Martha collaborative and unique. How do you work together?

Korn: Both of us believe that what we need to communicate is equally carried by the words and the visuals. A lot of clients don't understand that for words and images to mesh in a meaningful way, the process of writing and designing needs to start together. We need to generate the questions to ask the client together. And when the client answers them, and we develop a concept that reflects those answers, poetry can happen. Usually a concept will roll out naturally. This is a hard thing to explain to someone who's never been through the process with the right kind of team. Just hearing an explanation like this could seem overly academic or artsy, but it's strategically based. The correct solution allows a client to be brave. Because it's not just based on something that's blue and green, it's something that has meaning for them.

> "Educating" the client:
>
> Help your clients understand that to communicate effectively, the processes of writing and designing need to start—and progress—together.

How can you convince a large institution, where, as it's been pointed out, there might be thorny political issues, to be brave?

Korn: It's important, whether you work in-house or are an external consultant, to understand the chain of command and the approval process from the beginning. You have to know who needs to be engaged and included in the voyage you're going on together. Sometimes you find out that you've never met the key decision maker until it's too late.

McPherson: It's important to have everybody who can say "no" together in one room.

Tiedeman. Sometimes that's a lot of people.

Eddison: Our immediate clients at MIT got nervous at the approval stage. They didn't know what to do if any of the higher-ups on the tree of command said "no." So I said, "I'll take it to them." I took the piece, marched off to their offices, virtually read it to each of them, and more or less got their sign-off right there. It was kind of hard for them to disagree with me; they weren't going to throw me out; they'd gotten to like me by then, so there was a great advantage for my internal client to let me take that risk.

Congratulations. I'm impressed. Can we back up to the design brief? Your overall mission was to raise $1.5 billion for MIT. When accomplishing something of that magnitude, is that the problem stated by the client: "Martha and Denise, help us raise $1.5 billion," or are the deliverables more concrete: "We need a case statement, a newsletter, a website."

Korn: A campaign is an amorphous, organic thing. The project evolved out of a process of discovery. Over a five-year period it has taken several different turns. Originally, there was an RFP that stated, "We need collateral, we need a case statement that focuses on the following initiatives." We were brought in to produce those items. Martha undertook months of research studies, strategic analyses, and interviews with donors, and we came back and said, "You don't need this, you need that, and you're asking for way too much stuff." For example, donors don't want a big party, they want facts, they want to be engaged about what is compelling about this institution now. Some of the pieces that now exist evolved from the original list, and others were not even on their radar screen.

Do you bring written documentation, so that the strategy you're recommending cannot be considered an opinion, but is based on research?

Korn: Yes and no. A lot of what's going to work is intuitive as well as based on research. The solution might be based more on an understanding of the soul of the institution, in this case, an understanding of MIT's alumni and what would be needed to get their financial support. We shared a lot of documentation with the client, but in the end, it was the combination of Martha's content with the design solution that delivered that.

As just one example, MIT's colors are maroon and black. Every piece in this campaign is green and blue. People get very emotional about color. Did you have to fight any battles on this?

Korn: They wanted the brand identity for the campaign to be robust and bold. This is an identity for a five-year campaign. It was gutsy to go with that.

Eddison: There's an advantage in not having an organized design culture. So why not do green and blue?

Korn: Can I just add that the color green is never an easy sell?

Tiedemann: Clients hate that green.

Overall, there is a strong theme and look to these MIT pieces: the color scheme, the typography. Did you set out the parameters of the identity first and then design the individual pieces?

Korn: We inherited the mark for the campaign and refined it and made it functional, big and small, on the web, in color and black-and-white. We wove it into all the materials, moving forward in an organized way in terms of an identity structure. We posted a palette with colors and typography on the MIT Intranet for everyone who would be producing campaign materials over the five-year period to subscribe to. We created templates that people can pull down to create brochures. There's no design police, but there is a tool that many people in the institution can use to keep up the consistency.

Caroline and Rob, you are both employees of Northeastern University. You're doing some strong work together, and I suspect that until hearing from Andy and Michael, most in-house designers thought that outside design firms have all the fun. Not true, right?

Davison: Not at all. Like Andy's situation at Harvard, we have requests for twice the number of jobs we can do in a year. We select the projects we want to handle internally and work with outside freelancers to produce the rest. There are lots of interesting projects to go around.

The work you've done together also has a very strong look, a lot of red. Do you believe in having a campaign look or a color like Coca-Cola's red, a forever look?

Davison: Red is Northeastern's color. For years, numerous Northeastern reds were being used, and it was interpreted loosely at best. Sometimes it was crimson, sometimes more orange or even maroon. We standardized the color, creating a special ink mix that is distinctive and specific to Northeastern, so I'd like to think there is a parallel to Coke's red.

When can a look go from fresh to tired? How do you keep it fresh?

Jorgensen: Students go to college fairs and pick up materials from twenty, thirty different schools. A student has expectations about what an institution should look like, and it's up to us to keep them interested and excited. If a ten-year-old brochure looks similar to the one we have right now, students will pick up on that.

Davison: The materials we develop have to be an accurate representation of the university at a moment in time. A university is a fluid entity, and the challenge is to capture and package its spirit. Our goal is to showcase not only who we are, but what we're becoming. Projects that were effective even a couple of years ago often don't hold up as well as we would like.

Rob, you previously ran your own firm. Can you characterize the difference between being a design firm principal and managing an in-house department?

Davison: I've worked in several environments, from small design firms to larger agencies, as well as having my own firm. Whenever you connect with a good client, you hope for continuity and the opportunity to evolve things over time, but it's never guaranteed. Northeastern has been my first in-house experience, and I've had the chance to really look at the nuances here. While my work now revolves around a single institution, it's not too different to having my own firm. Working with design and branding standards reminds me of the Paul Rand essay, "Design and the Play Instinct." A limited pool of ingredients challenges you to bring out the richness in your design solutions.

The goal of your capital campaign was to raise $200 million. And every year, you need to recruit nearly 3,000 students. How do you evaluate design work, whether it meets certain design criteria or achieves those goals?

Jorgensen: The goal of an admissions office is to have a successful and talented class enroll, exactly the number we want. We had the highest number of applications in history last year, and we're seeing more higher-ability students than ever before. Our retention numbers are up as well. Our publications play a key role in this, and we see a direct effect on the caliber of students. Recruiting is not a passive or standardized process. We have a sophisticated communications strategy. We're implementing a system that can track the distribution specifics of our publications: who receives them, how many times each student gets a publication, what kind of student they are, and whether they apply and enroll. There will be an opportunity to test various communications and get a sense of our success rate in certain markets and with different types of students. This feedback will be an invaluable indicator of how well we are doing.

Davison: Caroline and others in admissions often share comments from students and parents about what they respond to in our publications, as well as what they would like to see. For high-level projects, we often use research firms that run focus groups. In terms of fundraising, development officers pass along comments on our capital campaign materials from prospective donors. There is very direct feedback, and we learn if a publication was persuasive or if it fell flat.

We designers love to create brochures; they're like our children. But what if you learned from some higher power that you didn't need print materials, photography, any of that stuff, to raise funds? I attended UCLA and designed UCLA development materials for several years after graduation. But now, students call and make the annual fund pitch on the phone, and that seems to work pretty well.

Davison: Print plays a vitally important role in informing and persuading people to make important, often emotional, decisions. Is it necessary to print data sheets? Probably not. Certain kinds of data are best accessed online. But we continue to hear that folks want a brochure they can hold in their hands: a viewbook that can be passed around the kitchen table, a capital campaign piece to display on the coffee table. A phone call may be able to successfully close a donation from an alum, but recruiting is a more complex process. For our primary audience, high school students, the game is how to get their attention and then keep it. Good photography plays an increasingly important role, as it quickly sets the tone and leads them into the piece.

How important is the website to recruiting?

Jorgensen: It is important, but there are a lot of ways for prospective students to connect. Part of reputation-building is looking at every point of contact as an opportunity to shape and evolve perception. It could be the site, a meeting at a college fair, an open house, campus tours, or word of mouth. Research shows that with all the media options available, students still want something physically in hand to carry with them when they visit a campus, to reference throughout the day during an open house. I don't believe even the best website would be as effective without printed material.

What is the best way to manage projects internally? The big complaint I keep hearing from in-house people is, "Our internal clients don't listen." How do you get them to listen?

Davison: As Denise, Michael, and Martha have said, by getting all the decision makers in the room at the beginning of a project. We host brainstorming sessions with the deans and selected faculty so they feel invested, have a sense of ownership, and so the approval process will go much more smoothly. Northeastern, like any large university, is decentralized. Various offices and

If there's only one thing you learn from this book, it's this:

Before you start designing, get all the decision makers—at least everyone who has the power to say "No"—in the same room with you.

departments create their own communications, some of which have no connection to the university brand. There are isolated fiefdoms around campus that are not interested in our design or messaging standards. We in the publications office can act as a consultant, educating them about the value of embracing the standards. This process can include a communications audit of their materials and strategic plan for improvement. There's often resistance, a lot of fear. But when they see that they can maintain their individual identity while working with us, it's a win-win situation.

When my son was a high school junior, the recruiting materials were coming to our house fast and furiously. But he sometimes wouldn't even open an envelope, saying "That's a dorky place" (he'd read all the *Insiders' Guides to College*) and he'd throw the brochure in the trash. Or he'd open the envelope and look at the pictures and say something like, "They have old computers," and then throw it away. From your perspective, what is it that causes a prospective student to choose one college over another?

Jorgensen: Our job is to demonstrate to prospective students and their families how we can be the right match. One of the best ways to accomplish this is to have them visit our campus. The majority of students who do so end up applying. Our marketing promotions create a window onto what they will see, feel, and experience once here. In choosing a college, students want a personalized experience. We are developing a whole new interactive experience: personalized URLs. Applicants will be able to check their status and be given information specifically about what they're interested in.

Davison: Word of mouth is everything in academia, so any way we can create positive buzz is worth it. Students are savvy and pick up on visual cues quickly. They want to get that big-picture overview of campus and its proximity to things. They see things like technology hardware and what students are wearing as signals to what a place is about. They want to see how they would fit in. Each year I push for an ample photography budget to ensure we have an updated pool to pull from—no old computers! How an institution's defining characteristics are represented visually is pivotal. We are located in the middle of a city. We have 14,000 students. We link classroom liberal arts learning with workplace experience. These aren't things that you want to gloss over. We make the most of them. When you truly capture the spirit of the institution in a way that speaks to the student, you bring him or her a big step closer to making that choice. ∎

20 The Visionary

SCI-Arc
AND April Greiman

Los Angeles native **Michael Rotondi FAIA** is a 1973 graduate of **SCI-Arc**, Southern California Institute of Architecture, which he helped found in 1972. He was the school's director for ten years, remains on the faculty, and lectures at architecture schools around the country. Now located in downtown Los Angeles, SCI-Arc is one of the nation's few independent architecture schools, offering undergraduate and graduate programs. Mr. Rotondi also heads the firm RoTo Architects, which he founded in 1991 after working independently and in various collaborations. He won the AIA Gold Medal in 2009.

April Greiman studied at The Kansas City Art Institute and Allgemeine Kunstgwerbeschule in Basel, Switzerland. She opened her Los Angeles practice, Made in Space, in 1976, and has been an innovator and leader in advanced technologies in graphic, environmental, motion, and interactive design. She creates, in her words: "explorations of image, word, and color as objects in time and space, grounded in a fusion of art and technology." Her work has been the subject of international solo exhibitions.

Michael Rotondi is the kind of client every designer wants, but few can have. He understands the ambiguities of design and doesn't tremble in fear—or change his strategy—when his colleagues criticize a new piece. He sticks to his guns and lets people engage themselves, take their time, and learn to appreciate the work. He is articulate and visionary when it comes to broader issues, too. For example, on the subject of typical corporate identity manuals, he says: "That kind of fixed identity comes out of a static culture that believes things have to be immutable; a culture in which very few people make decisions that affect very many." April Greiman says that the most valuable lesson to be learned from her relationship with SCI-Arc is that "it's possible to collaborate creatively on an idea and an aesthetic that pervades not only the various formats and applications of design, but enters into the bloodstream of the client's environment." She and Michael Rotondi became life partners, too, so this is a story of personal and professional synergy.

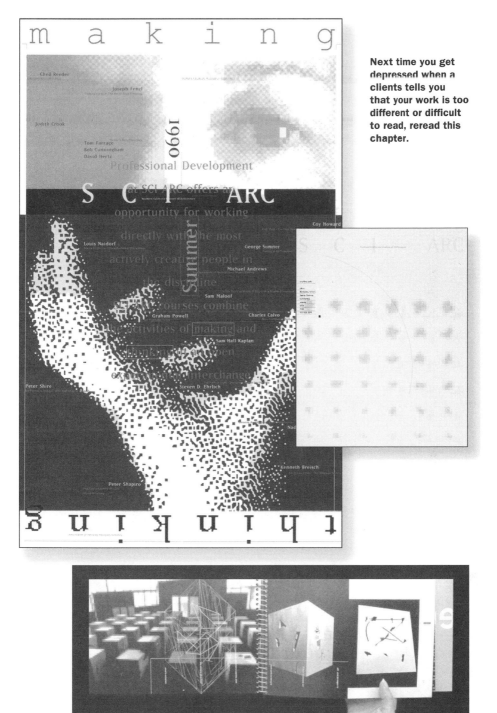

Next time you get depressed when a clients tells you that your work is too different or difficult to read, reread this chapter.

[I spoke with April Greiman in her studio just east of downtown Los Angeles.]

Q: You have commented that you "built an entire career on accidents." What, exactly, did you mean by that?

A: Greiman: Although I'm a rational, reasonable, sometimes articulate person, my main foot forward is intuitive, inspired by the Basel School, where I studied. I've never hired marketing consultants or gone after clients, mostly because work that is market driven is quite different than work that is a true integration between culture and commerce. I still prefer to put the design at the fore, and then figure out how to work within a budget or specific financial constraints. So far, it has proven successful.

Actually, I thought you were referring to computer accidents—an image that might suddenly appear or transform itself.

Greiman: That's true, too. I've always subscribed creatively to the chance principle. Before computers it was video. One time, I traded half-inch video cameras with a colleague who said, "Don't forget to adjust the white balance." I asked, "What's white balance?" He said, "Now I know how you get that great color!" Do you see what I mean? Often I'll watch an image take shape on the computer and have to go back and capture it so we can create it again for another project or purpose.

Are your clients concerned about fees?

Greiman: Is there a client who's not? Usually, they'll give us a budget rather than having us work on a proposal we have to revise three times. I ask every potential client if they're getting other bids, and can tell by who they're dealing with how educated they are about buying design. We know who's in our league.

How did SCI-Arc become your client, and what was the situation at the time?

Greiman: When Michael Rotondi was newly appointed director, he was a partner at the architecture firm Morphosis, which had hired me to do the Japan PGA Golf Club identity. At the time, SCI-Arc was an architecture school with an identity that looked like someone had put it together at an instant printer: a photocopy of a photocopy of a rubber stamp.

Michael felt that the school couldn't get to the next level of professionalism without a professional image. He trusted me and identified with the kind of communications work we did. He felt I was a world-class designer who could help him achieve his objectives. I toured the school, talked to staff and faculty, looked at student work, absorbed the philosophy —which is that architecture is part of a bigger culture, that buildings can be read as icons of other, bigger ideas. Architecture is about transformation and should emanate from ideas, rather than stylistic or decorative notions.

Tell me about the letterhead, which seems to be a cornerstone of the identity.

Greiman: I've always considered a letterhead—any piece of paper—a "space." And I wanted to transform it. We scanned an airbrush gradation and I kept enlarging it. I wanted to see the deeper structure of that gradation—like discovering the DNA. We used the anti-aliasing feature, and the pixels for each dot, instead of being hard-edged squares, softened and broke into at least sixteen million different colors. No two dots were alike. It really was architecture. I wanted to speak to technology, since architecture and design have always been aligned with technology and new materials.

Do you usually present more than one direction or solution?

Greiman: In my career, I've rarely showed more than one thing. But sometimes I present more than one version when I need the client's input to ascertain which is the most appropriate, since the details can be quite subtle.

How do you develop relationships that engender that kind of trust?

Greiman: I go to lectures and events at SCI-Arc, which gives me greater insight into the diverse ideas that are prevalent. I've worked with quite a few architects and architecture firms on color, finishes, and materials, signage, and environmental graphics, and therefore have become immersed in that world. Michael and I socialize, have lunches, meetings, talk about the various cultures and contexts of design. We discuss things such as, "Will the world need more architecture as it moves rapidly into the virtual world?" "Can there be great buildings any longer that do not reintegrate spirit and sensuality?" I feel that in past decades, time and money were wasted on building for skewed reasons. Signature work (architecture with a capital A) had no higher ideals or purpose. I truly believe architecture—and design—can inspire and transform people at the cellular level.

For example. . .

Greiman: Spaces that have powerful symbolism that combine the material, physical worlds with the spiritual, like Chartres, many Louis Kahn buildings, the Salk Institute as a prime example, Frank Gehry's Vitra Museum, Michael Rotondi's home, especially his studio.

Graphic designers often wonder whether they should be having dinner, going to shows or ballgames with clients, especially women designers with male clients? That kind of client entertainment seems artificial, possibly problematic, but occasionally a business necessity. You seem to be talking about socializing at a very different, more cerebral, level.

Greiman: I tend to be pretty antisocial. Shy mostly. I never enjoyed doing those kinds of things. I was never motivated by strictly business or money, although I love both. I socialize with people, clients, whom I feel connected to ideologically and spiritually. At a certain level, if you will, I don't have much competition, so I attract unique, perhaps unusual, kinds of clients, and they tend to be the kind of people I'll have to my home for dinner and vice versa. Again, there seems to be an affinity towards the ideological. It would probably be a good idea for me to go to a ballgame sometime!

You sprint between three or four different computers overseeing several projects at once. Can you describe your relationship with your staff? Can you define how much of a solution is "you" and how much is "them?"

Greiman: It's all me, and it is truly all them as well. We have such a small staff that I can spend a majority of my time doing design and not administration. My main responsibilities are concept and design, meeting and presenting to the client. Others in my studio are responsible for picking up on my lead and developing, enhancing, or managing the project once the main direction is set. While SCI-Arc is "my" identity and carries a particular spirit of that concept, everyone who works with me is either directly or indirectly part of the whole. It is a team and collaborative effort. That is the paradigm here: sharing, networking, and creative pluralism.

Does anyone ever complain that the SCI-Arc pieces are hard to read? Do you ever get comments like, "Students won't be able to tell what time the class is offered."

Greiman: No, not really. They're designed to be copy-light and image-strong. We're never interested in disregarding legibility. I'm not of the destroying-the-word ilk. I'm interested in fine and refined typography. But we push it to the limit, sometimes by doing things like printing olive green ink on fluorescent pink paper. You do have to work harder to read it. It's always the same conflict: readability versus memorability. I go for memorability, but not at the risk of losing readability. But if we were on press and something was illegible, I would pull the job. And you have to remember that the majority of this work is designed for potential students. They like to be stunned and want to see more image. For younger people, word is image. It's all about image. SCI-Arc has lower budgets and is less endowed than other schools. But perhaps its philosophy is stronger; its message more relevant. One could spend a lot on high-end photography, six-color printing, and still not have a clear message to communicate. Everything that comes out of SCI-Arc speaks with one voice. However, we are speaking about unity through diversity. It reinforces itself and builds on itself.

Do you ever come across clients who ask for dark type on light-colored paper, or

demand any particular sorts of things? What do you say to them?

Greiman: My clients never insist on anything. If there's something they're insistent on, it's usually something I notice myself, and we decide on it together. You usually don't notice these details until you comp up the piece at the last minute, and the client asks, "Do you think the type is big enough?" I'll say, "No." Those concerns should not be theirs. Having identified with my aesthetic, ideologically, they give me freedom. My clients have done their homework in terms of which designer they've chosen. I don't interfere with the way they manufacture their products or run their organizations. They don't question my aesthetic or interfere too much with my design. And I invite the client into the process, "We feel it could be red or green." Then we may show them two different files on the computer and ask for their participation: "Let's look at them and decide." But I don't invite them on day one. I wait until I've gone through all the preliminary exploration and I have a reasonable concept at work.

Can you describe an example of a project in which you had creative freedom, but also invited the client into the process?

Greiman: *The SCI-Arc Student Workbook.* This was the first time SCI-Arc published student work, although all major architecture schools do it every year. It's used for recruiting, but it's also sold in bookstores. Rizzoli was interested, but SCI-Arc published it themselves, and it became the second-best-selling book on architecture. People read it from cover to cover: in the undergraduate section, the emphasis on process, the philosophy, the assignments, and basic exercises. In the graduate section, the work product is treated with more reverence. We used "zap-shot" images with a still video camera to capture the texture of technology. Michael requested every spread to be a poster, which is exciting, but which ultimately was very time-consuming for me. Never to be repeated!

Once upon a time, you published a nude image of yourself in *Design Quarterly*. What effect did that have on your career?

Greiman: I understand it was fairly scandalous at the time and caused a lot of debate, but I ultimately only got positive feedback, and of course it was a sellout issue for the Walker Art Center. I guess it is now a landmark piece in the history of graphic design.

> **What is the client seeing?**
>
> Don't dictate, but invite clients into the process. Show two variations and ask for their participation: "Let's look at them and decide."

The questions it brings up are, "What's personal, what's professional?" and "What's fine art, what's graphic design?"

It was a big deal to decide to use a digitized portrait of myself. But it isn't "me," it's ink on paper, a representation of the female form. If I'd wanted to be a pin-up, I would have made it a whole lot hotter. I think the sad thing is that the main point has been lost, which is that this project represents a revolution. It was designed in cyberspace, output onto 8.5" by 11" bond paper, and printed "life size." Even more importantly, it signaled the end of "tangible art" and the beginning of working entirely digitally and manipulating light. With it, design was no longer reminiscent of the past, but indicative of the future.

In an article in *Communication Arts* magazine, "Women in Design Speak Out," one of the panelists said, "All the really famous women in this profession—you were named—don't have families." The panelists seemed to agree that women can't have children and put in the time it takes to do innovative or distinctive work. If you had been present at that event, what would you have said?

Greiman: Many famous women designers have families! Look at Sheila de Bretteville and Lella Vignelli. I never consciously made a decision not to have a family; it was just that the men I was with weren't into it. I guess you could say my work is my family; it's what I created. And I never set out to be famous. I was always interested in my work, which was the big adventure of my life. But if I'd had children, I wouldn't have let it hold me back. My career would have been different; I might not have been so prolific. But you get famous for quality, not for quantity.

[Later, in a SCI-Arc classroom in a former Hughes Aircraft plant on one of LA's last remaining tracts of undeveloped land, I spoke with Michael Rotondi.]

SCI-Arc began here with fifty faculty and students and is now considered to be one of the leading architecture schools in the world. How did that come about?

Rotondi: SCI-Arc is a place where a lot of the most active practitioners in LA work. It's like a laboratory where a lot of experimentation is going on. Teaching is an outgrowth of research, and by that I mean any time you have an idea, you can pursue it and give it form. It's a place of experiment and invention. The dominant group of students and faculty are doing experimental work. Because of this reputation, people who are among the best students and faculty around the world come here to search for and test out their ideas. When those activities are happening in a teaching and learning environment, surprising things arise.

Is there enough demand for experimental work for your graduates to find jobs?

Rotondi: It's easier to get a job when you're inventive and you've found your own voice. Your work is identifiable. The passion comes through. Clients want to work with somebody who's committed. They also require the skill level, manual and intellectual. We are teaching young architects to think and make simultaneously, to be good with both their minds and hands.

The kind of work that you do attracts clients. Period. Those who don't grasp this simple relationship continue to wonder how to get better projects. If you do cheap, crummy work, you attract cheap, crummy clients. If you push the limits, then you attract clients who also expect this.

This morning I was looking through *Architectural Digest*, which is not an architecture magazine in a sense that would be recognized here. Nevertheless, especially in light of my conversation with April, I was struck by how wealthy people have used architecture and interior design to create fictional environments for themselves. "I might be just a schmuck who made a lot of money," seems to be the thinking, "but if I surround myself with pilasters and pediments, marble and gold, the right draperies and paintings, then I will be like European royalty." Do you think that catering to that impulse will remain part of the role of architects?

Rotondi: There are a lot of different ways to practice architecture. I've staked out my way, which is to make buildings that reflect the way our lives really are, not the way we'd like to pretend they are. First, visualize your whole life; second, ask what the "big idea" is; and third, construct it of parts that will perform spontaneously and with similar purpose. Continuity, integrity, and generosity are essential aspects of any system—life, mechanical, or aesthetic—and will perform the best for the longest duration. We have been exploring every corner of contemporary life, and to be able to do that for other people is a great reward. The building or interior that clients get might not be something they recognize as familiar. It might be at the same time something strange and comfortable. They've never seen it before, but they can live in it.

> Takeaway message:
>
> If you do cheap, crummy work, you get cheap, crummy clients. If you do great work, you get great clients.

How did you meet April, and how did you present your design brief?

Rotondi: I knew her work. It was one-of-a-kind, yet not repetitive. A graduate student who had spoken to April about a lecture series poster introduced us. We met at a restaurant I'd designed and talked for hours. Part of the conversation was about SCI-Arc's need to grow to a higher and more sophisticated level in every way.

I felt strongly that the aspirations of the school should be embodied in its entire graphics program—print and motion.

When April describes herself and her work, one has the impression of being on a different plane from other graphic designers—even the most well-known ones—who might still be at the effect of carrying out clients' wishes. April says that her clients never "demand" anything. In a world where graphic designers are sometimes viewed as being between word processors and interior decorators, what is it that makes her different, that commands that level of respect?

Rotondi: Her spirit. She's an evolved spirit. She's energy. You go near her and it's like you plug yourself into a wall socket. It feels good. You just want to keep doing it. It's pure energy, somewhere between sexuality and spirituality. The quest is tapping into that. You just look at her work and know it's the way it should be. Her work is about ideas. It's not about selling or about marketing, although it ultimately does that. SCI-Arc has a very definite structure, but it's as invisible as possible. One event bumps into a second event to create a third event. You can look at one of April's posters, and it seems to be complete chaos, too. But the more you look at it, the more you can see the order and reason. It's a process of discovery, a terrific feeling.

What do clients see when you present your work?

If they say, "It's hard to read" (and it isn't), you can suggest that they sit down with it and engage themselves. Everything doesn't have to be a quick read.

Does anyone complain that SCI-Arc's materials are hard to read—parents, alumni, trustees? If so, what do you say?

Rotondi: Yeah, some of them do. I say, "Don't be so impatient. Everything doesn't have to be a quick read. Sit down quietly, spend some time with it, and engage yourself."

Remember, we're not doing these materials for sixty-year-old CEOs. They're for eighteen- to twenty-five-year-olds who can take in and process information faster than you or I can imagine. I asked April to learn about the school, who we are, what we do, and what it means. Then I asked her to make a student workbook accordingly, which outlined the curriculum and the projects in a way that requires all senses to be engaged to read it. Just like an experience with architecture, it should be an experience of the school, not merely the ideas of it. This workbook has attracted many students. The board of directors is pleased with the enrollment statistics.

Can you describe how you work together with April, and how you evaluate the results?

Rotondi: I start by discussing, generally, the ideas and feelings I have and then in some detail the nature of the problem. With some designers, it's wise to let them help define as well as solve the problem. April is an excellent collaborator. When you work with her you don't have to worry about the quality or precision of the outcome. You may wonder what it is you are going to end up with, but if you remain open and flexible and have the wonder of a child, the results are surprising and enchanting. The more she has done—postcards, brochures, books, and websites—the more the quality of this work has influenced our students. It did not take long before the students petitioned me to ask her to permanently teach.

Did you appreciate the letterhead design when you first saw it?

Rotondi: I had asked, "What if you made a piece of stationery that made you feel like the page is already covered, like an aerial view or a map of the city?" Then April said, "What if I were to put a line through it so it looked like someone had put their hand to it?"

When I'm outside architecture, I always try to suspend judgment as long as possible, but when I saw the design I thought, That's it! I knew you didn't even have to put a letter on it to convey a message. In the beginning, everybody complained about it: "You can't write a letter on it." "It looks messy, like somebody spilled their lunch." But eventually it engaged people. It's interactive. We've reprinted it many times.

When many people think of corporate or organizational identity, they still think immutable logo, a palette of colors, a guidelines manual, and so forth. How are the paradigms of identity changing?

Rotondi: Many institutional structures are predicated on systems theories that have time structures that are static and synchronous. This exists only in our minds; our behavior is inherently more spontaneous and fluid. The type of fixed identity you describe comes out of a static culture that wishes for an immutable world.

Until now, we've lived in a society in which a very few people make decisions that affect very many. All that is changing. Print and digital are enhancing each other's performance and spheres of influence. The identity of an organization must be fluid and multifaceted, yet be an integral part of its character. Integrity is based on ideas, not the marketplace, so designers and clients will have to be clear on what the "big idea" is that gives a human organization a sense of real purpose—a purpose that is humanist, not merely economic. Throughout history, the best things with enduring life cycles have balanced culture and commerce for the common good. ◼

21

The Unlikely Risk-Taker

The Episcopal Ad Project AND Fallon

The Rev. Dr. George H. Martin, former pastor of St. Luke's Episcopal Church in Minneapolis, is executive director of the **Episcopal Ad Project**, an independent, non-profit ministry that offers print advertising for churches to use. The initial market for the ads was Episcopal churches, but interest from many other churches led the project to release its ads for use in all denominations. Rev. Martin is a graduate of Hobart College and Bexley Hall Seminary, and did graduate work at Virginia Theological Seminary, where he is a consultant to the national Episcopal Church in the areas of communications and new church development.

Fallon is the Minneapolis-based agency "for clients who would rather outsmart the competition than outspend them." Founded as Fallon McElligott Rice by account manager Pat Fallon, copywriter Tom McElligott, and art director Nancy Rice, the agency is owned by French media holding company Publicis Groupe. The ads on these pages were designed by Nancy Rice and **Dean Hanson**, a graduate of Minneapolis College of Art and Design, the seventh employee of the agency, who retired in 2009 after twenty-eight years.

Not too many agencies can claim that among the clients for which they did their best work is an Episcopal priest. Great work. Is its purpose to get a job done or to win awards? Let's get the answer from a higher authority. Certain firms, on their way to recognition, glory, and national clients, launched their reputations by doing free work for local merchants and nonprofits, who ostensibly gave creative freedom in return. Fallon got its start with ads for a Minneapolis barbershop that featured a stock photo of Albert Einstein, hair in disarray, under the headline, "A Bad Haircut Can Make Anyone Look Dumb." Ads for the Episcopal Church were equally smart and funny. The agency cleaned up at the New York Art Directors Club, and its next clients were FedEx and Porsche. That was the subject of a scathing advertising column in the *New York Times*. I was most interested in hearing from the client. Did he feel "used"? Or did the ads work as well for the church as they did for the agency? Rev. Martin retorted: "We have one of the most successful campaigns in the history of advertising!"

For fast, fast, fast relief take two tablets.

In the Episcopal Church, we believe that some of the oldest ideas are still the best.
Like the regular worship of God. Come join us as we celebrate this Sunday.
The Episcopal Church

This creative work is as groundbreaking as it is historic. Just like the subject matter, the principles surrounding how it was developed are as relevant today as they were on the day of their creation.

Will you come back to church if we promise not to throw the book at you?

In the Episcopal church we believe in a loving and forgiving God.
Come and join us this Sunday when we open up the Good Book in worship.
The Episcopal Church

2000 years later, Christianity's biggest competition is still the Lions.

Before you sit down for an afternoon with the Lions, Bears, Dolphins, Rams, Cowboys or Vikings,
come spend an hour with some very new Christians in the love, worship and fellowship of Jesus Christ.
The Lutheran Church

[The interview began with a phone conversation with Rev. George H. Martin.]

Q: Reverend Martin, what inspired you to first think about advertising?

A: Martin: I wanted to reach the unchurched people in the immediate neighborhood of the church I served. The original purpose of the campaign was to change people's Sunday morning habits. We had a community newspaper, and I figured some good advertising might set us apart and bring badly needed attention to our church.

Here's one ad that shows Moses and the Ten Commandments. The headline reads, "For fast, fast, fast relief, take two tablets." Some people would say you are selling religion like Alka-Seltzer. Do you think that's a necessity in a culture brought up on TV commercials?

Martin: When I read the prophets, the sermons of Paul, and the parables of Jesus, what I find is a language that was contemporary at the time. I don't think we're doing anything new under the sun. I mean, you don't have to use religious language to communicate about God. You use ordinary language and ordinary examples. Jeremiah once took a pot and smashed it and said, "This is going to happen to us if we don't change our ways." That's great advertising.

Did any of your congregants or clergy at other churches object to the ads?

Martin: There are always people who look at things from a myopic point of view. They're too concerned with appearances. For me, if we disturb some of the purist types within the institution, it's almost like a litmus test that says we must be doing something right. Getting people upset is not our primary mission, but I've learned not to be disturbed by it.

> **Does your work touch their hearts?**
>
> Humor connects with people in ways that a serious tone often can't. It cuts through barriers. Very few people can resist humor.

How did you begin working with Fallon McElligott Rice? Who approached whom?

Martin: I went to Tom McElligott, we had lunch together, and I presented the case, as it were. At the time, my urban congregation wasn't in a terrible section of town, but it certainly wasn't in a growing area. We needed to attract new people.

I presented an advertising problem, and he was intrigued by the idea. Our first ads were done on the side.

Done on the side of what?

Martin: On the side of their regular work. At the time, Tom was employed at the Bozell and Jacobs agency. He and Pat Fallon had a side business called something like, "Lunchtime Limited," with a few clients they took on the side, and we were one of them. An initial set of six ads was developed, and we've kept within the same basic format. There has been evolution and change and, I think, greater sophistication throughout the history of the project.

When they presented those first ads, what was your initial reaction?

Martin: I really enjoyed them. They had a sense of humor and a fresh, snappy quality. They addressed the key issue we identified, which was how to get people who are not in the habit of going to church to at least give it a try. As time went by, we also confronted some of the more troubling aspects of our secular culture and its values. We also turned our attention to certain people within the religious world who were giving religion a bad name.

Have you ever rejected any headlines or visuals as too far out?

Martin: Yes. There was one that showed a picture of the devil. It was an attempt to say something about free speech, which wasn't an issue we needed to deal with at the time. Another one had a picture of Jim Jones back in the days when we were questioning cults, and I remember the headline saying something like, "Before you accept Christ into your life, make sure it's really Christ." It was just too blatant.

Can you usually tell what's right or not from a gut reaction?

Martin: Yes. Here's an example: we had a monumental struggle with the agency folks over an ad headlined, "Where Women Stand in the Episcopal Church." It took them two years to understand what I was saying; why we needed an ad that addressed the fact that women participate fully in the ministry and life of our church. In many churches, especially the Roman Catholic, women are excluded from the ministry. We needed to make our position clear and positive to people with feminist concerns. The struggle with the agency was over the visual. They wanted a pulpit and I wanted an altar, and we went round and round. They kept saying, "It's got to be a pulpit." I kept saying, "You don't know who we are if you say that." I wouldn't give on it, and we finally shot it as an altar. It was an award-winning ad that has really worked well. They were real stubborn, but I wouldn't go along with them because we're not a pulpit-centered church; we're a sacramental church.

Can you explain the distinction?

Martin: In a pulpit-centered church, like many Protestant churches, the most important thing that happens is the sermon. In our church, the most important thing that happens is the Eucharist or the Communion. In the Catholic tradition, whether Episcopal or Roman, only an ordained priest can celebrate.

Did you want to show a woman offering a wafer or wine at the altar?

Martin: The neat thing about that ad, and what makes it work so well, is it doesn't show anybody. It just shows an altar—a very clearly identifiable Christian altar. In the parlance of the trade, it's a quick read.

You say it was an award-winning ad. I'm going to read you a quote from a *New York Times* article headlined "Ad Agencies' Obsession with Winning Awards":

> Many executives also detect a frenzied effort among agencies, particularly new ones, to do work strictly for its award potential. The strategy, they say, was perfected by Fallon McElligott in Minneapolis ... "Part of Fallon's strategy,' executives of other agencies said, 'was to seek out small clients and pro bono accounts (among them a Minneapolis barber shop and, more recently, the Episcopal Church) for which the agency could do highly creative, even daring, work without risking the client's rejection. The strategy paid off in a spate of Gold Pencils at the One Show. It also helped the agency win *Advertising Age*'s 1983 agency-of-the-year award."

There are a lot of questions that come to mind. First of all, I want to address the phrase, "highly creative and daring work without risk of the client's rejection." The assumption is because they did the work for free, you had to accept it. You just told me that you weren't in that position.

Martin: I wasn't. It's true that Fallon and McElligott don't want to work through layers of committees. They want to know who has the responsibility for approval, and if it involves a huge process that takes months and various meetings, they avoid that client. In terms of our relationship, I'm the only one who says "Yea" or "Nay" to things. But I do, occasionally, reject things.

According to that article, there was a feeling in some agency circles that the work they did for you was used to attract national accounts—that you were used, so to speak.

Martin: We have one of the most distinctive campaigns in the history of advertising! I like Fallon's commitment to awards. That's how we know that they think, "We're not just in it for the bucks; we're in it for our quality." There's a freedom, too, for the people who work on our campaign. An account like this turns on their creative juices. And it has not all been easy. Once you move beyond creating ads to doing a successful campaign, there has to be a momentum to keep it going. We struggle to keep freshness in it because the history of advertising is the history of campaigns losing their edge.

Then you don't see awards as creative people patting each other on the back? To you they really are a mark of excellence, acknowledged excellence.

Martin: Absolutely. What's interesting is that when Fallon McElligott goes to pitch a client like Dow Jones or Armour Foods, they take our religious stuff along. You might think they would say, "We better not show that God work."

Here's another quote from the *Times* article, "Awards create imitation." They show a couple of award-winning campaigns and how they were knocked off by other agencies, other products. Did other churches or nonprofit organizations copy your advertising concept?

Martin: Not directly. There are a few other examples of sparkling religious advertising. But that's it, very few. I'm surprised that we have had the field to ourselves for so long. But we have a willingness to express a sense of humor. Some people say, "You shouldn't laugh at religion." There's a risk factor that we assume most institutions are not willing to take on, which is why so much advertising with institutional connections is bland and boring and dull.

Did you meet your initial objectives?

Martin: The ultimate tragedy is that we have these wonderful materials, and yet, in terms of individual churches, there still is the issue of, How do we begin to make use of them?

Do you mean that they can't afford the ad space?

Martin: Yes. We're dealing with small organizations, individual churches, that for the most part have limited discretionary budgets. It's too bad, because my experience is that when we do run an ad, the results are astounding. When our diocese could pay for it, we had the ads blown up into billboards at our local airport. I have seen the arresting quality of this work. It literally stops people in their tracks in the middle of a busy airport. Their heads jerk back and they say, "What did I see?" And they stop and they read it.

The Episcopal Ad Project was founded at St. Luke's Episcopal Church. There's kind of a success story there, too, correct?

Martin: We started by running the ads in a community newspaper. Then we saw the average age of the congregation gradually drop lower and lower; the hair in the congregation turned from gray to varying colors as they exist in God's world. We saw the Sunday school grow. People would say, "I didn't know much about the Episcopal Church before, but I came to check this church out because I wanted to see if you really matched up with what the ads were saying." Or, "I'd been away from church; I didn't think that anything could get me started again, but gee those ads were good."

Was your thinking that if the ads spoke the current American vernacular, people would sense that the priest would, too? That the church would, too? And that the people who'd be attracted might not be Episcopalians to start with?

Martin: Exactly. They were all kinds of Christians who had left the fold, so to speak. We do have some people who are still part of the old, stuffy Episcopal Church, and they'd like to keep it that way.

So it wasn't just that you ran some ads. You made some fundamental changes in the church.

Martin: That's true across the board. The Episcopal Church had been changing. It isn't just the church of the establishment anymore. The irony of this is that we have no control over accuracy. The Episcopal Ad Project distributes these ads, and we have no way of saying, "You can only use these ads if the reality of your particular church matches what the ads say." But I think there tends to be a fair correspondence between a church that has vision enough to use our ads and what goes on inside. I know that there are some real medieval places, but they're probably not going to use our materials.

Let's say you were addressing people with administrative responsibilities for other churches or service organizations that weren't attracting enough people. What advice would you give about advertising and promotion?

Martin: I'd say, you've got to be willing to be provocative and approach things with a sense of humor, or you're not going to get people to pay attention. We really err when we take ourselves so doggone seriously all the time. But the willingness to provoke and to ask the tough questions has got to be there. And you always have to keep up the struggle to keep the campaign fresh.

[I followed up with Dean Hanson, one of the campaign's art directors.]

Dean, how long were you with Fallon?

Hanson: I was one of the original hires. It was more than twenty-eight years.

You saw the agency grow from a five-person shop to a $1 billion global agency. What were some of the biggest changes on the creative side?

Hanson: The public has become much more sophisticated, less tolerant of bad ads, and more appreciative of good ones. Technology has made our job much easier technically and more difficult from a turnaround standpoint. There are shorter deadlines. Copy length has shortened dramatically, in both print and broadcast.

When people, like newspaper advertising columnists, presuppose that doing pro bono work means never risking the client's rejection, what do you say?

Hanson: For a small client, it's a challenge to communicate in a way that anyone notices. Your budget just doesn't let you outspend anyone you're up against. So you've got to push things a bit to get noticed. Balanced against that is the reality that just about every client has a group you can't afford to offend in the process, so that means walking a fine line. And inevitably, if you're doing your job right, sooner or later you're going to push up against somebody's comfort zone.

Besides having the opportunity to do those fresh, snappy, award-winning ads, were there any other rewards working for the Episcopal Church?

Hanson: No matter which client we're working for, we try to accurately reflect their personalities and their value systems. With this client, we were fighting misconceptions. It was an interesting exercise to shake the public's perception that the Episcopal Church was a staid, humorless, judgmental entity. And to communicate that it has tremendous relevance in the modern world for the way people live today.

What do clients see in your portfolio:

If you're not happy with what *you* see, find a local nonprofit and do great pro bono work. As Dean says, every good creative follows this route to some degree.

Does Fallon still do pro bono work?

Hanson: Yes. It's always been an important part of the culture. A couple of examples are the Children's Defense Fund, a children's advocacy group, and Camp Heartland, a camp for HIV kids and their families. Actually, the work for Camp Heartland goes way beyond communications. Every spring, the entire staff spends a day at the facility, building and maintaining the camp. Think art directors with chain saws.

How do you convince institutional clients, who can be very conservative, to take a chance on humor and other creative strategies they may think are risky?

Hanson: If it's done correctly, humor connects in ways that a serious tone often can't. The average person can easily put up a mental barrier to ad copy and visuals that play on tragedy or guilt. Very few people can resist humor.

I've been advising young designers who complain that they have nothing good in their portfolios to find themselves some local nonprofit clients—or retailers or barber shops—and do great work. Do you agree?

Hanson: It's worked since the beginning of the industry. I've never met a good creative that didn't follow this route to some degree.

What is your advice to young people who would like to be art directors at agencies like yours? How should they get started?

Hanson: Pretty simple. Study *Communication Arts* and other award-show annuals. Memorize them. Find a good partner to collaborate with to develop your book. Get the best job you can out of school and then work nights on your own stuff. Don't be afraid to jump jobs frequently. If you're not doing better work each year, you need to move on. ■

22

The Bureaucracy

Des Moines Metro Waste Authority AND Pattee Design

Catherine Huggins, now principal of Huggins Consulting Group, was previously communications administrator for the **Des Moines Metro Waste Authority (MWA)**, a $12 million organization that manages a regional collection center for household hazardous waste, a landfill, a compost center, and a transfer station on behalf of its twenty-one member communities. A graduate of Drake University, Huggins is a past president of the Central Iowa Chapter of the Public Relations Society of America and was formerly chief speech writer and deputy press secretary for Iowa governor Terry Branstand.

Past president of the Art Directors Association of Iowa and of AIGA/Iowa, **Steve Pattee** founded **Pattee Design** in 1995 with designer Kelly Styles. Pattee's work has been recognized worldwide in design exhibitions and industry publications. Two of the firm's annual reports for MWA have been on view in an environmental exhibit at the Smithsonian in Washington, D.C. A graduate of the University of Iowa, Pattee is a member of Trout Unlimited and the Federation of American Rivers.

It was a typical client dilemma: how to continue commissioning groundbreaking design within the growing political and budgetary constraints of a municipal agency. Three-quarters of the way through these interviews, I realized that this story could serve as a paradigm for the battle of Designers (Pattee Design) vs. Philistines (Iowa Waste Haulers): dedicated designers work miracles with impossibly low budgets in short timeframes; spend late nights mixing shreds of newspaper and grass clippings into paper pulp; sweet-talking printers into running the results through their presses; getting local binderies to make special dye-cuts; hand-knotting twine. The results are met with wild acclaim in the design community. Haulers don't see things the same way. To them, the reports are examples of spending excess. Battle lines are drawn: the client is told by board members to "curtail those designers." The story has happy ending, though. Designers are given mandate to blend educational content with fiscal responsibility and produce "green" design that won't make the audience see red.

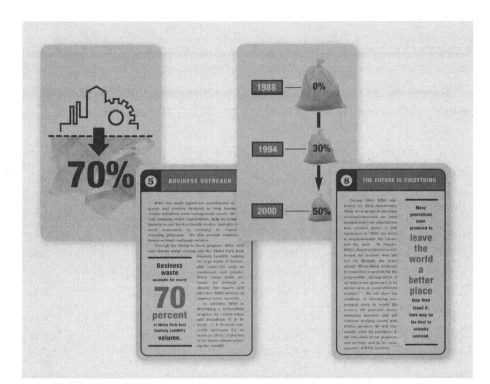

These flash cards first functioned as an annual report. An enclosed letter asked members of the business audience to forward them—after they were done reading—to schools for use in science classrooms. The students were asked to send them to graphic design schools, and from there back to the client. 80 percent of 5,000 sets of cards came back: a true recycling-in-action success story.

[The conversation began with a phone interview with Steve Pattee.]

Q: At an AIGA/Minneapolis competition, the annual report for the Des Moines Metropolitan Solid Waste Authority just jumped out at the judges. It seemed to be unique, as well as appropriate, for the client. How did you meet the MWA and start working with them?

A: Pattee: They were working with another design firm and something went haywire, some timing issue on a newsletter, and we got a call. Generally, we don't do newsletters, we're involved in business-to-business collateral. But this time we thought, "Hey, why not? This might be a good entree." The next project was the annual report, which also started with a call: "We need 300 annual reports."

Did the assignment to produce such a small quantity signal that you had the opportunity to create something virtually handmade?

Pattee: All of a sudden, you're in a different world of production criteria. And because the MWA's image—progressive-minded, ecologically up-to-date—had to be demonstrated as well as projected, the worst thing anybody could do would have been six colors on virgin bright white paper.

Was the client open to unusual ideas from the beginning?

Pattee: Because they had no experience creating communication tools, they were very open. So the first thing I said was, "If you only need 300 reports, we're going the stop at grocery stores and pick up boxes." We built a paper dummy and had it Wire-O'd.

You built these books from real corrugated boxes?

Pattee: Uh-huh. The inside cover might read, "Charmin" or "AA Large Eggs." Because these books are published by the organization that manages the city dump, the mandate has always been to use as little virgin material as possible, cut out the steps, simplify the process. On this project, we operate the same way. We make our art from laser prints, photocopies. In terms of press OKs, we say, "Just run it." There are no color matches or trapping issues.

Another report had a torn cover. Was that intentional?

Pattee: I can't tell you how many people asked that! We wanted to reintroduce the orange color and have the report look a little, well, trashy. In the office, we tore all 300 covers one by one to achieve what we were after. But there were quite a few calls, like, "We really like this report, but our copy came in damaged."

I imagine all the time you spent tearing those covers was done for love, not money.

Pattee: Yes, ma'am.

Tell me about the book with the cover line: "This Annual Report Is Trash." Are there pieces of old newspaper incorporated into the cover stock?

Pattee: The paper maker, Jerusalem Paper Works in Omaha, manufactured it to order for us, using thousands of old copies of the *Des Moines Register*. The challenge was, "What can you come up with this year? Can you bring us some other ideas?" So we hand-punched the reports and tied them with jute twine.

> Ask yourself on every project:
>
> What can we do to protect the environment; what steps can we take to save resources and reduce waste and landfill?

Isn't all this handwork very time-consuming?

Pattee: You can do it when the press run is 300 to 500 copies. We spent five to six weeks—tops—on each of these reports from start to finish. And the budget has ranged from $11,000 to $18,000, including design, writing, and production. We've let some serendipity get into the process. Two weeks before the deadline, my partner Kelly Styles and I were beating our heads against the wall to come up with an idea. She threw some paper samples down in frustration, we loved the way they looked when they fell, and said, "That's it!" The guy who printed it was one step up from a quick printer. The red tabs are waste from the red sheet. Again, we tied the string on ourselves.

It sounds like working for this client has meant a lot to you.

Pattee: MWA has made us more conscious about what we can do for all our clients. You can't be 100 percent environmentally correct on every project, but you can be more sensitive. For example, our biggest client is Principal Financial Corporation, an entirely different mind-set. Their press run is 300,000 copies. Last year, we cut the trim size by one-half inch and saved the equivalent of 44,000 pages. So we're always asking ourselves, "What can we do that saves resources?" When I talk to prospects, these pieces demonstrate that they're not going to get a canned look from us.

Another year, you used a pretty big embossing die on the cover. Is there ever a perception that these techniques are too expensive?

Pattee: Embossing is just as environmentally correct as you can get! You're not using any ink at all, just changing the shape of the material. And that book is 5.5" by 8.5", half-size. That year we had to reestablish ourselves with new marketing people who had come in from ad agencies and were used to a certain kind of process. Also, the reports were sent out to the public for the first time, so the report had to reflect the agency's decree: reduce landfill by 50 percent. Every year, the message has become more pointed: You—the consumer—have got to think differently and behave differently. We reasoned, "How do people learn? Flash cards!" That was the germ of the concept. We created a series of icons that identified the facilities citizens needed to become familiar with. Readers were asked to forward the reports to a school when they were finished with them, and over 80 percent did. The books were reused in classrooms.

You said that new marketing people came in. What happened?

Pattee: We were let go on the account! They wanted to consolidate everything at this high-test agency who'd come in with a big dog-and-pony show. We got the annual report back, but they said to us, "You have $11,000 to produce 3,500 copies." Seven times as many copies for two-thirds of the cost! I said, "We'll do it." Then I had to get as down-and-dirty as you can get. The result is this "To Our Trashholders" book.

Which looks like it's printed on your average 50-lb. offset.

Pattee: It's hard to convince printers that we don't mind all the show-through. But it's part of the effect. Things that would be considered mistakes or imperfections in another kind of job are part of the nature of the beast. We made the illustrations out of public-domain clip art, did Monty Python things with it, cutting by hand and collaging it. It was like three or four people in our office were playing Scrabble with pictures.

Am I looking at grass clippings in the cover stock this time?

Pattee: Yep. The same manufacturer, Jerusalem, used over 750 lbs. of real yard waste to make the paper. And the printer was not too happy about running it through his press! Our suppliers know their presses will get gunked up, so we're always cultivating relationships so they'll be willing to work with us and make these things happen.

It looks beautiful enough to sell on Etsy as photo frames and lampshades. Maybe they can recoup their losses that way. In addition to the annual reports, you've also done informational brochures.

Pattee: They're all about managing waste without adding to the waste stream.

What about the logo? Have you been hiding it from me all along?

Pattee: That was the agency's doing. Speed lines! I was so steamed I got the client on the phone. They said, "We needed an identity that made us look progressive and strong.'

Some people might say it looks like a late seventies cliché.

Pattee: They spent about $70,000 on that thing!

How did that make you feel after you spent all that time cutting corners by hand, literally and figuratively?

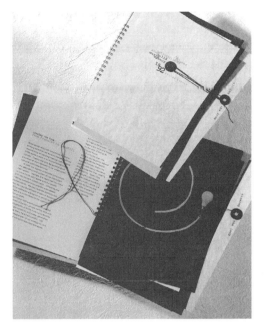

Pattee: Well, I'll just say that the MWA is now positioned in the industry as leaders. The message is going out all over the world. They are an example to their peers in other municipalities and states. We've demonstrated how good, solid creative has value and achieves results.

What's ahead for next year?

Pattee: We're looking into these guys who are making plastic board, kind of like compressed bubble wrap, out of used disposable diapers.

[Later, I spoke with Catherine Huggins.]

I should start with a friendlier question, but Steve Pattee says that you were one of the people who came in from the agency side and burst the bubble on the annual report. What happened?

Huggins: It was a different era. In the early nineties, the organization had a stable financial future and could afford the luxury of reports of that stature, with unique materials and design. A Supreme Court decision changed all that; they struck down "flow control" laws that had in essence given municipalities and states virtual monopolies so they could count on a certain revenue stream. Waste disposal is now interstate commerce, so if haulers can get a better deal in the next county, they'll take the trash there. In one year alone, we lost over $1 million in fees. Plus, there are increased regulations; we have to reduce the amount of waste in landfills by 50 percent. We've spent $26 million on curbside recycling programs, teaching people how to compost yard waste and creating byproducts that can be used by other industries. So we can't have a perception that we're spending a lot on the annual report.

I also understand that $18,000 was the top budget for any of these reports. To a typical corporation, isn't that number minuscule?

Huggins: You have to look at the cost per unit. If we're printing three hundred copies, that's $60 per book. We had to reassess those costs, and have brought it down to $5 to $7 per copy, which is in line with what corporations spend.

Didn't those earlier reports have a benefit to the MWA that can't be measured in dollars, positioning the organization as a leader?

Huggins: Yes. The best example of that is the flash cards. They were written up in the *Des Moines Register*. The report had three audiences. The reports were first sent to our usual audience: business leaders, regulators, board members, elected officials, the general public. An enclosed letter and label asked them to send the reports—after they were done reading them—to middle and secondary schools for use in science classrooms. Then the students were asked to send them to graphic design schools. And from there they were sent back to the MWA. About 80 percent of 5,000 came back. It was amazing and wonderful. A recycling-in-action story.

Several months ago, the *New York Times Magazine* ran a cover story claiming that recycling is one of the biggest frauds ever pulled on the American people; that it costs much more to recycle than to dump waste in landfills, there's plenty of land available, etc. What do you make of that thesis?

Huggins: Encouraging people to change their lifestyles does cost money. Recycling is expensive—it costs us more than $2 a month per household recycling bin for education and maintenance and transportation, and we only get 13 cents back. But it's an investment in our future.

> **What do clients not want?**
>
> A fear that at every meeting they'll be "knocking heads with the creatives."

There may be plenty of land, but it's not permittable land—we're not going to get permits to dump on it—and the airspace has to be maintained. Recycling now diverts over 5 percent of the waste stream, and it's finally becoming engrained in our culture.

What's it been like to work with Pattee Design?

Huggins: Steve and Kelly like to take creative risks, but they're easy to work with. You don't think, "Oh, here's another meeting where we'll be knocking heads with the creatives." And when you go into their facility, everything is very environmentally conscious. The floors are recycled textured wood. The desks have brushed metal bases. The walls are plyboard. They reuse their layouts as wallpaper.

To you, what's the key different between working with an ad agency and a design firm?

Huggins: With a design firm, there's less layers and more accountability. You can just sit down and talk. Designers can't push the accountability onto other layers: "Such-and-such was the copywriter's fault" or "the account service team didn't tell me about that." Often, it's the difference between a larger and a smaller firm. At a large firm, you can always find someone to talk to. If the account supervisor's not there, you can talk to the president. A smaller firm can make you more nervous at deadline time because the principals may be serving other accounts, and sometimes you have to wait patiently until they get back from a meeting. But Pattee Design has never missed a deadline.

Steve told me they got temporarily fired when the agency people came in.

Huggins: Not true! Several years ago, we wanted to pull together our advertising, public relations, and design, and put out an RFP to 100 agencies, most of them local. Pattee Design was one of them, continued to work for us on an ad-hoc basis, and in fact ended up among the six finalists.

What was the process like?

Huggins: The RFP had an eight-page questionnaire that covered such questions as, "Describe your strategic planning process for clients." "Does your firm possess environmental design experience?" "Do you have an in-house recycling program?" "What is the one strength of the account team you would assign to the MWA that sets it apart from its competition?"

All the agencies were rated in the areas of stability, solid waste industry knowledge, average billable rates, depth and expertise of the account team. We undertook an exhaustive search in which we reviewed the formal proposals , took agency tours, and had what we call a dog-and-pony show by each contender. CMF&Z, a local Young and Rubicam affiliate, was designated agency of record.

Did you ask any of the agencies for spec work?

Huggins: The agencies were more than welcome to bring in whatever they wanted to.

Did they bring in anything that surprised you?

Huggins: Not really. One group brought in some confetti, as if the whole thing were a festive event; another, some brown paper bags. I took great care to make sure there was a level playing field, and that even though I had worked at CMF&Z, that wasn't going to influence our decision. The first thing we undertook with the agency was a communications audit; the board thought Des Moines Metropolitan Solid Waste Authority (DMMSWA) was too bulky.

So we conducted benchmark research—focus groups—first asking whether it made sense to change the name, then identifying eight to ten possible names and positioning statements. It was ultimately decided to change DMMSWA to MWA. The logo was created by Bill Fultz at CMF&Z. His forte is developing symbols; he's just great at it. The decreasing lines communicate a subtle message of waste reduction. We use Pantone 576 green, which is an environmentally appropriate color, and Proterra paper for a consistent look.

Do you know what Steve Pattee thinks of the logo?

Huggins: No.

Well, not much. It sounded like he was more than a little upset that after they put in all that time doing $18,000 annual reports and tying on strings by hand—and not charging the MWA for the time—you were able to find $70,000 for that logo.

Huggins: It was $47,000 for everything, including focus groups and the name change.

> **What does the client see:**
>
> Projects that are memorable and exciting to designers (and even that are relatively inexpensive to produce) sometimes can be seen as excessive by the target audience.

Graphic designers are very sensitive to the fact that PR agencies, ad agencies, everybody else, seems to get bigger fees. In the past few years, there has hardly been a design annual—type directors, communication graphics—that one could open without seeing an MWA annual report. What do awards mean to you, if anything?

Huggins: It's fun to do award-winning design and have your work acknowledged by your peers at industry conferences. It's great when somebody says something is really neat or when the *Des Moines Register* writes up your report. Awards make us feel like the partnership works. But right now, we're into cost-effective creativity. We have to prioritize our limited dollars while respecting the audience's perceptions. When we do the right things with our budget and educate the most people, then I consider the project a success.

Are you saying that it could be a problem for you if something looks expensive that was actually done for free?

Huggins: Yes! The early reports were perceived as excessive. The ultimate-end audience did not see the value. In fact, those reports made them hostile. It was a real love-hate thing. The reports were memorable to designers and to business and civic leaders, elected officials, and the general public. But they were sore spots to our board members, waste handlers, city administrators, public works directors, regulatory officials—important members of our constituency. They said, "You've got to curtail those designers!" There was a public outcry. Years later, we still get letters; they're still talking about them.

What do you think accounts for that disparity?

Huggins: The people who hate them are the people who pay our disposal fees! In 1985, the fee was less than $5 per ton. It was more than $30 ten years later. That's a sixfold increase in a decade.

So they made the annual report into the scapegoat?

Huggins: Those people do their own reports in-house—they're real boring—but the thinking is, "All I need is a printout of the financials and that's X less dollars I'll have to pay."

That must put you in a tough position.

Huggins: It's a challenge. Our most successful projects will have an educational component rather than being created to look flashy or win awards. People need to be able to see the purpose. Now we have a standard communications work plan, which includes identifying areas such as: "Who is the target audience?" "What awareness or action do we want to communicate?" "What benefit should the communication promise?" "Why should the target audience member believe us?"

The mandate in government from Washington is, "Create a government that works better and costs less." For us, it's reuse and recycle. We are doing 4" by 9" brochures. Instead of sending a resource directory, we'll ask what the caller is looking for and fax or email the relevant page. We aim to maintain the quality level without going over the top. ∎

23

The Curator

The Wadsworth Atheneum AND Cummings & Good

Art historian **Patrick McCaughey, PhD** came to the US in 1990 from his native Australia to chair the Australian studies department at Harvard. He was soon appointed director of American's oldest public art museum, the **Wadsworth Atheneum Museum of Art** in Hartford, Connecticut. The Atheneum has grown into a five-building complex with more than 45,000 works of art, including American and European paintings, sculpture, and works on paper. Dr. McCaughey received an honorary doctorate from the University of Melbourne in 2012. He currently teaches at Yale.

Cummings & Good, located in a historic gallery-studio-shop in Chester, Connecticut, was founded by **Janet Cummings** and **Peter Good**, who met when they were studying for their BFAs at the University of Connecticut's School of Fine Arts. In addition to being a graphic designer, Cummings is a painter, printmaker, and fashion entrepreneur. Good's award-winning graphic design for corporations, museums, and arts organizations has been exhibited in museums internationally and reproduced in all the leading design periodicals.

Wouldn't it be marvelous (to use one of Dr. McCaughey's favorite words) if each of us had the opportunity to learn art history—instead of from slide shows in snooze-inducing, darkened lecture halls—from an energetic museum director like him? You'd follow flying coattails through the galleries and would be transfixed when he said things like: "Just look at this Thomas Cole. It's about finding the real truth in the American landscape. Is America a wild, untouched place, or is it cultivated, tamed, the road paved to expansion and commerce?" And all of a sudden, you'd see so much more in that painting. Perhaps at museums like the Wadsworth Atheneum, such a stroke of luck is possible. And wouldn't it be marvelous if each of us had the opportunity to be the graphic designer for such a museum? Other designers—and leaders of nonprofit organizations—can learn much from how Cummings & Good met the museum's challenges within the constraints of institutional tradition, local politics, and tight budgets—and won the client back after a hiatus and several changes of leadership.

A director, a committee, a board of directors, a history, a future, and the public . . . and a design firm who can put it all together in a way that all parties can appreciate.

The identity of a complex
institution is communicated
with a family of symbols used
in a free yet connected way.
Each is a based on the museum's Gothic facade.

Docent Council

Film Programs

School and Teacher Programs

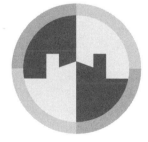

Museum Café

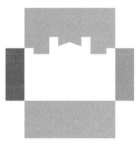

Family Programs

Wadsworth Atheneum
Museum of Art

Wadsworth Atheneum
Museum of Art

An Artificial
Wilderness

The Landscape in Contemporary Photography

August 31, 2013 – January 5, 2014

2013 SUMMER
FILM PROGRAM

WADSWORTH ATHENEUM MUSEUM OF ART

JUNE 21 – AUGUST 25   AETNA THEATER

CAPEFEAR, JUNE 21

PRESENTED BY DATA-MAIL, INC. AND THE MANDELL FAMILY

American Moderns on Paper

Masterworks from
the Wadsworth Atheneum
Museum of Art

The museum and the art
are the stars, not a design
style. Typefaces reflect the
period and feel of each
exhibition or program.

[I met with Dr. McCaughey in his Modernist office in the Wadsworth Atheneum complex.]

Q: You're known for having made quite a difference to this museum. Which of your accomplishments are you most proud of?

A: McCaughey: It's an evolutionary story. We raised seventeen million dollars. We renovated the galleries and cleaned lots of pictures. We installed new access ramps for the handicapped. I'm quite proud of our collections of African-American art; 85 percent of the residents of Hartford are minority, and it's their museum. But I guess I'm most proud of exhuming the basement. Did you know that there's enough art in the basements of American museums to go around the world three times? It's about time we got it up and let the public have a look at it. I've had one major disappointment: I put forth a proposal to make museum admission free to residents of Hartford. I mean, if they can borrow a book at the public library, why can't they come here for free? And the foundation refused. We did get a grant, however, for $150,000 for the "Colt 4," artists working around Hartford. So you count your blessings.

And your plans for the future?

McCaughey: To make the museum absolutely sing. To raise the level of seriousness of the temporary exhibitions. To mount more traveling exhibitions from our collections, such as "200 Years of American Painting," which went to Paris a few years ago.

When J. Carter Brown resigned as director of the National Gallery in Washington, newspapers reported, "The age of the imperial museum is ending." Is this a tougher decade for museums ?

McCaughey: Museums will have to do different kinds of things. Because there will be less money for blockbusters, there will be more emphasis on the permanent collections. New resources are being explored, for example, theme exhibitions. We might do an exhibition on American Impressionism, drawing on the resources of three or four museums here in New England.

And the importance of graphic design in all of this?

McCaughey: Oh, enormously important. Hiring Cummings & Good was one of my key accomplishments.

You've written: "Cummings & Good was chosen from a group of highly gifted graphic designers working in Connecticut . . . largely through the designers' inspiration and vision, the Wadsworth Atheneum now boasts one of the liveliest quarterly magazines produced by any museum in the northeast of America . . . It has won awards for its innovation." You go on to praise Peter Good's "gifted mind" and "imagination." How rare that clients publicly praise their graphic designers! Tell me about how the firm was chosen.

McCaughey: When I first came here the situation was graphic anarchy. The membership office would get its designer to do certain things. The public information office would get another designer to do something else. The museum projected a graphically disjointed, incoherent message. We wanted to find graphic designers who could give a real sense of unity to everything from catalogs to posters to the newsletter to gift cards and tote bags—the whole thing. The pioneer and great model for this is of course the Museum of Modern Art in New York. You can tell a MoMA catalog or poster from fifty yards away, and it was with that idea in mind that we set out to find a designer.

And it so happens that in and around the Hartford area, there were at least three or four very able graphic designers. They all knew each other and competition was fierce, so we held what we frankly called a beauty contest. We wrote to each of them and explained what our graphic needs were. We were very up-front about the fact that we were approaching the others, and asked, "If you're interested, would you like to come in and make a presentation?" We felt that Peter Good made the best case.

Do you hear what the client is saying?

Many clients don't want a designer who will impose a viewpoint or style. They want you to develop a style that mirrors the goals of the organization itself.

How were the designers' presentations? Did you find them similar or dissimilar?

McCaughey: Oh, they were very dissimilar, indeed.

In what way? What kinds of things did people do or say that caused you to respond positively or negatively?

McCaughey: One designer came in and told us virtually how he thought we should be running the place, what should be the focus. Well, there are a lot of very able people around here who think very hard about our nature and mission, and we really didn't want a designer who was going to try to impose his views on us. Some graphic designers have a slightly Napoleonic view of what their roles are or should be. Other designers had a very distinct house style, which, impressive as it might have been, made us feel like we would be absorbed into that style, and that wasn't a particularly attractive option. What was really attractive about Cummings & Good was that their terrific sense of the dynamics of the institution, what happens here, what our goals are. They let us know that they wanted to find a design style for us that mirrored the goals and ambitions of the institution itself.

The work the museum produces is of consistently higher quality than usually associated with nonprofit organizations on small budgets. How do you keep up the quality?

McCaughey: If you get great designers, you also try to live up to their expectations. Cummings & Good keeps our expectations high as to what the graphic design should be like. We've got an annual budget of just over five million dollars. We're not rich but not starving. It was quite a conscious decision—and now one which is part of the basic culture of the institution—that our graphic communications should be of high quality and maintain our image in the surrounding community upon whom we depend for financial help. Cummings & Good has helped us enormously from time to time by knowing people in the trade who can donate paper and so forth. But at other times we pay. They give us a very favorable rate, but we've learned to pay for quality.

When you say you've learned to pay, was there some resistance to that in the beginning?

McCaughey: Not exactly resistance, but it certainly caused some general adjustments around here. And not all good design is necessarily expensive, so we have sessions where we sort out what's really happening.

If one of your publications hadn't been in the *CA Design Annual*, I would never have heard of the Atheneum. That would have been my loss, but it would have been a shame. Almost everyone driving to Boston or northern New England from New York or points south goes through Hartford. But as far as I know, very few people say, "Let's stop at the Atheneum and see the art." Why is that?

McCaughey: Usually because there are no signs on the highway. There is one now, thank God. In some circles, this museum has tremendous, tremendous fame. We expend an enormous amount of energy turning the walls outward to get people to come in. The rates to advertise are very heavy indeed, and it's difficult to get and hang onto those pockets of dollars. One has to apply the resources of the museum to its priorities. And Hartford isn't on most people's tourist maps quite yet, but we're working on it.

What are your plans for the future in terms of graphic communications?

McCaughey: Our five buildings were sort of banged together over almost a hundred and fifty years, and as you've seen, the museum is the most glorious maze that gives you long wonderful vistas and eternal multiple choice. But one doesn't know which way to go because there is so much to see and look at. Now I love this idea of the maze, but we also do have to take pity on the visitor who needs a sense of how the place works. We need a signage program, a really good graphics system running through the building, so when people turn up, they're able to find their way to the Barbizon School without having to search the whole museum to find it.

Let's say you were addressing a group of graphic designers who were interested in working for museums. What would you say to them?

McCaughey: I'd say: the first job you have to do is to talk to people in the museum and become familiar with the style of the museum or the style it wishes to have. You have to think hard about what these people want to achieve, what this curator wants to do with this exhibition, and so forth, and then ask yourself, how can I make that idea really speak in a catalog, in a flyer, in a poster, and so on. Peter Good is an absolute object lesson to people in his field, to young graphic designers, and that's because of his tremendous ability to listen and to understand other people's ambitions.

[Later, I spoke with Janet Cummings and Peter Good.]

Patrick McCaughey characterized the process that was used to select your firm as a "beauty contest." How do you feel about that? What was the selection process like for you?

Good: I'd rather that they'd used a term that was more professional than "beauty contest," but the selection process was handled very professionally. I made a presentation to a committee, expressed my philosophy of design, showed about ten projects, and spoke about what I thought was important to the museum. I emphasized that I'd grown up in Hartford and had always loved the museum. My first experiences of the applied visual world were there; it was there that I saw my first Picasso, my first Caravaggio, my first Egyptian mummy. I tried to make two specific points: One, the museum presents a unique identity problem because it doesn't have a singular specialty. It's like a mini-Metropolitan: there's a major twentieth-century collection with terrific experimental stuff, as well as Renaissance art and collections of almost every other period. The identity must express this wide breadth. Two, the identity should evolve over time from a lot of different materials, rather than only be a rubber-stamp logo.

Tell me about the committee. Have you been required to satisfy a committee all along? That can be tough.

Good: The committee consisted of seven or eight people, including Patrick and his assistant, two outside consultants, and the president of the board of trustees. Although the committee was very involved in selecting the design firm, it hasn't gotten involved with approving designs. Patrick and a few others are the only people who do that, and since the beginning, there have been very few changes to our work. In terms of committees, the only people I have difficulty with are those who consider themselves "marketing experts." I usually find them too focus-group driven. Focus-group results should be one element a designer can consider, but not the driving force. In designing a T-shirt, for example, they can get caught up in issues like, "which T-shirt will sell" rather than "which T-shirt will make a great image." Because of thinking like that, there is a lot of mediocre design around. I also have difficulties with those who ask for work on spec: "Just show us how you might approach this . . . " I was worried that this might happen in this case.

Were you asked to work on spec?

Good: Fortunately, no. Before our presentation, I called Patrick to let him know that speculative work is against our policy, and he said that it wasn't necessary to show what I would do if we were hired. He said he just wanted to hear our general ideas. That made us want to work for him. But I did some sketches for my own benefit, to clarify ideas before coming in to speak.

Did your presentation include examples of work for other museums?

Good: No.

You've got to give any prospective client credit for not insisting that they see something exactly like what they're looking for in a designer's portfolio.

Cummings: We've lost projects because of that kind of myopic thinking. A client should be able to have confidence in you as a generalist. Our firm does a wide range of work; the only thing we don't do is retail advertising, other than for our own gallery and products.

A potential corporate or institutional client looking at our portfolio should be able to say, "This is a well-rounded firm that could move over a wide range of design problems." For the Atheneum, we were able to demonstrate our history of work in the arts, such as corporate posters for exhibitions at the Atheneum sponsored by United Technologies. One project we were very proud of—and still are—is "The American Experience" sponsored by Aetna. We did all Aetna's graphics, posters, mailers, and national ads, and this project demonstrated the application of a look or system to all kinds of visual materials. We were able to show a range of pragmatic solutions, the organization of complex information.

Let's return for a moment to a previous point, that you thought a singular logo would have been wrong for the Atheneum. Why?

Good: It would have been easy to come up with something that looked marvelous. But I think it would have been irresponsible. A symbol would sway the perception of the museum, which goes from Rubens to Rauschenberg. Should the logo look contemporary? Should it be Gothic or classical? At the meeting, I expressed my feeling that the museum should have a more open approach to identity. And, luckily the museum board agreed; they stressed the importance of continuity of design. It's usually the opposite: people insist that they just want a logo, something they think will make everything neat and simple.

We ultimately did design a logo, an icon based on the Gothic facade of the main museum building, but that did not substitute for a cohesive identity and publications program featuring the museum's art and complemented by classic typefaces like Baskerville, Bodoni, and Futura.

How do you keep up the quality on a museum budget?

Cummings: We keep up the quality by hard work. We do things over and over. We're very, very fussy. Our office has that dedication, and once you establish a certain level, you can't fall back. Doing it within the budget is a constant battle.

I'm impressed by the quality of the art and photography. Designers always cringe at getting that file of old photos when they begin a project for a nonprofit organization (and sometimes even for a for-profit organization).

Cummings: We do all the illustrations here, and the photos are supplied by the client. The art is picked up from resource books, or we'll do line drawings, sketches, silhouettes, anything to save a photo. We work at finding the right balance between text and art. All this effort is worthwhile because we, and all the people at the museum, have a common goal: to make everyone in and outside Connecticut aware of this exceptional museum. There are people in Connecticut who still don't know about it. Yet it has an incredible legacy: the Atheneum was the first American museum to install a Picasso exhibition, the first to buy a Mondrian and a Dali.

Building public awareness is a slow process, isn't it?

Good: It is, especially when you're limited by funds. When it comes down to whether you'll run an ad or fix the leaking skylights, you fix the skylights.

Many designers say that they would rather do a great design for nothing than do a bad design for a lot of money.

Good: When someone trusts you and gives you that opportunity, you'll work

> **Are clients hearing you?**
>
> "I have an idea I'd like to discuss" works a lot better than, "Here's what you should be doing."

harder. You accept the challenge to do the best possible work for them—and yourself. On the other hand, if your work is scrutinized by a board of trustees, if you feel there are multiple agendas to please, you lose interest, because that kind of critical overview inhibits intuitive solutions.

More and more designers are positioning themselves as marketing consultants in addition to visual communicators. Patrick made it clear that he rejected designers who wanted to advise the museum about what it should be or how it should promote itself. How do you think people at the museum would react if you recommended an ad campaign or something like a way to get more publicity in tourist guidebooks so that more people would know about the Atheneum?

Good: I think they would be open to it, but that would depend on how it is presented. If someone comes in and says to a scholar, "This is the way you should do things," it might be viewed as insulting. Having that kind of attitude is a mistake a lot of designers make. You have to remember that trustees and curators know their subject matter a lot better than you do. But if someone comes in and says, "I have an idea I'd like to discuss with you, how do you feel about this?" it would probably be well received. For example, a commemorative poster we did for the museum's 150th anniversary was entirely our concept, and it was accepted enthusiastically. We welcome collaboration.

Your work is elegant, clear, and classic. Tell me about your approach to style.

Cummings: I like to think we have no style. Style is created when a problem is solved. To us, there is enchantment in expressing ideas in a simple way. The art and the glory of the institution should be the stars, not Peter's or my way of working with images, type, and color. If we did anything that seemed to announce, "This was done by a trendy designer," it would be self-serving. We get our satisfaction from doing something that gets people to come to the museum, for example, a calendar that's clear and informational.

How is it running a design business in a smaller town outside a major metropolitan area?

Good: I previously worked for major New York design firms, including Chermayeff and Geismar. I loved Manhattan, but after we had children, we didn't want to live there. We wanted the convenience of small-town life. It wasn't easy to start a business in a place no one knew about, especially back in the pre-fax, pre-FedEx days. Our client base was more limited then.

Cummings: Over the years, we've branched out. Our work—particularly posters, which are a special love of ours—has been reproduced in periodicals, exhibited in international competitions and invitationals. We have worked for clients in France and Japan. The way communication is today, one can easily work for a company for years and never visit its offices. For us, electronic communications has opened a much larger world.

[I recently reconnected with Janet and Peter in their art-filled studio/ gallery/retail shop in the picturesque village of Chester, Connecticut.]

I understand there were several years during which the Wadsworth Atheneum was not your client. And that now you're doing important work for them again. How did that come about?

Good: At one point, I actually was on the search committee to find our replacement! For budgetary reasons, they wanted to turn everything over to anin-house designer. After that, we entered into a dry period when we weren't doing any work for them.

Cummings: A few years ago, many clients thought they could do it all in-house. Many in-house designers are excellent, but especially in a tough economy, some organizations try to rely on people who aren't qualified, who weren't trained as designers. Unless they put together design departments like Apple's, with enough people to handle all the work, they eventually learn they are wrong.

How did things get turned around?

Good: George David, the CEO of United Technologies, became the Atheneum's board chairman. He donated all kinds of corporate resources to benefit the museum. We were one of United Technologies' key suppliers, especially in relation to doing posters for exhibits they sponsored. With him there, our name was getting mentioned again. But it was a time of considerable chaos at the Atheneum, with various changes of directors and board members.

How do clients think?

There is virtue in patience. If your work created value for the client, even if there's a "dry period," they may call you again.

Cummings: Then a longtime curator, Betsy Lornhauser, hired us to design an exhibition catalog, which was very successful. And then came several books.

Good: Two years ago, a new museum director, Susan Talbott, came in. She said, "We must do something about our identity!" They had let go of the in-house designer and were using freelancers. The quality had disintegrated.

Had they returned to the "graphic anarchy" Patrick originally described to me?

Good: Yes. The curators and membership people also wanted a more cohesive look. They started calling us again and having us do exhibition graphics, banners, membership materials, film programs, even the menu for the museum cafe. But with such a complex institution, everyone started realizing that even if one piece was well designed, that without any kind of system. things weren't working in concert with each other as well as they could.

Cummings: One of the museum's major initiatives is its educational programs for teachers and students. That was the first system we created. We transformed the original logo we designed for the museum, based on a silhouette of the iconic Gothic facade of the main building, into a system of departmental identities that work together.

Were you asked to develop a comprehensive brand identity system?

Good: No. We did it surreptitiously. Piece by piece, we demonstrated how the logo could be expanded, yet used in a much looser, yet connected, way. Each logo—School and Teacher Programs, Family Programs, Films, Docent Council, Museum Café—is a variation of the facade symbol. None of them is in a lockup relationship with the typography, giving us a lot of flexibility.

Surreptitiously?

Good: Yes. You just start doing something and it becomes accepted. Let's call it transitional evolution.

I see in all your work a lot of craft, hand work. How does that fit into being a twenty-first-century design firm?

Good: Communication in general is more satisfying when it employs all the senses, touch, textures. Our work employs drawing, printmaking, painting, sewing, collage constructions. There is a satisfaction in doing this work that I don't get when manipulating a keyboard or choosing colors from an online palette. There is knowledge that comes from putting something together with your hands. But we also have the knowledge of what technology can do to enhance this work and make it part of a communications system.

Next to your iMac you have a drawing board with decidedly nontechnological tools: T-square, triangles, colored pencils.

Good: Yeah, it's where I still do a lot of my work. Our longtime assistant, Kirstin Desnoyers, takes those sketches and transforms them into digital files.

Cummings: And we are working on things that are dependant on technology, like collaborating with the Atheneum on a system in which you use your cellphone keypad to access audio information about selected works.

If you were asked to advise designers who were frustrated because they'd lost a client they loved, what would you say?

Good: Like most design firms, we've lost clients, and I was actually happy to see a few of them go, especially certain corporate clients. It was a pleasure working with a CEO who had taste, a sense of quality. Then a new CEO came in who was a bottom-liner.

Cummings: "Loved" is the key word. We just can't accept any work we're not excited about.

And now you are involved with other ventures you love, a gallery and shop.

Cummings: Chester is a mecca for artists, restaurateurs, musicians, writers. There are no fast-food places here and the nearest mall is fifteen miles away. This is where we wanted to live, work, and raise our two sons. We had the opportunity to buy this building, which looks like a bank, but was really the original dry goods store in the village, for a song. It was a mess. Little by little we gutted and renovated it, doing a lot of the construction ourselves. Luckily, there was an architect in town whose specialty was Greek Revival and he designed the major addition. It's now our second-floor studio and gallery, where we sell our posters, note cards, fine-art prints. The first floor, now Cummings & Good Unparalleled Apparel, evolved. At first, we weren't sure what we would do with it, but I'd always designed and made clothing, so we thought we'd make it into a beautiful retail space for a curated collection of clothing and accessories. And it's become a very successful part of the dining and shopping experience of Chester. Customers come from all over.

You are examples of everything coming together: work, life, family.

Good: People ask us all the time how we've managed to work together all these years. I guess it's a matter of complementary skills and personalities. Usually I'm the intuitive one and Jan is the analytical one. We are each other's strongest supporter—and critic. We don't always agree, but it works.

Cummings: When you love it, it works.

How do you apply that philosophy to the graphic design business?

Good: Work for those people whose missions you feel you can contribute to. If you are aligned with their principles, it will show in your work, and the work will have real intrinsic value. ∎

> **The last word:**
>
> When you work for clients whose missions you can contribute to, it will show, and your work will have real intrinsic value.

index

Books from Allworth Press

Allworth Press is an imprint of Skyhorse Publishing, Inc.
Selected titles are listed below.

Advertising Design and Typography
By Alex W. White (8 ¾ x 11 ½, 224 pages, hardcover, $50.00)

AIGA Professional Practices in Graphic Design
By Tad Crawford (6 x 9, 336 pages, paperback, $29.95)

Brand Thinking and Other Noble Pursuits
By Debbie Millman (6 x 9, 336 pages, paperback, $19.95)

Business and Legal Forms for Graphic Designers, Fourth Edition
By Tad Crawford (8 ½ x 11, 192 pages, paperback, $29.95)

Design Disasters
By Steven Heller (6 x 9, 240 pages, paperback, $29.95)

Design Firms Open for Business
By Steven Heller and Lita Talarico (7 x 9 ¼, 256 pages, paperback, $24.95)

Design Literacy, Third Edition
By Steven Heller (6 x 9, 288 pages, paperback, $22.50)

The Elements of Graphic Design, Second Edition
By Alex W. White (8 x 10, 224 pages, paperback, $29.95)

The Graphic Design Business Book
By Tad Crawford (6 x 9, 240 pages, paperback, $24.95)

The Graphic Designer's Guide to Pricing, Estimating, and Budgeting, Third Edition
By Theo Stephan Williams (6 x 9, 256 pages, paperback, $24.95)

How to Start and Operate Your Own Design Firm
By Albert W. Rubeling, Jr. (6 x 9, 256 pages, paperback, $24.95)

How to Think Like a Great Graphic Designer
By Debbie Millman (6 x 9, 248 pages, paperback, $24.95)

Selling Graphic and Web Design
By Donald Sparkman (6 x 9, 240 pages, paperback, $24.95)

To see our complete catalog or to order online, please visit *www.allworth.com.*